Cocktail Party

ECONOMICS

Cocktail Party

ECONOMICS

The Big Ideas and Scintillating Small Talk about Markets

EVELINE J. ADOMAIT
University of Guelph

RICHARD G. MARANTA

Pearson Canada
Toronto

Library and Archives Canada Cataloguing in Publication

Adomait, Eveline J

   Cocktail party economics / Eveline J. Adomait and Richard G. Maranta.

Includes index.

ISBN 978-0-13-266600-8

   1. Economics—Popular works. 2. Economics—Humor.

I. Maranta, Richard G. (Richard Gino), 1961– II. Title.

HB171.A36 2011   330   C2011-900398-8

ISBN: 978-0-13-266600-8

Vice-President, Editorial Director: Gary Bennett
Editor-in-Chief: Nicole Lukach
Acquisitions Editors: Gary Bennett, Claudine O'Donnell
Marketing Manager: Leigh-Anne Graham
Developmental Editor: Karen Townsend
Lead Project Manager: Avinash Chandra
Production Editor: Susan Broadhurst
Copy Editor: Susan Broadhurst
Proofreader: Patricia Jones
Compositor: MPS Limited, a Macmillan Company
Art Director: Julia Hall
Cover Designer: Miriam Blier
Interior Designer: Miriam Blier
Cover Image: iStockphoto

17 17

Printed and bound in United States of America.

To students everywhere, especially those who
like economics ... or who want to.

Contents

Each memorable verse of a true poet has two or three times the written content.
Alfred De Musset (1810–1857), French writer

About the Authors

Eveline Adomait was born to Dutch immigrants in rural Ontario. She attended the University of Guelph, intending to become a doctor until she realized that she couldn't use a scalpel on anything alive. This required a change in direction. Fortunately, she was taking an introductory economics course and fell in love with the ideas (and *look, Mom ... no blood!*). She has a master's degree in Economics from the University of Guelph and for the past 20 years has made her career as a teaching professor at her alma mater. By her calculations, she has taught the equivalent of the population of a small city various economics courses at the first-, second-, and third-year levels. Her favourite is the first year, with class sizes ranging from 300 to 600 students, because this is the year in which many students experience "aha moments" when it comes to economics. Their 18-year-old minds also keep her young.

Richard Maranta grew up in Brampton, Ontario, and graduated with a Master of Arts in English Literature from the University of Waterloo, focusing on critical theory and self-destructive American authors such as William Faulkner. Richard went on to obtain a Bachelor of Education from the University of Ottawa with the goal of becoming a secondary school teacher. However, he eventually ended up working for the dearly departed Nortel Networks in technical education and communications. He went on to co-found a company called Pinched Head, which develops innovative online courses for corporate clients. Richard continues to write and work with writers to say what needs to be said. For fun, he plays video games but has reluctantly come to realize that that he will never be as good at them as his two sons, who he used to let win.

Making Introductions

Either write something worth reading or do something worth writing.

Benjamin Franklin (1706–1790), American politician and polymath[1]

I am a woman[2] who is optimistic, extroverted, and an economist. (Oh dear, this sounds like one of those profiles in a dating service. All it needs is ... *who enjoys long walks on the beach and going to parties*.) As frivolous as it sounds, I really do enjoy going to parties: cocktail parties, wine and cheese parties, dinner parties, and ordinary barbecues. Dress-up parties hold a special place in my heart. The more haute[3], the better. It's not just the party itself that I enjoy, but I find getting ready for the party fun as well. I can spend hours deciding which of my many little black dresses I should wear; I have more than I need but that doesn't stop me from buying another. These dresses call to me from the store window as I pass by them. (Let's not mention shoes, shall we?) Black is such a slimming colour, and it can be accessorized with elegant shawls and jewellery of all kinds. I favour bigger, flashier pieces right now. If writing a book called *Cocktail Party Economics* requires experience at cocktail parties, then I have it.

So, how did I come to the write an economics book? It wasn't on a dark and stormy night or in a land far, far away. Rather, it all started after attending different social gatherings where, as an economics professor, I am often asked economics-type questions such as

- "Have interest rates bottomed out and should I lock in my mortgage?"

- "As a recent grad, what can I do to get a good job?"

- "Should the government bail out the car companies?"

- "What is the subprime mortgage market anyway, and why has it thrown Wall Street and the global economy into disarray?"

Usually, in order to do these questions justice, I find myself having to embark on a five-minute mini-lesson in economics. Since I am at a social affair, I'm not sure people want to spend a lot of time on this. In these kinds of situations, I feel like I end up arming people with random bits of ineffective economic knowledge without providing the

---

[1] A polymath is a person who has expertise in many and diverse areas. Benjamin Franklin was an inventor, writer, scientist, postmaster, printer, civic activist, and diplomat, as well as a founding father of the United States. I think it's safe to say he did things worth writing about and wrote things worth reading.

[2] This book follows the tradition of *Freakonomics,* which is the result of a writing partnership between economist Steven Levitt and author Stephen Dubner. Good writing requires both something worth saying and the ability to say it well. We thought that the use of a single voice—that of the economist, Eveline Adomait—would improve the book.

[3] *Haute couture* is French for "high sewing" or "high dressmaking" and refers to the creation of exclusive custom clothing.

necessary context within the big picture. However, big pictures require time to create—time that's not always available at a cocktail party.

On other occasions, the encounters are more confrontational in nature (this can happen after a few too many drinks). During the usual small talk at a cocktail party, an individual might make a bold statement that has something to do with economics. This person might assert any of the following while frantically waving a swizzle stick:

- "We should stop buying all this cheap stuff from China. It's costing us jobs."
- "How can you drink anything other than fair trade coffee?"
- "The government is selling the environment down the river by letting power plants buy pollution permits."
- "It's outrageous how much money athletes make."

It is a difficult party for me indeed if I hear all of these statements on the same night. At some point, I have to decide whether to enter into the fray. If I choose to respond, the ensuing debate can often feel like a "hit and run" encounter that I am sure to regret the next morning. (I have on more than one occasion told my husband to nudge me if the conversation goes on too long or becomes too intense.)

ECONOMICS + COCKTAIL PARTY = A BOOK

Economics is the study of mankind in the ordinary business of life.
Alfred Marshall (1842–1924), British economist

I find that any answers I provide, both to the polite questions and during any ensuing conflicts, end up being unsatisfying mostly because of their brevity. This dissatisfaction with my own ability to communicate economics clearly and concisely during cocktail parties has motivated me to write a book that fleshes out the various conversations I have started at social functions. When I told my friends what I planned to do, they thought it was a great idea for their own separate reasons. But one thing was common: They were all tired of feeling lost when presented with complicated economic news stories or financial discussions. Since most of them do not have the time or inclination to take a university course to learn more, I decided to offer this book as an easy way for them to gain a more complete understanding of economic principles.

My friends kindly warned me that the book would have to be fun to read or no one would buy it. *Gasp* … I definitely did not want to write a book that no one would want to buy. I am an economist, after all. So I asked myself, *How can I write a book about economics that is also entertaining to read?* To be honest, I didn't really know. So, I solicited friends, family, colleagues, and even random strangers I met at parties for help, and help me they did. Their every critique, comment, and question caused me to edit my manuscript. (This book has been rewritten more times than I want to think about.) One particularly helpful comment came from my darling husband, who reminded me: "People like stories, and you should add as many as you can." I took his advice to heart and decided to start every chapter with a party story that in some way connects with the ideas in that chapter. What is unusual about these stories is that I have placed you, the reader, in them. Don't worry, the scenarios are relatively ordinary party situations and involve believable conversations, so you shouldn't feel uncomfortable. There's nothing outrageous.

As well, the book contains illustrations and real-world examples to help make the economic concepts relevant. The footnotes are extensive, sometimes expanding a thought and other times offering a bit of relevant trivia. I also happen to be a "quote-aholic" and have littered the pages with quotations[4] that are sometimes discussed directly in the text or are obliquely connected. (If a quotation doesn't make much sense to you, I wouldn't worry about it. There will be plenty more.) I have tried to make my examples and illustrations accessible and make the text as entertaining as possible. I hope it works for you.

Thinking Like an Economist

Art consists of limitation. The most beautiful part of every picture is the frame.
Gilbert K. Chesterton (1874–1936), British author

Although one of my goals is to make economics fun to read, this book follows the pattern of a typical introductory text in terms of logic and topic progression. The logic of economics requires a systematic approach in order to truly understand what is going on. Because economics is fundamentally a way of thinking rather than a collection of idiosyncratic examples, after 20 years of telling a particular story I can't really write an economics book that doesn't build from the ground up. I want people to learn something about the elegant framework that surrounds all of the interesting applications found in the popular economics books on the market today. Like a great little black dress, basic economic concepts are timeless—relevant during both economic crisis and economic calm. Therefore, while I wrote this book to be understood by people who have never picked up an economics textbook, those who are taking or have taken an introductory economics course will recognize the flow of ideas but without the mathematics. Think of this book as Econo-Lite—enough to give you a buzz but not enough to have your keys taken away from you. For those of you who have no background in economics, don't worry. This one's for you. My friends made sure of it.

Reconcilable Differences

Burn the mathematics.
Alfred Marshall (1842–1924), English economist

We have to thank the eminent economist Alfred Marshall for the mathematical direction that economics textbooks have taken, although—as we can see from the quotation—even he felt that analysis had to be more than just high-powered math. Out of necessity, most economists have become pretty good at math, which can be a conversation killer at parties if the economic conversation drifts toward calculus or algebra. (A bit of advice:

---

[4] In order to satisfy copyright laws, most quotations are from people who have been dead for at least 50 years or who are quoted in a book. This eliminated great quotations from speeches, television or radio interviews, songs, poems, and general hearsay. I hope the loss isn't felt too keenly. Look at this book as containing a brief history of old thoughts!

Should you discover that an economist is coming to your party, hide the paper napkins and remove any pens from sight beforehand. This will prevent mathematical doodling.) Thankfully, this does not mean that the underlying ideas can be understood only with the language of mathematics. This book uses plain English and simple stories to explain the central concepts of economics that, in some form or another, we can find discussed everywhere—from media outlets to dinner parties. Sometimes the economics concept is accurately represented, but not always. I want to help you be able to tell the difference.

Having said that words and stories will be the main vehicle used to travel down this road of economic enlightenment, I must confess that you will find a couple of chapters (well, actually, more than a couple, if a couple for you literally means two) that will require you to look at a few pictures. Okay, okay, I mean *graphs*. But don't let that scare you. If you consider them equivalent to a root canal, you can detour around them to more palatable sections. However, I promise that if you persevere, you will be way ahead of others when it comes to understanding how markets work. I have tried to make these chapters as user-friendly as possible. To give you a heads up, I have designated them as Venti[5].

A Few Caveats

Again, most of the chief distinctions marked by economic terms are differences not of kind but of degree.

Alfred Marshall

We all know that how we use words makes a difference. Unfortunately, economists take everyday, ordinary words and use them to describe very specific economic concepts— words like *scarcity*, *costs*, *producers*, *firms*, *money*, and *investments*. Within economics, these words take on very precise and, some would say, peculiar meanings. The familiar is used in an unfamiliar way, which can cause some confusion until you understand exactly what is meant. If a word seems strange in the way it's used, try to suspend judgment about it until you have finished reading the book. I promise that the words will begin to take on new meaning for you in the context of economics.

Furthermore, like most social sciences, economics has some measure of the common sense about it. You don't need to understand economic concepts to live out your economic life any more than you need to understand psychology to be a good parent or boss. But "knowledge is power," or so they say.[6] By understanding the big ideas behind economics and getting to know the lingo, you can feel smarter, especially at a party. It will also give you another topic of conversation in addition to your work, family, or favourite sports team. Seriously, though, it can make your common sense work a little harder for you as you make important life decisions.

Finally, while it is very tempting to jump directly to the chapter that most interests you, I recommend that you read the book from beginning to end. I have sequenced the ideas in a logical progression to lay the foundation for the economic ideas that follow.

---

[5]   *Venti* means 20 in Italian and is the largest size of coffee (20 oz.) sold by Starbucks. Coffee helped me to write this book.

[6]   From the Latin phrase *scientia potentia est*, stated originally by Sir Francis Bacon in *Meditations Sacrae* (1597).

The goal of this approach is to help you better understand the underlying economics of any real-world situation. Hopefully your conversations at cocktail parties about economics will have not only sizzle but substance as well. Also, wouldn't it feel great to be able to move on to another conversation when some show-off at a party goes on and on about the markets—not because you don't understand what he or she is saying but because other conversations and people interest you more? I hope this book empowers you in this way.

The One-Liner Notes

> *All we are trying to do is give the public good entertainment. That is all they want.*
>
> Walter Elias "Walt" Disney (1901–1966), American creator of Walt Disney Productions
> Taken from *The Gospel According to Disney: Faith, Trust, and Pixie Dust*[7]

I truly wish I could say that my goal is solely to entertain, but that wouldn't be true. I also want you to learn some economics, and that can only happen if you read *Cocktail Party Economics* carefully. Because it can take some time to work your way through a chapter, it may be possible that you will lose sight of the main point once you reach the end of the chapter. To help prevent this from happening, I have included a feature called the Cocktail Napkin Note. This one-liner summarizes the main idea of the chapter—the take-away thought, so to speak. Here is this chapter's note. I hope by now (or at least by the end of the book) you will be able to agree with it.

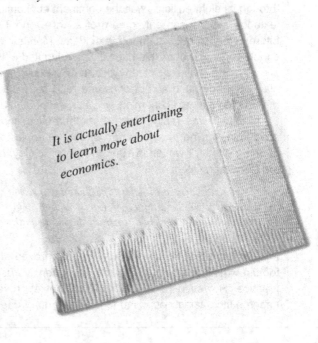

It is actually entertaining to learn more about economics.

Stargazing

> *Martyrdom ... is the only way in which a man can become famous without ability.*
>
> George Bernard Shaw (1856–1950), Irish playwright
> Taken from *The Devil's Disciple* (1901)

As an added touch, somewhere in each chapter I feature a famous economist in a section called Gossip Column. (This is the equivalent to name-dropping at a party.) I have

---

[7]   By Mark I. Pinsky (Louisville, KY: Westminster John Knox Press, 2004).

included many of the early economics writers along with a few Nobel Memorial Prize[8] laureates.

To get things rolling, let me introduce you to a man mentioned four times in this chapter. Unfortunately for him, he never won the Nobel Prize in Economics (worth 10 million Swedish kronor) because he died before the first one was handed out in 1969. Nevertheless, he changed how economics would be taught forever. His name is Alfred Marshall.

Gossip Column

Alfred Marshall was born in 1842 in London, England, and died in 1924 in Cambridge, England. He was one of the most influential economists of his time, teaching at Cambridge University. He wrote a textbook called *Principles of Economics* (1890) that, through its eight editions, was the dominant economics textbook for half a century. (Most textbook authors can only dream of such a run.) This book laid the foundation for all future introductory texts. In terms of ideas, Marshall was the first to draw a demand and supply curve in a book (although it was relegated to the book's appendix). These curves are now the mainstay of any economics book. He also contributed the concepts of elasticity of demand and of consumer and producer surplus.[9] For many years, a common saying among economists was "It's all in Marshall."

Marshall was really good at mathematics and could keep up with the best of academia, but he never wanted ordinary people to feel that economics was beyond them. In a letter[10] written in 1906 to Arthur Bowley, he laid out (in interesting grammar) the following system:

> *(1) Use mathematics as shorthand language, rather than as an engine of inquiry. (2) Keep to them till you have done. (3) Translate into English. (4) Then illustrate by examples that are important in real life. (5) Burn the mathematics. (6) If you can't succeed in 4, burn 3. This I do often.*

I like to think that Marshall would have approved of the non-mathematical approach I took in writing this book along with my extensive use of footnotes, which was also his practice. However, he would probably not approve of my career. It seems that he became increasingly opposed to the granting of degrees to women, which is quite odd

---

[8] This prize is technically not a Nobel Prize. Alfred Nobel, the inventor of dynamite, left funds for five prizes. They are awarded in Peace, Literature, Chemistry, Physiology or Medicine, and Physics, and were first awarded in 1901. Sweden's central bank established The Sveriges Riksbank Prize in Economic Sciences in Memory of Alfred Nobel in 1968. It is added to the mix with the other prizes and is awarded using the same system. Depending on the exchange rate, this prize is worth approximately US$1.5 million. The new prize is not without controversy, however. Peter Nobel, the great-grandnephew of Alfred, has criticized the creation of this award and its association with authentic Nobel Prizes. The Nobel Foundation refers to it as the Prize in Economics, with no mention of Nobel.

[9] See Chapter 9 for more on the concepts of producer and consumer surplus.

[10] The letter to Bowley was included in a book on Marshall, which was edited by Marshall's protege Arthur Cecil Pigou (another famous economist). The book is *Memorials of Alfred Marshall*, published by Macmillan in 1925, and the letter is on pages 427 and 428. Bowley took only a short course with Marshall but it changed the direction of his life. He became an economist who worked on economic statistics.

given that he married one of his students, Mary Paley Marshall. Mary was one of the first women to study at Cambridge University, but she was debarred from graduation because she was a woman. This did not stop her from doing the work of an academic. She lectured at Cambridge and was regarded as an excellent teacher, economist, and unofficial collaborator of Marshall's work. It is not entirely clear why he opposed the granting of degrees to women.[11]

Marshall was raised to enter the clergy but defied his parents and became an academic in mathematics and economics instead. I, on the other hand, was raised by a member of the clergy (like Mary and Arthur) but was never expected to become a minister, or to become an academic for that matter—especially in the field of economics. My parents are both surprised by and proud of my accomplishments. I am so grateful that universities now grant degrees to women.

---

[11] *The Oxford Dictionary of National Biography* offers more about the lives of economists Alfred and Mary Marshall.

CHAPTER 1

It's All about Scarcity

It is no crime to be ignorant of economics, which is, after all, a specialized discipline and one that most people consider a "dismal science." But it is totally irresponsible to have a loud and vociferous opinion on economic subjects while remaining in this state of ignorance.

Murray Newton Rothbard (1926–1995), American economist
Taken from *Making Economic Sense* (1995)

It has been a long day and you just want to go home and watch *American Idol,* but your employer has asked you to attend a networking cocktail party on behalf of the firm. As you enter the room, clusters of people catch your attention. Straight ahead, in front of the French doors leading to the patio, a group of men appear to conduct several simultaneous conversations with each other and with their BlackBerrys. You overhear their verbal competition about who is busier and getting less sleep. One thing they all do agree on: There are not enough hours in a day.

On your right, stationed near a food table, a group of well-dressed women gather, each with a martini in one hand and a plate of crudités in the other. Earlier in the day they wore jackets over sheath dresses, but for this event the jackets are off and high heels and "bling" have been added. *Vogue* would be proud of them for their transformation from office to evening wear using the same basic dress. Most of them nod in agreement as one woman states matter-of-factly, "Dating is so difficult. It seems all the good ones are taken."

Suddenly your attention is diverted by raised voices between two "suits" in the corner. Words like *idiotic* and *ridiculous* are volleyed back and forth as they argue over how the government should spend the taxpayers' money. It is clear that they unashamedly support different political parties. You start to wonder if both of them have taken their blood pressure meds—but, then again, that might not mix well with the 12-year-old Scotch they're drinking.

Before joining any of these conversations, you decide that it might be a good idea to get fortified for the evening ahead. As you walk to the bar you think to yourself, "What kind of party is this going to be, anyway?"

A SCARCITY MENTALITY

The first lesson of economics is scarcity. There is never enough of anything to satisfy all those who want it. The first lesson of politics is to disregard the first lesson of economics.

Thomas Sowell (1930–), American writer and economist
Taken from *Is Reality Optional?: And Other Essays* (1993)

Welcome to the fascinating world of economics. You might not notice this right away, but each of the conversations in the opening vignette in one way or another illustrates the idea of scarcity—a foundational economic concept. We have all heard that "a good man is hard to find," or that there is not enough time in the day, or that we need more government funding. All of these conversations say something about what is scarce. Let's look more closely at this idea.

A "Stones Story"

Suppose that, like Diane Keaton's character in the movie *Something's Gotta Give*, I enjoy meandering along a deserted beach and collecting perfectly flat, round, white, smooth stones. What if, on one particular occasion, I dig up 10 stones with an unusual black stripe down the middle and am so enraptured with them that I decide to bring them along to the party I attend that evening. Suppose that, while at the party, I feel generous and offer them to anyone who wants one, but to my surprise no one does? This exercise reveals to me that even though the stones are available in a finite number (10), they are not—and I repeat, not—scarce. Apparently I was the only one who thought the stones were worth collecting. Now, that is not really a big problem except for the fact that I have to transport them home again and I might feel a little embarrassed that my treasures were rejected. (I can just imagine the comments when people get home, starting with "What was she thinking?")

If, on the other hand, the stones create a sensation and 20 people clamour after the 10 stones, there would be a problem. We would now consider these stones a scarce commodity, because there are more people who want them than there are stones available. If 100 people wanted them, the stones would become even scarcer. Therefore, we can conclude that scarcity is fundamentally a relative term rather than an absolute one. It captures the idea of limited resources (10 stones) relative to multiple potential recipients.

The Implication of Scarcity

Find ... sermons in stones, and good in everything.

William Shakespeare (1564–1616), English playwright
Taken from *As You Like It*

This scenario of stones demonstrates that scarcity creates problems that need solving. You might ask, "What kinds of problems?" First, we have the problem of who gets the scarce item. If 20 people want the stones, then of the 20 who ask for one, only 10 will receive a stone. Second, we have the problem of distribution. There needs to be some kind of system that gets the stones into the hands of the right 10 people. Given that I own these stones, it seems reasonable that I make the decision on the means of distribution. But I have options, so there are choices to be made.

I could do any of the following:

1. Hand them out on a first-come, first-served basis (queuing).
2. Put everyone's name in a hat and draw the 10 winners (lottery).
3. Give them to 10 of my dearest friends or family members (favouritism or nepotism).
4. Set up some kind of contest where the top 10 take the prize (tournament).
5. Ask Miss Manners for advice on who ought to get them (social norms).
6. Auction them to the highest bidder (market).
7. Cut them in half and give a piece to everyone (rationing).

Or, the matter could be taken out of my hands completely if someone

8. Steals them from me and hands them out in the manner of Robin Hood.

Each method listed above can allocate these scarce stones. Markets are just one method in this rather long list of choices, yet it is the one allocation method that is most near and dear to an economist's heart. Here's why: The problem is not simply getting the stones into somebody's hands, but rather getting them into the right hands. I will talk later about what "right" might mean, but for now understand that economists generally see markets as the preferred allocation method because they can perform the task most effectively. This book unapologetically advocates for markets, but you will have to wait until Chapter 9 to get "the full Monty" on why economists think markets allocate resources better. This is not to say that the markets work in every situation. In fact, I devote Chapter 11 to market failures and possible solutions. Most of the solutions we prefer as economists are market-based. Only when functioning markets are not possible will most economists concede that one of the other methods should kick in and allocate scarce resources.

Gossip Column

Lionel Charles Robbins, or Baron Robbins of Clare Market (1898–1984), was a British economist of considerable influence. He is famous (among economists) for his classic definition of economics. Robbins also shifted Anglo-Saxon economics away from ideas put forth by Alfred Marshall and his followers (see the Gossip Column feature in Making Introductions) through the various essays he wrote and through his hires at the London School of Economics and Political Science (LSE) of great economists who thought differently than the Cambridge group. (He did become friends with Cambridge academic Lord John Maynard Keynes, or Lord Keynes[1], a very famous economist who changed the way governments spend money, so the issues were differences in views about how the economy works, not university snobbery. In fact, Robbins wrote a book titled *The Great Depression,* published in 1934, that decried the Keynesian stimulus spending approach. He would later recant his negative views on stimulus spending and in his autobiography expressed his wish that the book be forgotten. Generally, his wish has been granted.)

Robbins became the chair of the Economics department at the LSE in 1929, but was required by the university to resign in 1961 in order to take the positions of chairman of the *Financial Times* and director of *The Economist*. It seems that Robbins thought he could both be chair of the department and work for a newspaper. To his great disappointment, the university didn't agree and forced on him this opportunity cost. Fortunately, Robbins was able to devote his efforts to the paper and gave *The Economist* the academic credentials it needed to become the premier economics magazine it continues to be to this day. Robbins remained committed to the LSE, giving public lectures, teaching courses, and acting as the chair of its Court of Governors. In recognition of his efforts, the LSE named a building after him.

---

[1] Keynes was, like Robbins, a mere baron and would have been addressed as Lord Keynes.

Robbins was a man of considerable influence in many spheres of British life. During World War II he was director of the economic section of the war cabinet offices. He was also the chairman of the National Gallery and director of the Royal Opera House and Covent Garden. In 1959, he was given a life peerage (one of the first offered) and became Baron Robbins of Clare Market in the City of Westminster.[2] He was also responsible for the direction of the British university system because of the Robbins report (1963). Robbins was an academic economist who had a practical influence.[3]

THE CLASSIC DEFINITION OF ECONOMICS

Economics is the science which studies human behaviour as a relationship between given ends and scarce means which have alternative uses.

Baron Lionel Robbins (1898–1984), British economist
Taken from *An Essay on the Nature and Significance of Economic Science* (1932)

Although the above definition of economics by Baron Robbins is a classic, it certainly sounds dull—definitely not something you want to quote at a cocktail party. If you understand it, however, you will realize that it has profound implications. Robbins points to scarcity as the key idea in economics since, without scarcity, no economic problem exists because all people can have as much of everything as they want. (Heaven[4], here we come!) This means that nothing needs to be allocated, making markets, as one method of allocating things, unnecessary. Scarcity, therefore, sits at the root of all economics in general and markets in particular. Once something is scarce, it is no longer free for the taking, which creates an allocation problem that needs solving. Now we are definitely back on Earth.

So What's It Gonna Cost?

Where there is no choice, we do well to make no difficulty.

George MacDonald (1824–1905), Scottish author

Anyone who has spent a day at the mall—whether working or shopping—knows that acquiring things takes time, energy, and resources. Simply put, the greater the scarcity of something, the more it *costs* to acquire. Economists want to know what you gave up in order to acquire a particular item because people usually must give up something in order to get something else. What you forgo actually reveals the cost of what you chose. The official term for what we give up is *opportunity cost*.

---

[2] In the United Kingdom, life peers (as opposed to inherited peers) are created members of the Peerage whose titles may not be inherited by their children. Life peerages are created under the Life Peerages Act of 1958, always at the rank of baron, and entitle the holders to seats in the House of Lords if they meet certain qualifications such as age and citizenship.

[3] *The Oxford Dictionary of National Biography* is a good place to go if you are interested in learning more about Lord Robbins. It is now available online.

[4] Gordon, Scott. (1980). "The Economics of the Afterlife." *Journal of Political Economy, 88* (February): 213–214. In this paper, Gordon argues that scarcity could still exist in heaven.

Opportunity cost carries with it the idea that every choice you make implies a choice for an alternative that you did *not* make. Let me put it this way. If a situation involves a choice between two alternatives, the choice you finally make means that you have lost or given up the other possible choice. Opportunity cost is the choice you didn't make—the opportunity lost.

Here is an extreme example. In the movie *Sophie's Choice*, a sadistic soldier forces Sophie to choose which of her two children would live and which would die. In a gut-wrenching scene, Sophie finally chooses that her son live and has to live with that choice for the rest of her life. The cost to save her son was very real—the death of her daughter. The moral of the story is this: Every choice involves loss, and that loss is a cost. In Sophie's case, the loss was devastating. For most of us, the losses involved in everyday choices are minor. When I choose to have a coffee, I decide against having a tea. Not a big cost, but still a cost that represents an economic reality.

Let's see if we can find a lighter artistic example to illustrate the subject of costly choices. In Robert Frost's poem *"The Road Not Taken,"*[5] we find the narrator musing over the attractiveness of the paths ahead. If an economist attempted to analyze this poem, he or she would want to put a value on the road not taken in order to determine the cost for the one taken. Moreover, there is no universal cost to this road because the road not taken can be different for different people. For example, if I choose a coffee for my afternoon break, I might be passing up on a tea, whereas someone else might forgo a soft drink or bottled water. In other words, the personal (opportunity) cost for choosing a particular road differs from person to person. When observed from the outside, it is often very difficult to identify the true cost of someone's choice since most people's second option—the road not taken—remains a private matter.

Other times, however, the opportunity costs are quite public for all to see. Such was the case with two British men who lived around the same time. Each of them made similar choices but with very different costs. C.S. Lewis (1898–1963) and King Edward VIII (1894–1972) were both bachelors who decided to marry divorced women. King Edward chose to marry Wallis Simpson and willingly gave up his throne because of the laws surrounding divorce and the monarchy. C.S. Lewis, on the other hand, was required to give up only his bachelor pad at Oxford University, which he gladly did as well. It may well be that Lewis loved Joy Gresham as much as King Edward loved Wallis Simpson, but the truth of the matter is that King Edward paid the larger price for that love. In his mind, Wallis Simpson's love was scarce and worth the price.

Time Is Relative

The only reason for time is so that everything doesn't happen at once.

Albert Einstein (1875–1955), Nobel Prize–winning physicist

Getting back to the men at our cocktail party, they don't seem like the kind of guys who have a lot of time for romantic stories about the scarcity of love in the lives of King Edward VIII and C.S. Lewis. These men care more about the scarcity of time. They all

---

[5]   Robert Frost (1874–1963) published the poem "The Road Not Taken" in 1916 in his collection *Mountain Interval*. It was the first poem in the book and the first poem he printed entirely in italics.

agree on that. After all, who can argue with the facts that there are only 24 hours in a day and that death is 100 percent certain?

Even though we can agree that time is limited, that doesn't mean that the level of scarcity of time is the same for everyone. In other words, individuals have different opportunity costs for time. For instance, retirees who often talk of having *a lot of time on their hands* are much more willing to wait at the doctor's office than people who have to *take time off work* to do so. Some teenagers and young adults will camp out for days to get tickets for a concert or the latest game consoles, whereas busy executives might pay someone else to stand in line to purchase these items for them. Busy people look at time as a series of costly choices. Bill Gates captured this idea when he said, "Just in terms of allocation of time resources, religion is not very efficient.[6] There is a lot more I could be doing on Sunday morning."[7]

Bill Gates is right in stating that religion takes time away from an activity that makes him a lot of money. Anything other than work can be expensive to pursue if you earn a high salary. Research has shown that men with higher-paying jobs work more and sleep less then men with lower-paying jobs.[8] Economists explain this phenomenon by saying that men with high-paying jobs have greater opportunity costs for a little "R and R" than men with low-paying jobs. For them, it is a costly decision to not be working. A big paycheque is a form of "golden handcuffs" that keep well-paid men chained to their desks.

Cocktail Party Etiquette

Dear Miss Manners: What about Easter? I suppose you have etiquette rules that apply to Easter Day?

Gentle Reader: Certainly, and when the Day of Judgment comes, Miss Manners will have etiquette rules to apply to that, as well.

Judith Martin (1938–), American writer
Taken from *Miss Manners' Guide to Excruciatingly Correct Behavior*

For any of you who have resorted to multi-tasking as a time management solution, here's the skinny. You can't really do two *competing*[9] things at the same time. You

---

[6]   Now that Bill Gates has retired from Microsoft and technically has more time, he can rethink his Sunday morning activities, but even when he was running Microsoft it still might have been "efficient" to go to church. Part of efficiency is how much Gates values the experience compared to how much time he has available. The quotation simply reveals that Gates doesn't value religion enough to use his scarce time in that way. A change in his values would change what choice is deemed "efficient." See Chapter 2 for more on this topic.

[7]   *Time*, January 13, 1996.

[8]   Biddle, Jeff E., & Hamermesh, Daniel S. (1990). Sleep and the allocation of time. *The Journal of Political Economy, 98*(5), 922–943. Approximately one-third of adult life is spent sleeping, but these numbers are not the same for everyone. Biddle and Hamermesh found evidence that there is some variability in who sleeps how much. Women, on average, sleep 20 minutes less per night than men do. Higher wages reduce sleep time for men but small children reduce sleep time for women.

[9]   Strayer, David L., Drews, Frank A., & Crouch, Dennis J. (2006). A comparison of the cell phone driver and the drunk driver. *Human Factors: The Journal of the Human Factors and Ergonomics Society, 48*(2), 381–391. Chewing gum and walking are not competing activities. On the other hand, driving and using a

might think you can, but you can't. The amount of time you give to one activity simply means that there is less time for the other. Because time is scarce, you must make choices and these choices are going to cost you. The minute you spend on your smart phone costs you a minute of meaningful face-to-face conversation with the person beside you. The cost of face-to-face interaction is the text message you didn't read in that moment. The choice is very simple but meaningful in terms of understanding opportunity costs.

Now, here is the test. Tell me what you should do when a call comes in on your BlackBerry during a party. Do you take it or continue with your conversation? Which activity gets your precious time? Unfortunately, markets can't provide you with the solution in a social setting like this. Fortunately, someone like Miss Manners[10] could help solve this dilemma with one of her Gentle Reader answers. Of all of the allocation methods available to solve this particular time problem, I'm afraid that only social norms have a fighting chance of optimally allocating your time.

Here is some advice that Miss Manners would probably give: A cocktail party is just that—a party. It is a social thing, so you should keep it social. When you go to a cocktail party, don't be like the men in our story who are trying to talk and text at the same time, because you will end up doing neither very well. As Eckhart Tolle would say, "be in the moment" so the party doesn't turn out to be a boring, collective waste of time for everybody. Turn your ringer off and resist answering if you can. (Unless, of course, your wife is going into labour and needs to contact you.) This is the polite thing to do. Thank you. Thank you very much.

Single, Educated Female Looking for Soulmate

God give me a rich husband though he be an ass.

Thomas Fuller (1654–1734), English preacher, physician, and writer
Taken from *Gnomologia* (1732)

Now that we have dealt with the conversationally challenged men in our story, let's turn our attention to the well-dressed women who felt that all the "good ones" were taken. Are they? Well, given what these women might define as a good man, it is probably true.

Research has shown that educated women can be somewhat picky when it comes to finding a suitable marriage partner. In general, they want a man who has as much or more education as they do.[11] You've heard the phrase *beggars can't be choosers*?

---

cellphone seem to require the same faculties. Researchers found that using a cellphone while driving was similar to driving drunk.

[10] Recommended reading: *Miss Manners' Guide to Excruciatingly Correct Behavior, Freshly Updated* by Judith Martin (1938–). See the chapter on Electronic Communication. It should be noted that Martin's father was an economist with the United Nations.

[11] Susan Lewis and Valerie Oppenheimer, in their paper "Educational Assortative Mating across Marriage Markets," found that, in the United States from 1979 to 1992, 64 percent of "marriageable" women married. Of the women who married, 70 percent married "up" in terms of education. In areas of the United States that were more "thin" on educated men, women were more likely to marry "down," especially as they aged. In areas where men were not as scarce, women were more likely to wait for the right "educated" guy.

Well-educated women don't have to be beggars, because they tend to be financially independent and can afford to wait for Mr. Right or choose to stay single. However, if they have some urgency regarding marriage (saying that they are "desperate" to get married doesn't quite sound right), then the numbers don't work in their favour. On average, the college and university student population is about 60 percent female.[12] Furthermore, should our well-educated women require additional qualities in terms of height, religion, race, or other important traits, the search for Mr. Right gets even tougher. So it is true: A particular type of good man *is* hard to find; in fact, he is quite scarce. What do these women do when they want to marry an educated man? Can markets help? Let's find out.

Make Me a Match, Find Me a Find, Catch Me a Catch

Someone interesting ...

Taken from *Fiddler on the Roof* (1964)

Usually, when women want to get married, they put great effort into meeting men. Attendance at cocktail parties is one way to do this. I guess the hope is that, once they meet someone, sparks will fly and a match made in heaven will transpire. However, it's not always that easy. The scarcer these men become, the greater effort a woman must put into searching for them. Consequently, she must give up something of value in order to make this effort, which means that this effort has an opportunity cost. She can take her valuable time and go where the men are (which is like a queue) or join some kind of dating service to have it search for her (a market). Either way, it is costing her time and/or money.

If she thinks that the search for Mr. Educated Right is too expensive (i.e., the opportunity cost is too high), she can opt out of the market altogether and stay single or simply change markets and go after less educated men who are more abundant. Don't take this the wrong way, but these men are easier (and economists would say cheaper) to find. Essentially, these women find themselves engaged in what is called a marriage market, which has all of the usual features of markets. This market allocates scarce men to women who will pay the price to find them. It gives a whole new meaning to the term *meet market,* doesn't it?

The Politics of Choice

Real politics are the possession and distribution of power.

Benjamin Disraeli (1804–1881), British prime minister

When General John Vessey, Jr. served as the chairman of the Joint Chiefs of Staff under U.S. President Ronald Reagan, he commented that a "resource-constrained environment" was really another way of saying there wasn't enough money to go around. Vessey's observation still captures the economic tension involved in political choices and explains why the "suits" at the cocktail party in our opening story end up arguing about politics. Once a government has set its budget, it must still divide that budget

---

[12]   Christofides, Louis N., Hoy, Michael, & Yang, Ling. (2006). The Gender Imbalance in Participation in Canadian Universities (1977–2003). University of Guelph discussion paper.

between competing recipients. Supplying one rifle to one soldier might mean that an elementary school class doesn't get the publicly funded swimming lessons it wants. If that is how the government decides to slice the cake, the cost of the rifle can be measured in terms of swimming lessons not given. If you are a kid who wants to learn to swim, the cost is very disappointing. But it goes both ways. When a soldier faces an enemy, the government's decision to allocate funds to a classroom of 10-year-olds instead of arming her with a weapon becomes a very significant cost to her.

The reality is that government officials, who may or may not represent your personal wishes, make these spending decisions all the time. It's no wonder that government budgets get people riled up. They cause voters in democratic countries to support political parties in the hope that, upon a party's victory, their elected leader will represent at least some of their interests. Although this is an indirect way of getting what you want, sometimes getting involved in politics is the only alternative.

Governments use most of the allocation methods mentioned above to distribute the scarce resources they manage. They do everything from organizing people into queues in emergency rooms to rationing supplies during natural disasters. They are involved in market activities when they collect tolls on roads. Sometimes they employ nepotism, which tends to generate a flurry of letters to the editor from those who are "shocked and appalled" once it is uncovered, which is why politicians try so hard to cover this type of thing up. In less democratic countries, bribes and payoffs are the cultural norm in allocating scarce resources to particular people. Although this is a backhanded type of market, it is still a market.

Generally, governments tend to get more involved in the areas where markets don't seem to work well. In Chapter 11, the problem of market failures will explain why governments are necessary to provide the optimal allocation of scarce resources when unregulated markets cannot.

SO, HOW DOES ONE GET A DRINK AROUND HERE?

Be careful to trust a person who does not like wine.

Karl Marx (1818–1883), German philosopher, political economist, and revolutionary

Finally, you have made it to the bar! I think it's fair to assume that if alcoholic beverages were free, the number of drinks that people would want would exceed the number of drinks available. Wine, beer, and other spirits would therefore be scarce. This is just a more complicated version of the "stones story" earlier in the chapter. Allocating these drinks to drinkers now becomes the challenge. Let's look at some possible solutions.

1. If the party has an open bar that serves drinks on a first-come, first-served basis until they run out, the allocation method would be a form of queue where the early birds get the brew. I hate to tell you this, but in this situation you really will need to get in line and pay for that drink with your time.

2. If the establishment hands out one drink ticket per person (even to the non-drinkers), we have a rationing system. If at this point you happen to want two drinks, you had better try to find some abstainers and convince them to give you their drink ticket.

Here, you pay with the time it takes to search for these people and the effort it takes to negotiate with them.

3. It may be that Miss Manners has decreed that only one drink is socially acceptable at this kind of cocktail party. A social norm of this type will ensure that there's enough to go around as long as no one cheats. Here, you pay with guilt if you cheat—and, in that case, shame on you! For those who come to the bar and find the drinks are all gone—tough luck and don't get too angry about it.

4. The owners of the bar might randomly draw names from a bowl of business cards (lottery); only the winners get to drink, while the losers get to watch the winners drink. Here, it pays to be lucky.

5. The bartender serves drinks only to friends (favouritism). In this case, you might want to be friendlier to the bartender. (As a woman, I don't really want to think about it!)

While each of these methods offers possible solutions for allocating drinks and a few of them are quite common at social settings such as a retirement party or a wedding, this book is all about how markets can allocate the drinks among the drinkers.

Getting to the Swizzle Stick

When you go to a party that has a cash bar, you find yourself in a market setting. If you want a drink, you must take something of value to the bar and exchange it for your desired libation. This is not a good time to forget or lose your wallet. If you have nothing of value to bring to the bar, you will not get a drink even if you are desperate for one. This is the downside of markets, which will be dealt with in Chapter 9. For those of you who have the money for drinks, when you go to the bar you need to realize that whatever you offer to the bartender will no longer be available for you to purchase something else. Therefore, each drink has an opportunity cost.

Ultimately, it is a matter of personal choice whether you decide to buy a drink or not. Each of us must assess the subjective value of the drink relative to its opportunity cost. If the personal value of the drink is more than its opportunity cost (something you could have used the money for instead), you buy. If it's not, you don't bother. In other words, in order for you to buy a drink there has to be nothing else you would rather do with your money at that moment than to buy that drink. Again, if it isn't worth the opportunity cost, you will pass.

Pricing Policy

Flying might not be all plain sailing, but the fun of it is worth the price.
Amelia Mary Earhart (1897–missing July 2, 1937), American aviation pioneer and author[13]

The illustrations discussed in this chapter show that scarcity causes everything to have an opportunity cost associated with it, against which you must compare your subjective

---

[13] Earhart was the first woman to receive the Distinguished Flying Cross because she was the first female pilot to fly solo across the Atlantic Ocean. She set many flying records and wrote two books about her flying experiences, one of which is called *The Fun of It*, published in 1932.

values. Notice that markets have conveniently put numbers on the opportunity costs, which gives you a reference point when making choices. We call these numbers prices, and they are found everywhere and anywhere a market exists. Because the concept of value is related to the concept of scarcity and affects the outcomes of markets, it gets its own chapter. It's time to think about what it means to get some satisfaction.

Scarcity creates costly choices.

CHAPTER 2

Value: Where Emotions and Economics Collide

What is a cynic? A man who knows the price of everything and the value of nothing.

Oscar Wilde (1854–1900), writer of plays, short stories, poems, and novels

The journey to the bar was a long one. The day had progressed as a series of unfortunate events. First thing this morning, you were on the phone with a major client. He refused to pay his bill because he didn't feel your work was "worth it." Your boss found out and became irritated with you.

Mid-morning, your brother called to let you know that your annoying sister-in-law, an art history major, thinks she bought a Jackson Pollock painting at a garage sale over the weekend.[1] An older couple hadn't known what it was and didn't like it. It was taking up too much space in their small house and they were happy to get rid of it. Gritting your teeth, you insincerely say, "That's great. Wow. Congratulations. Hope she's right."

In the middle of the afternoon, you heard more bad news. Your recent round of in vitro fertilization had not worked, and the gynecologist wants to schedule next month's treatment. You think, I don't want to live through that again.

By the end of the day, you felt bagged and just wanted to go home and change into some comfortable clothes. It is just your luck that the CEO dropped by your office and said, "I committed to going to a networking cocktail party, but a client has just invited me to an NBA playoff game, so you will have to go to the party for me." You think, Why does this guy deserve to earn 200 times my salary when all he does is go to sporting events with clients and watch athletes make mega amounts of money for having fun?

Later, while slouching at the bar, you wonder about what makes something valuable. Why is the Pollock painting more valuable than the work you did for your client? Why is the CEO's and the star athlete's time more valuable than yours? These questions are quickly drowned out by the bigger, more personal, questions. Given that it doesn't seem to be working, is it worth all the money you are spending on in vitro, and when is it time to stop trying?

IS ANYTHING PRICELESS?

Honest disagreement is often a good sign of progress.

Mohandas Karamchand Gandhi (1869–1948), Indian political and spiritual leader

When it comes to what we value highly, we sometimes feel that it is in poor taste to put an explicit price tag on it. Those famous "priceless" MasterCard advertisements support our emotional sense that some things are beyond valuation. But I have to disagree. I'm probably going to offend a few people when I say this, but to most economists nothing is truly priceless.

---

[1] It might be far-fetched to think that an original painting could make its way into a garage sale, but sometimes it happens. *Who the #$&% Is Jackson Pollock?* is a documentary about a woman named Teri Horton, a 73-year-old former truck driver who may have purchased a Jackson Pollock painting from a thrift shop for $5. Some in the art community question the painting's authenticity.

Someone might protest: "Who can put a number on the value of a human life?" Be aware that human lives are reduced to a number every day, and rightly so. Authorities often call off searches for missing persons because they can no longer justify the cost of their effort. Doctors, in consultation with family members, pull the plug on patients in hospitals because it is too costly (on many levels) to keep them alive. Lawyers recommend living wills[2] precisely because family members may not see the value of your life in the same way you do. Even if your family is unified, the hospital may take the matter to court because it values your life differently. Ultimately, value is a number[3] and that number is not infinity. The question remains: "Whose number do we use?"

Value Is Subjective ... It's Personal

Things only have the value that we give them.

Molière (1622–1673), French actor and playwright

Just like fingerprints, the preferences, desires, and things that are appreciated differ from one person to the next. This means that people have different trade-offs they are willing to make for just about everything. You, for instance, might be willing to pay for something I wouldn't take even if it was offered to me for free. It seems to me that sometimes the fate of a particular item—be it a couch, bicycle, or teacup—depends on whether a family wants to go through the hassle of having a garage sale to get rid of it. I would much rather just put the item on the curb the night before garbage day in hopes that it "disappears" into a good home.

The older couple in our story obviously thought the Jackson Pollock painting was a problem and they wanted to get rid of it. They knew they didn't value the painting as a work of art in its own right. What they didn't know was how much others would value it. Consequently, not knowing has cost them money. But once things are bought or sold in a market, some of their hidden values are revealed. Prices play a role in separating people who have a high value for something from those who have a low value for it. In the case of the Pollock painting, a series of markets will eventually enable the individual who has the highest valuation for it to actually acquire the painting. The first market (the garage sale) allows the annoying sister-in-law—who values the painting more than the retired couple—to obtain it, but she will resell it to someone else who wants it even more than she does. The final buyer in this chain of markets will keep the painting because he or she values it so much. Without these markets, each person's value for the item remains hidden; however, once someone pays a price, some minimum value can be seen.

... It's More Than Personal

The people who make up various societies and cultures have strong opinions about what we ought to value, and this is expressed in our religions, morality, and cultural norms. However, each cultural group in the world may emphasize some values over others. For instance, some groups place a high value on the life of the unborn child while others

---

2   A document, made by a person when still legally fit to do so, expressing the desire for types of medical intervention when the person is no longer fit to express his or her preferences.

3   The U.S. Environmental Protection Agency default value of a "statistical life" is US$9.1 million (in 2010 dollars).

place a high value on nature in terms of the environment or animal rights. Each group will work tirelessly to promote its causes or values. This is why we see boycotts of existing markets for such things as cosmetics tested on animals or products made in a particular country where people's labour is deemed exploited.

Cultural norms, morality, and even religious convictions can change over time and, with them, so can our values. When societal values change, what we are willing to buy and sell also changes. For example, to people who live in the free world, the idea of owning another human being is morally repugnant. We cannot imagine how anyone could have thought that slavery—the buying and selling of human beings—was a good idea. However, 200 years ago, some seemingly decent individuals in the southern United States had no qualms about owning slaves. Fortunately there has been a shift in values prompting economic change as well.

Answering Questions That Have Answers

It is the business of economists, not to tell us what to do, but show why what we are doing anyway is in accord with proper principles.

Joan Violet Robinson (1903–1983), British economist
Taken from *Economic Philosophy* (1962)

Economists can say a lot about what individuals and societies value, but they have little to say about what *should* be valued. They are very good at holding up a mirror to society and showing it what it really looks like, but they rarely comment on the beauty of the reflection. From an economist's perspective, the main point is this: If you want a picture of what people value, check out their markets. The market tells the truth. You may or may not like that truth but it doesn't change how the real world works. Yes, CEOs of corporations and top athletes do earn "obscene" amounts of money compared to the average person's "pittance" of a salary. Paintings by famous artists do sell for "outrageous" prices while no one would pay a dime for one that looks similar if painted by your beloved child. You can't get away from it. Markets reveal all and serve as exposés on our collective values. Most economists see their role as one that uses market analysis to explain why something is valuable and to explain what forces are at work to change the revealed value, which is known as price. (Also, most economists would never use words like *pittance*, *obscene*, or *outrageous* to describe a price.)

SCARCITY REVEALS VALUE

In every child who is born under no matter what circumstances and of no matter what parents, the potentiality of the human race is born again, and in him, too, once more, and each of us, our terrific responsibility toward human life: toward the utmost idea of goodness, of the horror of terrorism, and of God.

James Rufus Agee (1909–1955), American author

If I were to ask parents to put a dollar figure on how much they love and value their children, they would probably be offended. I can see how my question would be offensive to them. Of course, parents think their children are priceless. But when we look at how most parents acquire children, we can see that they have not actually paid very much to get them. (In fact, the encounter that produced these children could have been quite pleasant!) So, before I begin an analysis of the value placed on babies (and before anyone sends me an angry email), let me state that I agree with the obvious platonic[4] idea that things can have intrinsic value. That value is not infinite, however, but it can certainly be very high. I accept the fact that parents love and value their children. I just think that "high value" means different things to different people. When markets become part of the process of acquiring a child, let's say through adoption or in vitro fertilization, the bottom end of how high parents are willing to go to acquire a baby becomes exposed. Hidden values become public because of monetary transactions.

Let's look at couples who have been diagnosed with infertility (my husband and I are included in this group). For us, the normal way of conceiving and having a child doesn't seem to work. To put it bluntly, for infertile couples like us, babies are scarce. The good news is that an initial diagnosis of infertility may not necessarily lead to childlessness. There are ways of acquiring a child, but because of the scarcity problem it will cost us to do so. Infertile couples pay in terms of time as they wait for appointments with doctors, in terms of discomfort as they endure painful medical procedures, and in terms of money as they have to pay medical specialists. If more and more couples experience infertility, the increased demand on a doctor's time drives up the cost to see that doctor. In the United States, which has a private health care system, infertility specialists' fees will rise; in Canada, which has more public health care system, couples will wait longer to see these doctors. These couples pay either with time (queue) or with money (market). Therefore, the value that potential parents place on a biological baby becomes evident to those around them as they pay, pay, and pay some more.

If medical science cannot produce a baby for these couples, they may shift their efforts toward adopting a child. Essentially, this is a shift to a substitute market. The couples pay even more, both with time as they wait on various adoption lists and with money for adoption services either at home or abroad. In fact, they end up giving money to everyone in the adoption process except the woman who actually gives birth to the child. Ironically, if a couple actually did pay the birth mother directly to give them her baby, many people would become morally offended since, in their minds, it turns babies into a commodity that you can buy or sell. (In some places, surrogacy has created a way for a woman to get paid to have a baby, although it is not legal everywhere.[5])

Every time a couple pays something to acquire a baby, they reveal how much this child is actually worth to them. Each of these payments is the result of the scarcity of babies to infertile couples. As babies become scarcer, the opportunity cost to acquire a child goes up. If it costs more and you pay the cost, then you reveal to those around you that this child is worth at least this much to you. If the child had not been worth the higher opportunity cost, you would have opted out of the market and not paid the price. Economists call this *revealed preferences*. We now have more information about how

---

[4] Plato (428/427–348/347 BC) was a Greek philosopher. He studied under Socrates and was a mentor to Aristotle. In this example, the value of a child is said to be of universal, not just particular, value.

[5] Surrogate mothers sometimes provide the egg, but other times they simply "rent out the womb" to a fertilized egg. If they provide this service for free it is called *altruistic surrogacy*. *Commercial surrogacy* provides the surrogate mother with an income for her actions. This is illegal in Canada but not in India, which is now the world leader in surrogate services.

highly these parents value their children. For some families, babies are the "pearl of greatest price."[6]

I don't think infertile couples are necessarily people who value children more than those for whom pregnancy and childbirth is easy (although "easy" is not how most women would describe the birthing experience). It is just that, for most couples, babies are not hard to acquire and so these couples don't end up revealing their preferences. On a personal note, both Martin and I are very thankful that we adopted our two sons. On a financial note, we are also thankful that we didn't have to mortgage our entire future to do so.

Acquiring children is one thing; raising them is another matter. With the advent of birth control, the decision to have another baby has come to depend on the value of that additional child to the parents and the opportunity cost to raise him or her. For both fertile and infertile couples alike, scarce resources must be used to raise a child. This is probably why most parents do not choose to keep having children until it is physically impossible to do so.

Valuing a Jackson Pollock

I can't change the fact that my paintings don't sell. But the time will come when people will recognize that they are worth more than the value of the paints in the picture.

Vincent van Gogh (1853–1890), Dutch painter

A Jackson Pollock painting sold in 2006 for more than $100 million. Wow. This is partly because Pollock died in 1956 and is obviously no longer painting. The number of Pollock paintings is fixed, although a new one could pop up in someone's storage locker.[7]

However, the concept of scarcity is driven by more than some fixed quantity available. Scarcity also captures the idea of how many people want or value an item. Jackson Pollock was recognized as someone who played a significant role in the development of American abstract art. Museums, galleries, and private collectors would all jump at the chance to get one of his paintings. The value of a Pollock painting has to do with the individual valuations placed on it by the potential buyers. Market value is about both sides of the fence: the quantity available and the valuations placed on that quantity. It is possible that Pollock's work could, at some time in the future, fall out of favour. If this happened, the quantity of paintings would not change but their market value would. The paintings have value only because someone wants them and, given the current market price of a Pollock, someone wants them pretty badly.

Put Your Money Where Your Mouth Is

In 2006, record executive David Geffen put Pollock's *No 5, 1948* up for sale. The painting sold in a private deal for $140 million. What does the final price of $140 million tell us, and what does it not tell us, about the value of the painting?

---

[6] Jesus tells a story in the Gospels of a man who discovers a pearl in a field. The man then sells everything he has to buy the field in order to make the pearl his own. Giving everything you have for something is about as close to priceless as economists are willing to go. Those with more resources have more that they can give up in order to get what they want.

[7] In May 2005, NPR reported that 32 unknown works were discovered in a storage locker belonging to Pollock's friend Herbert Matter.

To begin with, it tells us that no one else was willing to top this price,[8] and therefore no one else valued this painting at the $140 million mark. It also tells us that the Mexican financier who bought the painting valued the painting for at least that amount. He might have been willing to pay even more for it, but that wasn't necessary. We also know that David Geffen did not value this painting for more than $140 million or he wouldn't have sold it. Economists often equate the price of anything, in this case the painting, with its value. Although this is not strictly true, it isn't a bad approximation. The price paid for this item is called its market value and is about as good an approximation for the true worth of the painting as we can get. The subjective value that the buyer has for the painting is at least equal to the market value, but it could very well be more. Markets only reveal so much.

Gossip Column

Karl Heinrich Marx was born in 1818 in Trier, a part of the Kingdom of Prussia. He died in London, England, in 1883 and is buried in his wife's Highgate Cemetery grave. Marx was both a scholar and an activist. As a political economist, sociologist, political theorist, philosopher, and revolutionary, Marx is often called the father of communism. This doesn't resonate well with most economists, although his ideas have found a home in what is called Marxian economics. He proposed that the market value of a good should be based on the quantity of labour used to make it. This is in contrast to the idea put forth in this chapter that market value is a matter of scarcity.

When Marx died, he was essentially penniless (net worth of £250), but he left behind his ideas in *Das Kapital*. Only the first volume was published in his lifetime. The remaining two volumes were published posthumously by his good friend Frederick Engels. Engels was a very good friend, indeed. He supported the financially strapped Marxes (ironically using funds from the Engels family cotton mills) and even went so far as to claim paternity of a child—Henry Fredrick—born to the Marxes' housekeeper Helene Demuthin in order to keep Marx's wife, Jenny, from finding out the child was actually Karl's. Marx had six named children (one died before receiving a name) with his wife, and each of four girls was named Jenny, after their mother. Fortunately, they didn't go by Jenny. Imagine the confusion. At least two children, a boy (Henry Edward Guy) and a girl (Jenny Eveline Frances), died a year after birth, which must have been heartbreaking to the parents. Marx had to beg money (£2) from a friend to purchase a coffin for one of these children. The grief and marital tensions must have been unbearable, and this may explain how Henry Fredrick came into existence.

Through *Das Kapital* and *The Communist Manifesto* (co-authored with Engels), Marx's influence has been enormous. In scholarship, his work has appeared more frequently in the index of the *International Encyclopedia of Social Sciences* than

---

[8]   It is possible that someone who values the painting more didn't know about the sale, but I doubt it. The "big money" art community is pretty small.

anyone else's. As well, within 50 years of his death, about a third of humanity was ruled by governments devoted to Marxism.[9]

While I cannot claim sympathy with Marx's ideas, I do have sympathy for him (and the Jennys), especially since he named one of his daughters the same name as me.

WHEN PLAY BECOMES WORK: SPORTS AS A BUSINESS

Golf may be played on Sunday, not being a game within the view of the law, but being a form of moral effort.[10]

Stephen Butler Leacock (1869–1944), Canadian economist and author

Armed with ideas about value and scarcity, lets look at why sports stars (or any kind of star, for that matter) make so much money. Most obviously, the number of very talented people at the very top of a field is small. There are only so many athletes like golfer Tiger Woods[11] or basketball player LeBron James out there. That's half of it. The other half is explained by the excitement factor, which affects the size of the audience watching. Big salaries and endorsements go to sports stars who are successful at popular sports. They generate a lot of value because they have so many fans, who are each willing to give up something else to watch them and to buy a product they endorse. The sports star may be only marginally better than another athlete, but that's all it takes to create a following.

Athletes such as Tiger Woods and LeBron James have negotiated some of their value into their own pockets. They actually might be worth more than what they are paid but they are certainly not worth less, even though some critics may think so. Each team or company that employs these stars has a maximum price it is willing to pay them depending on how much it estimates the players will generate in revenue for the franchise or company. By the same token, the star has a minimum number he or she is willing to receive depending on what others have offered to pay. These other offers are an opportunity cost for making a deal with one particular organization. The market value for a player is usually some number in between the player's minimum and an organization's maximum. These deals are usually negotiated, so it helps to have a good agent working for you to get the highest salary possible.

(By the way, if you have a bad season, you will be re-evaluated, so make sure to play well and not get injured. If you need a clean-cut image to be worth something in endorsements, don't commit marital infidelity. Notice that I didn't say *don't get caught*. If you are a star, you will get caught! As Tiger Woods found out, your downfall has value in other entertainment markets, most notably the gossip tabloids.)

---

[9]   Even though Marx was born in Germany, he spent much of his life in England. This explains why he has a biography in the *Oxford Dictionary of National Biography*, just as the Marshalls and Robbins do.

[10] It used to be common for a Christian culture to abstain from working on Sunday. Thus, if golf were work, it would have been forbidden.

[11] In 2007, Tiger Woods had the highest endorsement income of any athlete, earning $100 million. LeBron James's endorsement income was third at $25 million. Woods would go on to be the first athlete to earn $1 billion.

From the perspective of free market economists, these top athletes are worth every penny they receive. The market has brought together those who value the athlete's performance and those who can perform. Everyone is happy until they start talking about salaries over a beer.

On the other hand, Marxist economists see the value of a worker as something intrinsic to being classed as labour, and no one labourer deserves this level of remuneration. It should be clear why most top athletes want to live in a free market economy.

THE SPECIAL CASE OF THE CEOS

My problem lies in reconciling my gross habits with my net income.

Errol Leslie Flynn (1909–1959), Australian-born actor

To many economists, CEOs are just another example of highly specialized talents that get the big bucks for being marginally better than anyone else in creating value for their shareholders. These economists believe that slight increases in the scarcity of executive ability elicit huge gains for these CEOs.[12] Other economists aren't convinced that executive compensation is an issue of simple scarcity and put forth alternate theories to explain the multi-million-dollar salaries given to top executives (mainly in the United States). Most of these theories have to do with the incentive structure of various compensation packages and how they motivate managers to behave in ways that increase the profits paid to the shareholders.[13] This example demonstrates that while the simple idea of scarcity is foundational in economics, sorting out what is actually going on with executive pay is matter of debate.

During the fall of 2008, U.S. President George W. Bush convened an emergency summit to look at a $700 billion bailout for American firms in the financial sector. The Emergency Economic Stabilization Act of 2008 limits the amount of compensation these failed companies can give their executives. Wall Street's mantra of "pay for performance" raises questions about how much pay the top executives deserve for really poor performance and why these bright (scarce) and mostly male executives in the financial sector got it so wrong.[14]

The Not-So-Special Case of You

Here is the depressing news: If you have a set of relatively common skills and you are not the topic of conversation at the annual shareholders' meeting, you are not particularly scarce. Unfortunately, your salary will reflect that fact. What can you do to change this?

A good way to increase your salary is to try to show your boss that you are valued elsewhere. Getting another job offer and then having a meeting with your boss about it might be a good way to stay at your current firm but receive higher pay. This tactic is a bit risky if you don't really want to leave your job because, while your boss may be

---

[12]   See Gabaix, Xavier, & Landier, Augustin. (2008). Why has CEO pay increased so much? *The Quarterly Journal of Economics, 123*(1), 40–100.

[13]   See the chapter titled "Why Your Boss Is Overpaid" in Tim Harford's book *The Logic of Life*.

[14]   Andrew Ross Sorkin's book *Too Big to Fail* is a fascinating read about the main characters in this saga. The salaries earned by these executives were in the tens of millions of dollars.

sorry to see you go, he or she will also help you take your things to the door if the company's value for your services is not as high as your other offer.

Another thing you can try is to make yourself more extraordinary and your skills less common. That will up your value in the labour market. By improving your education or work experience, your services become a scarcer commodity. If you can develop a skill that makes clients love to pay you because "you are so worth it," your compensation package should reflect that unique ability. Sometimes it also helps to play golf with clients. Whether you should win or lose the game is a decision you're going to have to make for yourself. Again, think about the opportunity costs.

THE PARADOX OF VALUE

When the well's dry, we know the worth of water.

English proverb

So far, we have looked at the price of things as telling us something about value. Economists call the price of something its *marginal value* or *incremental value* rather than its total value. The idea of margin or increment means that you are looking at items one at a time and treating them separately, as opposed to cumulating their values over all products in a category. Price is the marginal value of one painting, one athlete per season, a paid sexual encounter, or your services per paycheque. It is not, for example, the total value of all Jackson Pollock paintings. If Jackson Pollock had lived longer and painted more (and nothing else had changed), the price of one of his paintings would be less but the total value of all of his paintings would actually be higher. More people would get pleasure from his canon of work and society as a whole would be better off, even though the price per painting would be lower. Economists call this *the paradox of value*. The more abundant something is, the less we pay for it but the greater overall total value it has in the economy. One star athlete is paid a high salary but his or her overall contribution to society is much less than an army of daycare workers who each earn minimum wage. Adding up the value of low-paid individuals would result in a number higher than the sum of a few individuals who make a high income.

Of Cabbages and Kings: Value and Price

"When I use a word," Humpty Dumpty said in rather a scornful tone, "it means just what I choose it to mean—neither more nor less."

Charles Lutwidge Dodgson, pen name Lewis Carroll (1832–1898), English author
Taken from *Through the Looking-Glass* (1871)

People usually want the total value of a good or service to be reflected in its price. This is understandable, because it feels fairer to them. After all, important things should cost more and reflect their true value, shouldn't they? But prices are simply measures of relative scarcity—its marginal revealed value—and become a mechanism to get people to use those scarce resources wisely. Only those individuals who value a particular thing above its price will actually purchase it. Prices are not measures of total significance. Child care, the water we consume, and the cabbages we eat are cheap to buy, not because they are unimportant in the scheme of things but because babysitters, water, and cabbages are relatively abundant. The abundance of something may have large societal benefits overall, but its price reflects the fact that there is a lot of that thing to go around. In many ways, it is good that important goods and services like babysitting, water, and cabbages are so abundant and cheap to purchase. Think about what life would be like if or when they became very scarce. Who would look after our kids? What would we drink? Where would we get our cabbage rolls?[15]

TRADING VALUES

These first two chapters have given you the basics to understand how trade works and why so many people are willing to engage in it. When people have different values for scarce goods, trade is the next logical step. Let's take that step into the next chapter.

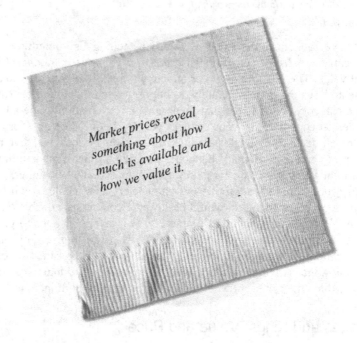

Market prices reveal something about how much is available and how we value it.

---

[15] On a less sardonic note, when natural disasters occur often the basics of life—clean water, first-aid supplies, and batteries—become quite scarce and cause untold heartache to those involved.

CHAPTER 3

Exchange: Supply and Demand, Take One

If economists could manage to get themselves thought of as humble, competent people on a level of dentists, that would be splendid.

Lord John Maynard Keynes (1883–1946), originator of Keynesian economics

With glass in hand, you saunter toward a group of men chatting and overhear one dad say, "What a night. I didn't realize how tricky Halloween could be when kids are different ages. My oldest son wanted to run and get to as many houses as possible. He was so frustrated with his kid sister who couldn't keep up with him, we finally decided that he would do both sides of the street and my daughter and I would only do one. He got twice as much as she did but they both seemed happy with it. Thankfully, it wasn't raining and my part was over by 9 p.m. It sure wasn't over for the kids, though. By the end of the night, their rooms looked like the floor of the New York Stock Exchange used to look after a day of heavy trading.[1] What a mess, and I hate to think about the dentist bill."

A NIGHTCAP ... I MEAN, RECAP

Teach a parrot the words "Supply and Demand" and you've got an economist.

Thomas Carlyle (1795–1881), Scottish historian

The road from scarcity to markets is surprisingly short—a hop, skip, and a jump, really. We have seen that scarcity leads to an allocation problem. Markets offer a great system to allocate goods. (The fact that markets are often the best solution to the allocation problem will be explained in Chapter 9.) The concept of scarcity combines the ideas of both subjective values and availability. When these two team up, choices need to be made. Scarcity makes decisions costly and markets conveniently put a numerical value on those costs. It's called price.

Suppose that someone gives you a gift certificate for a jewellery store. At the jewellery counter, you see a watch and a ring that would look just terrific on you. However, you discover that your gift certificate can buy only one of them. Don't you just hate it when reality hits and you realize that you can't have both the watch *and* the ring? You have to choose. How do you make the final decision? It all depends on your answers to a couple of simple questions. First, what are the costs? Second, what are the benefits? This is the classic cost-benefit analysis you often hear about. The (opportunity) costs in this story are easy. If you get the ring, it will cost you the watch; if you get the watch, it will cost you the ring. The benefits depend on your subjective values. Between the two accessories, you will buy the one that has a subjective value greater than the (opportunity) cost. If things are close, you will stand at the counter for a long time, potentially making the jeweller more and more nervous as the Mozer mantel clock ticks on.

---

[1] All trading is now done electronically.

Costs and benefits bring us to the concept of supply and demand, the buzzwords of economics. There are two ways to look at this topic. The first is a top-down approach and the second is (surprise, surprise) a bottom-up approach. This chapter provides a top-down broad overview of why markets usually work. For the bottom-up approach, Chapters 6 and 7 break supply and demand down into its component parts and look at them in nitty-gritty detail. Chapter 8 puts it all together and the supply and demand framework will be used to tell some stories that illustrate these market concepts. In particular, I will focus on auto sales and the housing market to help you see how supply and demand works.

The Basics Are Surprisingly Simple

Things should be made as simple as possible, but not any simpler.

Albert Einstein (1879–1955), German-born theoretical physicist

When you give something up, you are supplying or selling it.
When you get something, you are demanding or buying it.
Sometimes money is involved. Sometimes it isn't.

WHAT IS A MARKET?

Never underestimate the determination of a kid who is time rich and cash poor.

Cory Doctorow (1971-), Canadian author
Taken from *Little Brother* (2008)

On October 31 of each year, children in North America scurry through the streets, going door to door to collect junk food. It's called Halloween, and it can be a lot of fun. Just make sure you don't get between the kid and the candy. That's when you will see the real ghouls come out! On this night, you will find junior entrepreneurs working at the most organized form of begging there is. The evening rewards the swift because the window of opportunity (dictated by social norms) runs from about 6 p.m. to 9 p.m. and then it is all over for another year.

What a joy it is to dump the haul on the floor and begin the ritual sorting. Chocolate bars[2] in one pile. Chips[3] in another. Finally, candy in a third. (Apples are tossed before they make it into a pile. Halloween is about basic food groups, and fruit isn't one of them!) The compulsive child will refine the sorting into even more piles ... and probably even record them on some sort of spreadsheet.

Happy is the child who has siblings, because the evening's business then goes into overtime with major wheeling and dealing. Despite the differences in wealth (some kids cover more ground and hence have more loot), trading has its benefits. For instance, suppose that one child doesn't like chocolate but is addicted to chips and candy and that the other child likes everything. It makes sense that the first child would propose a mutually satisfying trade to the other, saying, "How about two chocolate bars for one bag of chips?"

---

[2]   The Hershey company and Mars Inc. are the largest manufacturers of chocolates in the world. Nestlé and Lindt are also big players. Mars Inc. is owned by members of the Mars family, making it one of the largest privately held companies in the United States.

[3]   Potato chips account for approximately one-third of the total savoury snacks market.

"It's a deal," the other child agrees. These two rational children (and all children are rational when it comes to candy), with their different value systems, engage in complex trade negotiations to improve their own personal situations. After all, no one freely trades something they like for something they hate ... unless, of course, we are talking about a mother trading with her children! Economists call the benefits of a mutually satisfying trade the *gains from trade*. Markets or exchanges[4] are simply the mechanisms that allow such improvements in happiness to occur. It is as old as civilization itself.[5]

After all of the trades are completed for the night, we can figure out the real price of a bag of chips for these children. We saw that one bag of chips traded for two chocolate bars. Therefore, we can conclude that the price of a bag of chips is two chocolate bars and, conversely, that the price of one chocolate bar is a half a bag of chips. (I hope you now recognize that these prices are opportunity costs for chips and chocolate.) Due to the nature of barter,[6] each player must be in two markets simultaneously (both the chips and the chocolate markets). One child cannot buy chips without selling chocolate bars. If one of the children didn't want to trade (we have all heard of some kid sister who refuses to deal), then neither the chocolate market nor the chips market would exist in that household. Markets require the willingness of both players to exchange something of value at a price they can agree upon.

Adding Money

All government—indeed, every human benefit and enjoyment, every virtue and every prudent act—is founded on compromise and barter.

Edmund Burke (1729–1797), Irish statesman

The concept of barter (for example, the exchange of chips for chocolate bars) is simple to understand, but what happens when we add the real-world complication of money? Money exists because societies may want to engage in wider trade beyond two parties.

Let's look at a complicated trading scenario: Wilma wants what Barney has, Barney wants what Fred has, and Fred wants what Betty has. Finally, Betty wants what Wilma has (and it's not Fred!). In order for barter to work here, as in the Halloween story, you would need to have all of these players in the same room doing some pretty complicated trade negotiations. From *The Flintstones*, we know that these people are couples and best friends, so barter would probably work. But what if the people are unrelated?

Actual or Potential?

Money is only as good as what you buy.

Gilbert Van Sligtenhorst (1934-), Eveline Adomait's dad

---

[4] For example, stock markets are also called stock exchanges. In the United States, commodities are listed on the Chicago Mercantile Exchange (CME).

[5] Trade of commodities seems to date back to least 5000 BC between the Mesopotamian and Indus regions.

[6] Barter is the trade of real things for real things. No money is involved. If someone agrees to babysit a child in exchange for a toilet installation, he or she would be bartering services. If both sides agree to this exchange, they are both getting a good deal.

Let's see how money can help. Suppose that Wilma sells her stuff to Betty, who pays her in money. Money then acts as a type of holding tank of potential buying power. Economists say that money is functioning as a store of value. This store of value (money) can sit in Wilma's purse until it is convenient for her to meet up with Barney and buy what she wants. However, once Wilma purchases something, she converts what is *potential* value into *actual* value. Her money buys something real that she can use. Barney, on the other hand, has given up something actual or real (which he values) in return for money, which hopefully retains its value for as long as he has it. This money now gives him potential value or buying power to be used to obtain what he wants when it is convenient for him to do so. He must use his money to buy something in order to experience the actual value of a dollar.

Money allows these Stone-Age characters to make trades without having to be in the same room together. As long as money holds its store of value, these players can take their time to make a purchase. Thus, complicated deals become much simpler. In addition, money allows people to be in one market at a time rather than require them to be in two simultaneously, as is the case with barter.

The simplicity of using money makes it seem as if money is actually real in and of itself. The use of money disguises the fact that all markets are eventually about real things changing hands, not about money. Money is just a way of storing value until it is convenient to purchase something real. For most people, the real trade is labour hours supplied in exchange for goods and services demanded. It could be a T-shirt slogan:

Life is simple:

Work (*real)*

Get paid (*money*)

Buy stuff (*real*)

The Real World

All perception of truth is the detection of an analogy.

Henry David Thoreau (1817–1862), American author

Halloween is a perfect illustration of real trade. The kids who work the streets have piles of junk food to either consume or trade. They trade (or supply) a part of their stash if they can get back (or demand) something they like better. If all kids do this, the world is a better place by the end of the evening. I can almost hear you now: "All of this stuff about *The Flintstones* and Halloween is kids' stuff. I get what you are saying about trade at this level, but how does this relate to the real world of international trading arrangements? Can this help me understand how countries trade with each other?" In the vernacular of Fred Flintstone—yes, it yabba dabba does!

For starters, it is a misnomer to say that countries trade with each other. Rather, individuals in countries trade with each other, and countries keep track of the numbers that move in and out of their borders. The governments of various countries are not major trading participants. An international story comparable to our Flintstones example goes something like this: The American company Walmart[7] buys clothing from manufacturers in China. With the money the Chinese companies are paid, they buy oil[8] from Canada. The Canadian shareholders of the oil companies use some of the money from the sale of oil to purchase Californian wine.[9] Finally, the workers at the winery buy clothes at Walmart that were manufactured in China. It's Wilma, Barney, Fred, and Betty over again. The situation only looks more complicated because we have added borders, three currencies (monies), and people who never meet.

While governments provide the environment that makes trade easy or difficult for the average citizen to engage in, they usually aren't big players in the actual buying and selling of goods themselves.[10] This fact can be lost when people talk about countries such as the United States, China, or Canada trading with each other. It is easy to think that presidents and prime ministers are trading clothes for wine, when in reality they are not. (They simply go to cocktail parties with each other.) Trade agreements set up the terms and conditions that allow citizens in their respective countries to negotiate these trades.

Getting into the Game

There are two great rules of life, the one general and the other particular. The first is that everyone can in the end get what he wants, if he only tries. That is the general rule. The particular rule is that every individual is, more or less, an exception to the rule.

Samuel Butler (1835–1902), British author

Some look negatively on markets and point out that not everyone participates in markets and therefore cannot benefit from free trade. This is the big criticism from the political left,[11] which is usually suspicious of free markets. (A communist approach would ration goods equally to all citizens.) Economists have to admit that market economies imply that only those with something to trade can reap the rewards. Let's take a careful look at our Halloween analogy to see who doesn't engage in trade and identify what they represent in the global economy.

First, children without brothers or sisters have no one to trade with. They still have their piles of goodies, so it is hard to feel sorry for them. However, if they could easily trade with someone, they would be better off. They could trade something they "sort of" like for something they really like.

---

[7]   Walmart is the largest U.S. importer of Chinese consumer products, sitting at 12% of the total amount originating from China.

[8]   China is the second largest consumer of oil in the world. Since 2005, China has been buying into Canadian oil companies in order to secure a stable supply of oil.

[9]   In 2014, 90 percent of U.S. wine exports were from California and totalled $1.49 billion in value. Canada bought approximately 30% of those sales, second only to the E.U.

[10] When governments purchase items from other countries, they are engaging in trade but acting like any other player. For example, the LCBO (Liquor Control Board of Ontario), an agency of the Ontario government, is a big buyer of alcohol on the world market and a big seller of alcohol (more than 50%) to Ontarians. Sales in the 2014–15 fiscal year were $5.2 billion.

[11] The term *political left* originates from the French Revolution and had a lot to do with the seating arrangements of the political parties. The nobility sat on the right of the president's chair and the liberal deputies sat on the left. The French assembly still seats its representatives from left to right in terms of their politics.

Any country that produces goods and services but doesn't trade with the outside world would be in this situation. This is called *autarky*, which means self-sufficiency. China was close to an autarky from around 1950 to 1978 because of policies established by Mao Zedong. Since 1978, China has steadily increased its use of markets and subsequently has more to trade. Also, with its accession to the World Trade Organization (WTO) in 2001, the volume of trade has increased significantly so that China is now the fifth largest exporter in the world.[12] Whether these gains translate into general increases in the standard of living for all of China's citizens is a question of some debate. It appears that urban[13] and younger people receive most of the gains from trade.

Second, sick children generally do not trade. This situation is sad. Through no fault of their own, these children cannot bring anything of Halloween-generated value to the economic table.

Similarly, countries that have had natural disasters, famines, wars, or epidemics have a smaller pile with which to trade. While free trade can take a terrible situation and make it slightly better, it cannot fix the underlying production problems.[14] For instance, the United Nations has set specific goals to reduce poverty in the world by 2015. However, these goals look unattainable for the continent of Africa due to civil wars, the HIV/AIDS pandemic, malevolent dictators, and drought. The situation in many African countries appears to be much more complicated than a simple trade problem.

Third, kids whose parents oppose "trick or treating" and prohibit this activity have nothing to trade. For religious reasons, some parents prevent their children from going out on Halloween night. Other parents inspect their children's stash for anything they consider *really* bad (although most of it is bad for you). Many dentists recommend that parents remove the candy or "buy it back." This kind of trade is usually not negotiated but rather imposed by the parent. In other words, it is *forced* trade rather than *free* trade.

These kinds of actions represent government policy, and international trade policies affect the ability of citizens, both at home and abroad, to trade with each other. Countries, through their laws and institutions, influence the environment within which markets operate. For example, the United States currently forbids any trade with Cuba due to ideological and political differences. Even when a country is a friendly trading partner, a single event can block trade. In 2003, the United States banned imports of Canadian beef due to one case of mad cow disease. Before the ban, Canada was the third largest exporter of beef in the world; trade was valued at $4.1 billion, with 90 percent of it going to the United States. After the ban, exports dropped to virtually zero. You can imagine the devastation this caused to the beef industry in Canada.

Finally, kids whose candy gets stolen unfortunately don't get to trade either. Think of it … all that hard work was for nothing. Trade or markets have no power to get back people's loot. What is needed is a system that protects private property, preventing theft from happening in the first place. On Halloween night, when there are tricks as well as treats, protection may come in the form of a parent or older sibling accompanying the child on his or her route, thereby protecting the goods from other unscrupulous imps.

---

[12] In 1980, China's volume of trade was valued at US$38 billion. In 2002, the volume had grown to US$620 billion. Over a period of 20 years the trade balance had doubled at least three times.

[13] In 2013, real per capita disposable income (income adjusted for inflation and taxes) grew by 7.0% in urban areas and 9.3% in rural areas. However, urban median incomes are 3 times that of rural ones.

[14] See Chapter 4 for issues facing developing countries.

On a grander scale, governments play a role in setting up and policing the legal systems that protect property from transnational theft. The Paris Convention for the Protection of Industrial Property is the most widely adopted international treaty in the world. This convention seeks to protect the holders of patents (and other intellectual property) from losing income due to theft and was first signed in 1883. Today, 173 countries have signed the treaty, giving a legal framework to the rights of patent holders.

Gossip Column

Adam Smith[15] was probably born in June 1723 (the month and year of his baptism), approximately six months after his father died. He was therefore raised by a single mother and was quite close to her, living with her when not at university or travelling. He entered Glasgow University at the age of 14 and, while he was there, won a scholarship to Balliol College, Oxford. At Oxford, it appears he may have suffered a nervous breakdown because he left before his scholarship was over. From then on, Smith maintained Glasgow's intellectual superiority over Oxford[16] as an academic institution. In 1751, he earned a professorship at Glasgow University, giving lectures in the fields of ethics, rhetoric, jurisprudence, political economy, and "police and revenue."

Smith was the stereotypical absent-minded professor who dressed strangely, spoke to himself, and collected books. (Sounds like a typical prof to me.) He loved his work and apparently was popular with students as well. In 1763, Charles Townshend made Smith an offer he couldn't refuse: to tutor and travel with Townshend's stepson Henry Scott, the Duke of Buccleuch. Smith resigned his university post in the middle of term and attemped to return the students' fees, but the students refused to take the money back.

Smith authored two historically important books: *The Theory of Moral Sentiments* (1759), which is based on his lectures at Glasgow, and *An Inquiry into the Nature and Causes of the Wealth of Nations*, commonly known as *The Wealth of Nations* (1776), which, interestingly enough, came out in the birth year of the United States. (In *The Wealth of Nations*, Smith refers to the American Revolution as "present disturbances.") In a letter to friend David Hume, Smith wrote that he had started to write *The Wealth of Nations* while touring "the Continent" with young Henry Scott because he needed something to pass the time in Toulouse, France. It took him more

---

[15] There are 20 pages written on the life and works of Adam Smith in the *Oxford Dictionary of National Biography*.

[16] Smith believed that universities and colleges should receive some of their funds directly from students (Glasgow type) rather than rely on endowments (Oxford type) because it puts the incentives in the right place. It forces the professor to care about the student when preparing course lectures. In *The Wealth of Nations*, Smith has a whole chapter on the education of youth. He writes, "In some universities the salary makes but a part, and frequently but a small part of the emoluments of the teacher, of which the greater part arises from the honoraries and fees of his pupils. The necessity of application, though always more or less diminished, is not in this case entirely taken away. Reputation in his profession is still of some importance to him, and he still has some dependency upon the affection, gratitude, and favourable report of those who have attended upon his instructions; and these favourable sentiments he is likely to gain in no way so well as by deserving them, that is, by the abilities and diligence with which he discharges every part of his duty."

than a decade to finish it. Once published, it was an instant success and the initial print run sold out in six months. Smith planned to write more books but died in 1790 after a painful illness. He ordered any of his writings that he considered unpublishable destroyed, which is truly unfortunate. On his deathbed he expressed regret that he had not achieved more.

Smith is known for his explanation of how rational self-interest and competition, operating in a social framework (which ultimately depends on adherence to moral obligations), can lead to economic well-being and prosperity. He used the phrase *the invisible hand* to illustrate how all of these ideas work together. Contrary to the way he is often portrayed, he wasn't a free market absolutist and did recognize some role for government.

Smith is ranked at number 30 in Michael H. Hart's list of the most influential figures in history. To honour Smith, the Bank of England put his portrait on £20 notes beginning March 13, 2007; he is the first Scotsman to be given this honour. Most economists point to Adam Smith as the granddaddy of modern economics.

LAYING BLAME

No society can surely be flourishing and happy, of which the far greater part of the members are poor and miserable.

Adam Smith (1723–1790), moral philosopher and political economist
Taken from *The Wealth of Nations* (1776)

While each of the situations discussed above place markets in a global context, markets are really about individuals, of any age, trying to improve their situations. However, when bad things happen, markets often get blamed for the outcome. I hope, from these examples, you can see that the existence of trading relationships is not the real issue. Blaming poverty, social unrest, and political upheaval on the market economy is like shooting the messenger rather than dealing with the root causes.

In the next chapter we will take the first step in helping us to sort out how societies create something of value and what players need to do to get into the game. Just as problems have root causes, so does wealth. I hope you will find the next chapter "a treat" rather than "tricky" to read.

Free exchange can make both people better off.

CHAPTER 4

Producing Wealth

It is not wealth one asks for but just enough to preserve one's dignity, to work unhampered, to be generous, frank and independent.

William Somerset Maugham (1874–1965), English writer
Taken from *Of Human Bondage* (1915)

A line of partially filled bottles obscures a part of your reflection as you stare into the mirror behind the bar. A quick shake of the head and you are out of your silent reverie. You raise the glass that was resting on the coaster in front of you to your lips. The first sip of the Cabernet Sauvignon is wonderful, rich and mellow with a hint of smoke. After a survey of the room, you realize that the conversations haven't changed much since you last eavesdropped, and you aren't really interested in joining any of them. Today was not a good day. Your computer crashed and all of this week's work was lost. You can't believe that you didn't back up your files, which is your normal practice. Your boss doesn't know about the fiasco yet and is going to be livid. Even though you are here to connect with potential clients, you feel sorry for yourself and brood at the bar, nibbling on peanuts[1] instead of networking.

The bartender catches your attention by vigorously shaking up two martinis. A waiter orders six different cocktails: a Bloody Mary, Singapore Sling, Manhattan, Fuzzy Navel, Daiquiri, and Margarita. Without moving from her position, the bartender swiftly grabs the appropriate bottles and pours and mixes the drinks apparently without much thought. You are fascinated by her speed and dexterity.

"You have all those drinks memorized?" you ask, attempting to make conversation.

"Yes, I took a bartending course and work here part-time. I have done this job so long that I can make these cocktails in my sleep!" she replies, happy to have someone engage her.

"So what do you do when you're not working here?" you continue.

"I'm a university student finishing up a degree in languages and linguistics. I couldn't get a student loan so I bartend to pay my way through school."

"Good for you!" you exclaim. "So what does a person do with a degree in languages and linguistics, anyway?"

"I speak four languages fluently and hope to work as a courtroom interpreter at some point. I'm also doing a minor in cultural studies, which should help me understand the immigrants who find themselves in court. Working here is great! I have made really good contacts with lawyers and a few judges. A couple of them said that they would be willing to give me a reference when I need one."

Another waiter comes with an order and the bartender quickly loads the tray with drinks. You think to yourself, *What an accomplished person she is. She will go far.* As she walks to the fridge, you notice that one of her shoes has a much bigger heel than the

---

[1] On July 13, 2005, while a guest on *The Tonight Show with Jay Leno*, Johnny Depp claimed that a study on bar peanuts had revealed 27 different types of urine mixed in with the nuts. He used this evidence to explain why he doesn't eat them. I have to admit that, even though this might be an urban myth, I am inclined to not eat them as well.

other and that she walks with a decided limp. Your admiration for her rises even more and you quickly decide to end your private little pity party. With your wineglass fully loaded, you do an about-face. It's time to work the room.

THE WEALTH OF NATIONS

We cannot seek or attain health, wealth, learning, justice or kindness in general. Action is always specific, concrete, individualized, unique.

John Dewey (1859–1952), American philosopher, psychologist, and educational reformer

In our society, we can easily assume that an individual or a country blessed with an abundance of natural talent or resources will inevitably be very rich. But this is not necessarily the case. We all know that there are many people who possess knockout good looks and are very intelligent but don't do much with their lives, whereas other people live with some sort of handicap and go on to do great things.

Countries aren't much different. Let's compare Japan and Zimbabwe. Both countries are about the same size, but that is about all they have in common. Japan lost World War II and has little in the way of natural resources, whereas Zimbabwe has fantastic natural resources and won its independence in 1980. You would think from this information that Zimbabwe should be the wealthier country. *Au contraire.* The United Nations reports that in 2007 the per capita income in Zimbabwe was US$261, while Japan's per capita income was US$33 632. Furthermore, the Japanese have the highest life expectancy in the world at close to 83 years, whereas Zimbabweans' life expectancy is close to 38 years. The numbers tell a different story.

While this chapter looks at the resources used to make goods and services, we need to remember that these resources are not enough to predict the standard of living in a country. Wealthy nations are not lucky countries but rather are productive ones. They take the *inputs* available to them, whether small or great, and efficiently make *outputs* from them. Economists call this the *production process*, where productivity is the key to a growing economy. Think of productivity as the conversion factor that translates inputs into outputs. For example, a bartender's "drinks served per hour" is one measure of how productive that bartender is. Another measure may be the aesthetic quality of the cocktails' presentation. (Who knew all those cute little umbrellas holding fruit on top of brightly coloured drinks could be called productive?) Whatever the productivity measure, it is still true that more inputs produce more wealth because they create more of something to value. If more goes in, then more comes out.

SO, WHAT ARE WE WORKING WITH?

God creates everything out of nothing—and everything which God is to use he first reduces to nothing.

Soren Kierkegaard (1813–1855), Danish philosopher and theologian

Anything that makes something else is called an input. Inputs can be complicated or very simple. For example, growing a tomato requires dirt, sun, rain, and seeds—the good stuff. We can make it more complicated by adding fertilizer, greenhouses, and genetically modified seeds. When brought down to the most basic level, inputs are resources, and these separate into broad categories, which we will look at in turn. Before we begin looking at each basic input type, let me make a few general comments.

First, most resources on earth are now relatively scarce and have an opportunity cost associated with using them. Second, each category of resources calls its opportunity cost or price by its own special name. Furthermore, inputs are typically sold in markets and as the level of scarcity changes, so do their prices. Third, the quality of an input is not necessarily uniform across any one category. This affects its opportunity cost. Fourth, inputs often need to be combined with each other to actually produce something. "No input is an island entire of itself"[2] and all that.

Let's look at the possible building blocks to obtain a high standard of living. (There is one resource that won't be discussed below but can be "relatively" important in terms of living well: your parents. You might want to think about treating them as valuable resources.) This chapter will feel a bit like reading an encyclopedia; I'm sorry about that, but it can't be helped. Understanding the basic terms goes a long way in terms of holding your own in any meaningful conversation about economics. It's hard to sound intelligent if you don't know the vocabulary. Here we go.

1. Land

Buy land, they're not making it anymore.

Mark Twain (1835–1910), American humorist, writer, and lecturer

Because historically the wealthy were mainly landowners, land was written about as a resource by all of the early economists. While it may seem obvious that land is a scarce resource because it has a fixed quantity,[3] it is not the finiteness of the quantity that actually makes land scarce. If the amount available exceeds the amount that people want, then land is actually not scarce. In fact, land across the plains of North America felt endless to the early pioneers. As they headed west, land was essentially free and there for the taking. This is not the case anymore. Somebody owns all of the land in North America; if you want it, you're going to have to pay for it. What you will pay varies depending on how scarce the land is, which also includes the scarcity of certain qualitative features. For instance, land in cities is scarcer and therefore more expensive than land out in the boonies. Swampland differs from areas with fertile soil. Land in the desert is different from a property with a lake or ocean view. In other words, as the cliché goes, land costs are about location, location, location, which is really code for scarcity, scarcity, scarcity.

When considering land as an input or resource, it does not always progress from abundant to scarce. When areas like those during the Gold Rush that were once booming become ghost towns,[4] land becomes relatively abundant again, enabling people to find a cheap place to rent or buy. However, it can be tough to find a job working for ghosts.

---

[2] "No man is an island entire of itself" is a line from John Donne's (1572–1631) *Meditation XVII*. The first part of the line—"No man is an island"—is cleverly but falsely attributed to Bon Jovi in the movie *About a Boy*.

[3] Although we've said that land is a fixed quantity, the Netherlands did reclaim land from the sea. Due to a system of polders and dikes, approximately 27 percent of the Netherlands is actually below sea level. More than 60 percent of the country's population of 15.8 million lives in this area.

[4] There are at least 180 ghost towns and historic places in the United States.

Economists call the opportunity cost of the land you use in the production of goods and services rent. You might say, "Hey, wait a minute, I don't rent my land. I bought it." That may be true, but if you write off your land as a business expense, or give up the opportunity to rent it out, economists call the cost of using the land in production the rental cost, even if you are paying rent only to yourself.

2. Raw Materials

> *One cannot fix one's eyes on the commonest natural production without finding food for a rambling fancy.*
>
> Jane Austen (1775–1817), English writer
> Taken from *Mansfield Park* (1814)

Raw materials are inputs that we need to put some effort into getting, but usually they are not fundamentally created by people. The best examples are wood, water, oil, metals, and minerals. Sometimes farm products like rice, coffee, wheat, and pork bellies (think bacon) are put into this category. They are essentially commodities. These commodities are priced according to their level of scarcity. Prices of raw materials are usually quoted as a price per barrel, bushel, tonne, etc., which we now know to be its opportunity cost.

Again, as with land, the level of scarcity of raw materials can change over time. For example, fresh water, which for hundreds of years was considered abundant on the west coast of the United States, is now starting to become scarce.[5] Saudi Arabia can produce high-quality oil by basically sticking an oil well in the ground whereas the tar sands of Alberta[6] require a major expenditure of resources to get the same quality of crude oil out of them. This means that the tar sands are a viable source of oil only if the scarcity price is high enough. Given the huge swings in oil prices, we can safely say that the level of scarcity of oil is not constant.

3. The Environment

> *Swigert: Okay, Houston, we've had a problem here.*
> *Duke: This is Houston. Say again please.*
> *Lovell: Houston, we've had a problem.*
>
> Apollo 13 (said April 13, 1970)

Whether it immediately comes to mind or not, the environment is a resource. Out of all of the scarce resources in this chapter, the environment raises some of the biggest concerns for humanity because it seems that many people feel it is being used in a completely irresponsible way. However, the economics of environmental problems is not simple. We will deal with environmental problems in Chapter 11, but for now let's just mention the environment's biggest complexity.

---

[5]   Seventy-one percent of the world is covered in water; however, 97.2 percent of it is salt water. Polar ice accounts for another 2.15 percent, which leaves less than 1 percent that is fresh water. Taken from Bjorn Lomborg's *The Skeptical Environmentalist* (2001).

[6]   Tar sands are found in extremely large quantities in Canada and Venezuela. Oil sand is often referred to as non-conventional oil or crude bitumen, in order to distinguish it from the crude oil traditionally produced from oil wells.

The biggest problem is that no one owns the environment. This phenomenon is known as *the tragedy of the commons*.[7] Because no one is directly responsible for the environment, people treat this scarce resource as if it were abundant. Consequently, no one pays the true price for using it. Most people don't purposely mess up the environment. They are essentially reasonable people acting in their own personal interests in a way that ends up destroying the planet, which of course is not in the collective interest of humanity.[8]

Markets handle most other scarce resources effectively, but the environment is not marketable ... to its peril. However, if someone did own the environment, he or she would ensure that all who used it paid the true opportunity cost. When we treat something that is actually scarce as if it were free, we run the risk of overusing it or degrading it to the point that it is no longer worth anything. Unfortunately, doing nothing makes things worse, but it is logistically difficult to do what needs to be done to make things better because of this lack of ownership.

4. Physical Capital

Capital is that part of wealth which is devoted to obtaining further wealth.

Alfred Marshall (1842–1924), British economist

Capital is made when some inputs are used to make machines or buildings. One input leads to another one. Usually, these machines or buildings are only useful in producing something else and are not consumed by people for pleasure. After all, most of us would never drive a tractor to the movies or live in a factory as a home; they are used to create or produce other things. Of course, there are exceptions to this generalization. The same kind of car can be both an intermediate capital good (taxi used to generate cab rides) or a final consumption good (family vehicle). Many small business owners have a home office, which is analogous to a factory. This space may be the only room in which they live, but technically it's a work-space when they are working and a home space when they are not working. This is starting to feel like a home and garden channel. They always call rooms "spaces."

Capital also has a quality aspect to it. Top-of-the-line machines differ from basic models. In addition, capital depreciates when machines wear out and buildings run down. Rusty, broken-down trucks and vacant, dilapidated barns no longer function as useful capital. Furthermore, technological advancements can make certain kinds of capital worthless unless they're in a museum. For instance, we generally no longer use typewriters, even if they are in mint condition. The typewriter has become an obsolete technology replaced by computers and printers.

Costing Capital

If it isn't the sheriff, it's the finance company; I've got more attachments on me than a vacuum cleaner.

John Sidney Blyth Barrymore (1882–1942), American actor

---

[7] "The Tragedy of the Commons" is an article written by Garrett Hardin and first published in the journal *Science* in 1968.

[8] Elinor Ostrom, the first woman to win the Nobel Prize in Economics (2009), does outline eight design principles that can stabilize the management of a common property. Needless to say, these principles are easier to achieve on small local problems than big global ones.

When economists speak of capital, we usually mean *physical capital* such as machines, inventories on hand, and buildings. These are the things that can actually produce goods. They are real. However, when we hear the term *capital markets* in the business news or issuing from the lips of pundits,[9] it is usually associated with paper assets such as stocks, bonds, loans, or mortgages rather than the real assets such as machines, buildings, and inventories. Economists call paper assets *financial capital.*

Why the confusion in the use of the word *capital*? It has to do with the connection between physical capital and financial capital. In order to purchase a machine or build a factory, business owners usually borrow[10] money. The "borrowed" funds generate a paper trail in the form of stocks, bonds, mortgages, and so on, to keep track of the financial arrangements. On the flip side, people's savings represent the funds that are available to lend in financial capital markets. These funds search for good investment[11] opportunities, and these opportunities are found in real capital making real products.

Here is a concrete example: Canadian company Research In Motion (RIM) created a great product called the BlackBerry. In order to get the device to consumers, RIM needed to pay developers, marketers, retailers, and whoever else could make this happen. RIM's owners didn't have the funds to do this on their own and basically had two alternatives for funding: They could either borrow the money or issue some stock in the company. If the funds came as a loan, the lender would get signed loan papers with a payment plan that specified a certain rate of interest. If the company sold stock, the buyers of that stock would get a piece of paper that represents their part ownership of the business. These papers keep track of the sources of funds and remuneration required to take an idea and make it a reality. Start-up companies usually have difficulty convincing a bank to lend them money and therefore rely heavily on equity financing. Without a doubt, RIM's early stockholders are very happy that they parked their financial capital with that company.[12]

Touched by an Angel

The four most dangerous words in investing are "This time it's different."

Sir John Templeton (1912–2008), American-born British financial investor and philanthropist

Essentially, financial capital acts as the grease that keeps the gears of real capital turning. The funds provided by those with savings purchase the real assets sitting on the factory floor, which generate the real goods. Without these angel investors,[13] many small businesses wouldn't have enough financial capital to get their product to market. A credit crunch occurs when no one wants to provide the funds that business owners need, therefore restricting their ability to generate real goods and services. No angels for them.

---

9   The term *pundit* originates from a Sanskrit word meaning learned and is first found in English in 1672. The term's contemporary usage may have its origins in a Yale University society known as The Pundits founded in 1884.

10 I use the term *borrow* loosely and, some would say, incorrectly. Borrowing is strictly about debt financing, which stocks are not. A stock is part ownership of a firm but is still a source of funds that require a repayment of sorts. Either way, the business owners are using funds that don't belong to them.

11 Technically, businesses invest (real capital) and people save (financial capital).

12 RIM was originally financed by Canadian institutional and venture capital investors. Since 2011, RIM's fortunes have changed because of increased competition from other producers.

13 Angel investors typically invest their own funds, whereas venture capitalists manage the pooled money of others in a professionally managed fund.

This was the big concern during the global financial crisis of 2007 to 2009. Central banks around the world worked hard to keep bank credit as a source of funds flowing precisely because it is so connected to the real economy. Chapter 12 will look at the financial crisis in some detail, but for now I want to make sure that capital—both physical and financial—gets its rightful place when the credits start to roll on any production.

I Owe, I Owe

Ambition is an illness in Italy, and no one wants to catch it.

Marlena de Blasi, American-born Italian writer
Taken from *A Thousand Days in Venice* (2002)

The vocabulary of high finance can leave one bewildered, but many of these words find their roots in how early entrepreneurs thought about their businesses, especially their machines and buildings. Suppose that you borrow $1 million (a nice, round, big number) at 10 percent interest per year to buy a machine. In order to get the cool million, you have to sign a piece of paper called a contract that commits you to give the bank $100 000 per year in interest payments and to some repayment plan for the principal. With sweaty hands, you sign the papers. After a brief panic attack, you rush back to the factory and march down to that new piece of machinery. Once there, you stare into its expensive blinking lights and think, *You had better be worth it!*

So, what will make this machine worth it? Simply put, if the 10 percent interest you must pay to the bank (which is called the cost of capital) is less than the return on investment (sometimes called the rate of return) of the machine, then you're good. In other words, if the machine makes you more money from what it produces than the money you have to pay to use it, then all is well. If not, you will live with a few regrets, not to mention some sleepless nights.

A Capitalist?[14]

The rate of interest acts as a link between income-value and capital-value.

Irving Fisher (1867–1947), American mathematician and economist

What if I already have the money and don't need to borrow funds to buy the machine? Does that mean I don't have any costs and the revenue the machine makes is all gravy?

No, it doesn't. Why? Because the money is not free. Remember when we talked about opportunity costs earlier? When I use my own money, I am—in a real sense—lending the money to myself; this implies an opportunity cost, because I could have loaned the money to someone else just as easily and made interest income. Therefore, even if I use my own savings, I need to think about such things as the interest rates that the banks are paying when I make an equipment purchase. Whether I borrow from an outside source or from myself, the equipment needs to make a rate of return at least equal to the rate of interest to be a worthwhile investment.

---

[14] The word *capitalist* was minted by William Thackeray in the sense of one who owns capital and was more precisely defined by Karl Marx in *Das Kapital* as one who owned working capital, including machinery, and made money by letting others work on those machines. Here is what Marx said about capital (I couldn't resist including it): "Capital is dead labour, which vampire-like, lives only by sucking living labour, and lives the more, the more labour it sucks." You have to admit, he certainly had a flair for the dramatic!

However, there are a few positives with respect to lending the money to myself, and they shouldn't be discounted. I am unlikely to foreclose on myself if I get behind on the payments, and I require a lot less paperwork. This is probably why so many corporations like to use their own money (called retained earnings[15]) to finance capital expenditures rather than go to the bank or stock market for the funds.

5. Going into Labour

Opportunity is missed by most people because it is dressed in overalls and looks like work.

Thomas Edison (1847–1931), American inventor and businessman

The concept of labour, the human sweat portion of production, is self-explanatory so I won't bore you with the obvious. However, I do want to point out that working to feed your family is just that: working. It is not slavery, even if it sometimes feels like it. While you may feel you do not have a real choice about whether to work, most of you do have some choices with respect to employment. Slavery offers no choices because the slave is the property of someone else. Now, if someone is forced to work at gun-point, we can safely assume that the person is no longer a worker but a slave. However, if a person is a free agent, he or she would be classified as a worker and not a slave whether the work that he or she does is enjoyable or not. That person may also feel underpaid and overworked. This is still not slavery.

So, why all this melodramatic talk of slavery, and how does it relate to the way most of us think about employment? I've noticed that, once we start to compare working conditions around the world, the phrase *slave labour* is thrown around quite a bit. While there are real human rights issues when it comes to working conditions around the world, wage differentials between developed and less developed countries have nothing to do with the concept of slavery. The fact that a worker in a developing country makes less than a worker in an industrialized country does not make that worker a slave. If they voluntarily show up for work, put in a long, hard day, and take home a paycheque that feeds their families, they are workers and not slaves.

Slavery, properly so called, is the establishment of a right which gives to one man such a power over another as renders him absolute master of his life and fortune.

Charles-Louis de Secondat, baron de La Brède et de Montesquieu (1689–1755), French social commentator and political thinker

Child labour is one of the most complicated labour issues we face today, stirring up powerful emotions and moral indignation. Due to extreme poverty, children all over the world are forced by their parents to work in what many refer to as "sweatshops"—jobs where the children work in difficult conditions and have no choice in the matter. The children are, for all intents and purposes, slaves who work in order to generate an income for their parents. For those of us who live in the developed world, it is an unthinkable reality and something that most of us would like to see ended. However, it is not a simple matter of closing down these sweatshops. Poverty is a symptom of a greater

---

[15] In Canada, even in a recession, at least 40 percent of corporate capital needs are met with internal funds. In most years the number is higher than 60 percent. See Chapter 16 of *Principles of Macroeconomics*, 4th edition, by Frank, Bernanke, Osberg, Cross, and MacLean (McGraw-Hill).

problem that requires something other than simply shutting down "the corporation" in that country. This sort of "feel good about yourself in the West because you joined a campaign to shut down the big boys and did something" solution usually reduces the options of the impoverished individuals involved and can actually cause circumstances to go from bad to worse for a child. There is no doubt that sweatshops are abhorrent, but this is a complex issue. One thing is certain: Removing the productive capacity of a developing county will not make its people better off.

We need to get away from our Western assumptions for a moment. Contrary to what we might think, most parents in developing countries love their children, but economic survival can take its toll. We need to remember that these parents are not forcing their children to give up playing with Lego in order to work in a sweatshop. Playing with Lego was never a viable alternative. These children have to work because, without their income, the whole family would be in dire straits. It turns out that when sweatshops are shut down, these children often end up as prostitutes, maimed beggars, or even dead—not exactly what human rights–minded individuals hope will happen and certainly not good news for the children or their parents. Removing a place of employment doesn't free them to a better life. Don't get me wrong: I would love for these children to be free to play with Lego all day without any economic responsibilities. The best way to accomplish that is to make their countries more productive with more alternatives in an economic sense. The richer a country becomes, the better the lives of its children are. That means encouraging economic growth. What we think of as childhood is really a phenomenon found in the world's richest countries. Maybe corporations, who know something about producing, can be part of the solution.

Quality Assurance

Education alone can conduct us to that enjoyment which is at once best in quality and infinite in quantity.
Horace Mann (1796–1859), American education reformer and politician

Labour also involves the issue of quality. Highly skilled workers are different from low-skilled workers. Economists talk about acquiring human capital[16] through education, experience, and networks. It is both who and what you know that pays. When people invest in their education, they earn a rate of return on that investment. However, because that education becomes embodied in a person who usually cannot be repossessed[17] as a machine can be, borrowing to fund educational pursuits can be difficult. In economist speak, the credit market to acquire human capital is incomplete.[18] Remember that the bartender in the opening story was working her way through university because loans are tough to get. Despite the difficulties, she strategically invests in her education in hopes that her future will be brighter because she will know something that others don't know or have skills that others don't have. After all, not many people can speak four languages as she does. The fact that she is also establishing a Rolodex of contacts will help her become

---

[16]   The term *human capital* first appeared in a 1961 *American Economic Review* article titled "Investment in Human Capital," by Nobel Prize–winning economist Theodore W. Schultz.

[17]   In previous times, a person could be repossessed and put in debtor's prison or taken as a slave.

[18]   When markets are "thick," there are a lot of buyers and sellers. When markets are "thin," they can sometimes be incomplete with one side—either the buyer or the seller—missing.

more valuable to the marketplace. Employers love workers who can connect people to save them money or who can enhance business opportunities for the company.

However, human capital can also depreciate. This means that the quality of labour goes down. For instance, leaving school to work at a job for an extended period of time before returning for postgraduate education is not normally a good idea, because you naturally forget what you learned the longer you are away from it. My advice to students is to keep going until you are ready to stop formal education for good. Alas, sometimes breaks are unavoidable. For example, maternity leaves take women out of the workforce for a time. If the woman's job relies heavily on business contacts or if some new technology transforms the industry while she is away raising kids, then coming back to work can be daunting. She can feel both unappreciated and depreciated when she is passed over for promotion.

Workers can also get sick, retire (someday), or die (hopefully not too soon). All of these events affect the quantity and quality of labour available at any given time. Both Japan and Zimbabwe have declining numbers of workers. However, the reasons for those declines are very different. For instance, Zimbabwe's problems are due to the fact that AIDS/HIV and other diseases have decimated the workforce, whereas Japan's problems are due to an aging population because of declining birth rates and tough immigration laws. Japan's decline signals a looming problem for that country's future.

Getting Paid

The misery of being exploited by capitalists is nothing compared to the misery of not being exploited at all.

Joan Robinson (1903–1983), British economist[19]
Taken from *Economic Philosophy* (1962)

Labour is generally paid in the form of wages, salaries, commissions, and bonuses. However, these wages have meaning only in relation to what those wages can buy, which economists call earning *real wages*. For instance, if a worker in another country earns a low wage but those low wages provide an adequate or even good standard of living in that person's country, then the real wage is great. International comparisons between countries are only sensible if we take both wages and prices into account. Here is how it works: Suppose that I live in a country that pays $100 per day but where bread costs $10 per loaf. Now suppose that you earn $10 per day but bread costs $1 per loaf. While my income is supposedly 10 times yours, it has the same purchasing power—10 loaves of bread per day. We both earn the same real wage.[20]

6. Entrepreneurial Ability

A gardener, who cultivates his own garden with his own hands, unites in his own person the three different characters, of landlord, farmer, and laborer. His produce, therefore, should pay him the rent of the first, the profit of the second, and the wages of the third.

Adam Smith (1723–1790), Scottish moral philosopher and political economist

---

[19]   It is thought by many economists that Joan Robinson should have been the first woman to win the Nobel Prize in Economics.

[20]   Usually international comparisons are made in purchasing power parity, or PPP U.S. dollars. Purchasing power parity is an attempt to get at the idea of real standard of living.

There are basically two ways in which someone can own a company. The first seems obvious: A person starts a business. This entrepreneur combines all of the resources we have discussed previously, takes the risk of bankruptcy, and runs a business hoping for big returns. He or she gets whatever is left over after everyone else receives payment. These returns are called profits, and profits are the only cost of doing business that cannot be written off as a business expense.

Let me underscore an important point. Economists have the concept of what is called normal profits. These profits are the amount needed to convince entrepreneurs to start a business. Depending on how much the entrepreneur could make elsewhere, the level of normal profits varies from individual to individual. This is where accountants and economists differ. Suppose that an accountant told a client who gave up a job making $50 000 working for someone else that they made profits of $30 000 in a given year. An economist might frame it differently to the same client, "Sorry, but you actually lost $20 000." Economists always see profits in terms of opportunity costs.

The second way for a person to own a company is less obvious but really important nonetheless. A group of shareholders can hire managers to act on their behalf. They do this when they buy stock in a company. These individuals provide the funds for the managers to work with, and in turn they require a return on their investment. This return is paid out of profits in the form of dividends. If you happen to think that the amount of profits should be legislated downward and get upset at reading headlines about a particular company making obscene profits, consider this: Without the ability to make profits, our society does not provide an environment to promote entrepreneurship or give people a reason to save. Business owners and their investors are the backbone of what most people think of the free enterprise system and the productive engine of our economy. These individuals are the risk takers and will take those risks only if the rewards (which come in the form of profits) are high enough.

Gossip Column

Wassily Leontief (1906–1999) was born to a Jewish family and raised in Russia. His father was an economist and Wassily must have been a natural, because he finished the equivalent of a master's degree in economics by the time he was 19. At the end of his studies, he opposed communism and spoke out for free speech and academic autonomy. The KGB detained him several times because of his views, and he was able to leave Russia in 1925 only because of a medical misdiagnosis. He then went to Germany, where he earned his Ph.D. at the University of Berlin in 1928.

In 1932, Leontief went to work at Harvard University in the Economics department. It was there that he finished his work on the input-output tables that won him the Nobel Prize in 1973. These tables were generated by a series of mathematical equations that modelled the U.S. economy in what economists call a general equilibrium framework. Using real data and the newly invented Harvard Mark II computer,[21] he

---

[21] The Harvard Mark II was a computer built at Harvard University under the direction of Howard Aiken and, fortunately for Leontief, finished in 1947. Like many high-tech inventions, it was funded by the United States military.

was able to provide empirical evidence for his theoretical ideas. Leontief was fundamentally against "theoretical assumptions and non-observed facts" and he believed
that economists should get their hands dirty with real numbers. This input-output
approach has been used by Western, socialist, and developing countries alike as they
engage in economic planning. Leontief's ideas sit on the shoulders of other great Jewish economists, namely David Ricardo, Karl Marx, and Piero Sraffa.

DOTTING THE I'S: INVENTION, INNOVATION, AND THE INDUSTRIAL REVOLUTION

Invention is the mother of necessity.

Thorstein Bunde Veblen (1857–1929), American economist and sociologist

For most of human history, economic growth, in terms of output, was miniscule. There
was subsistence living for a very long time. But somewhere around 1750, all that
changed with the arrival of the Industrial Revolution. At that time, human beings had
accumulated enough knowledge and capital to reach a critical mass, which caused an
explosion in practical inventions—things like the steam engine, weaving machines, and
electricity. Finally, Mother Necessity could give birth to her inventions. The world
hasn't looked back since and now takes rapid technological growth for granted.

Technology has progressed to the point where one thing is for sure: Education is at
the heart of any future advancement. Education is what trains the brains (human capital),
which in turn invent the equipment (physical capital) that fuels our economy. For example, Intel's Andrew Groves earned a Ph.D. in chemical engineering from the University
of California (Berkeley) in 1963. Under Grove's leadership, Intel became one of the
world's key players in microprocessors. All that math training was good for something!
It helped him to multiply Intel's value from $18 billion to $198 billion.

Patiently Crossing the T's

With inventions came patents … and patent lawyers. The thinking behind the establishment of patents was that patents would give the originators of ideas a temporary return on
all of their hard-earned thinking. However, intellectual property is not like physical property in that it is less tangible and therefore it is harder to catch and punish those who steal
it. The arts industry has been trying to prevent illegal downloads of music, films, and pictures without much success. Intellectual property is also not like physical property in that
society as a whole benefits from these inventions when they are "stolen." This might seem
like an odd thing to say, but consider generic drugs. Once a drug is out of patent, that
helpful drug can be made cheaply and distributed to people who need it. Patents limit the
production of socially beneficial products. I'll discuss intellectual property in a different
context in Chapter 11 but, for now, it's easy to see why individual inventors would want
tough patent laws and why society might not want those laws to be quite so ironclad.[22]

---

[22]   Malcolm Gladwell, in his book *What the Dog Saw*, provides what I think is a very cogent argument for
why society would not want to stifle creativity with strict copyright laws in the chapter titled "Something
Borrowed." I must confess that he is one of my favourite authors.

The Domino Effect

Contrary to popular opinion, society's "middlemen" do serve a useful function. They provide convenience to the customer, saving time or offering specialized skills in the production process. Intermediate companies take the outputs of a supplier as an input to their own businesses, add value to it, and then sell it to the next player in line. For example, a chemical company sells silicone gel (input) for a breast implant (output)[23] to the plastic surgeon, who performs the breast augmentation (input) on a movie star (output), who wants to have big breasts to improve her career. The movie star takes her new body (input) and gets a lead role in a new film (output). Theatres get the rights to show the film (input) and display it on opening weekend (output). I don't think eliminating the "middlemen" would be a very good thing in this case. Slapping a glob of silicone gel on a movie screen would not look very appealing without all of the steps in between.

Beyond the Basics

The test of our progress is not whether we add more to the abundance of those who have much; it is whether we provide enough for those who have too little.

Franklin Delano Roosevelt (1882–1945), American president

All of the scarce resources or inputs we have discussed in this chapter, when used in combination with each other, produce things. Economists call this thing *output* because this word captures the idea of both a physical product such as silicone gel and a service such as plastic surgery. People buy these outputs and experience the standard of living that these "things" bring.

Fundamentally, there are only a few ways to get out of poverty and into a decent standard of living:

1. Find more inputs to use. The recent discovery of new oil resources off the coast of Brazil is a good example of this effort.

2. Improve the quality of the inputs.[24] For example, labour can improve through education, training, or better health.

3. Change technology[25] and use existing inputs better. Improvements in agriculture labour productivity due to advancements in fertilizers, machinery, and genetic modification of foods are good examples.

---

[23] In 2015, Americans spent a total of approximately $13.5 billion on cosmetic procedures. Of that number, $8 billion were spent on surgical procedures and women account for approximately 90% of the total (data from the American Society for Aesthetic and Plastic Surgery).

[24] Sandra Black and Lisa Lynch in "Human-Capital Investments and Productivity" (*AEA Papers and Proceedings*, May 1996), found that development of computer skills significantly increased productivity. (Remember, this was the 1990s.)

[25] The paper "The Economics of Has-beens," co-authored by Michael S. Weisbach and Glenn MacDonald, appeared in the February 2004 issue of *Journal of Political Economy*. In their study, the researchers argue that while experience may offer the older worker a certain amount of income protection, technology advances "always turn them into has-beens to some degree." Unless older workers can easily update their skills, new technologies will tend to depreciate their labour value.

4. Get government to administer effective programs. From a strictly economic point of view, let alone from a humanitarian one, it makes perfect sense that countries educate children and immunize them against debilitating diseases. These public programs produce a high-quality labour force; since each highly skilled, healthy worker produces more output than a low-skilled, sick one, this is a good idea. In contrast, the AIDS pandemic has devastated developing countries because it kills off the most productive workers, leaving behind a population consisting of the very young and the very old, who are unable to produce enough to sustain a decent standard of living, not to mention invest for the future.

Researchers Sheggen Fan and Neetha Rao, in their paper "Public Spending in Developing Countries: Trends, Determination, and Impact,"[26] conclude that not all government spending has the same impact on growth and poverty reduction. In developing countries globally, the best thing to spend money on is agricultural research, education, and roads, whereas the worst thing to spend money on is defence. In Africa, spending on agriculture and health has the biggest impact.

While inputs are the building blocks for generating wealth, there is still the question of what you should make with the inputs you have. The next chapter will revisit trade; but instead of looking at what gains can be made from trade, we will look more closely at who should produce what in order to have something to trade. Given that individuals can use their inputs to make different outputs, we need to figure out what people should do for a living.

You need inputs to make outputs.

---

26   Fan, S., & Rao, N. (2003). Public spending in developing countries: Trends, determination, and impact. *EPTD Discussion Papers 99*. International Food Policy Research Institute.

CHAPTER 5

The Absolut(e)[1] of Comparative Advantage

> *There is hardly anybody good for everything, and there is scarcely anybody who is absolutely good for nothing.*
>
> Philip Dormer Stanhope, 4th Earl of Chesterfield (1694–1773), British statesman

From the bar, you see a flurry of activity at the door as a group of Shakespearean actors walks in, high on the evening's performance. This was the opening night for a production of *Hamlet*,[2] and the audience showed their appreciation with multiple standing ovations. At the encouragement of the host, the actors head straight to the bar for a celebratory drink. It seems that a patron of the theatre has already instructed the bartender to give the actors a drink …on him.

The actor who plays Horatio orders in a suave manner: "A Black Dane, please." His colleagues roar with laughter.

Once everyone has a drink, "Hamlet" raises his glass to make a toast. "May plays always be the thing!"

"Hear, hear!" the thespians agree.

You overhear "Laertes" comment to "Ophelia", "To think that my parents wanted me to have a normal job. An accountant, actually, but as I always say, 'To thine own self be true.'[3] It looks like my hard work is paying off. I just got a major role in a movie."

"Ophelia" displays a slight sadness as she tries to gather up a big smile and congratulate "Laertes." In the back of her mind, she wonders where her own career is going. That very morning she took a pregnancy test and the result was positive. She and her husband are ecstatic about the news, because they really want children, but the rational part of her is already wondering how this is going to affect her career. One thing is certain: Now is not the time for her to audition for a role in a movie.

SO, WHAT DO YOU WANT TO BE (OR NOT TO BE) WHEN YOU GROW UP?

> *My mother had a great deal of trouble with me, but I think she enjoyed it.*
>
> Samuel Langhorne Clemens, pen name Mark Twain (1835–1910), American writer

If you want to spark fear in a helicopter parent,[4] suggest that his or her child could grow up to be a failure. The parental drive to produce successful children has caused many

---

[1] In 2008, Absolut vodka was sold by the Swedish government to the French company Pernod Ricard. Absolut is the third largest brand of alcoholic spirits in the world after Bacardi and Smirnoff. More than 40 percent of the imported vodka in the United States is Absolut.

[2] William Shakespeare wrote more than 40 plays. *Hamlet* is one of his most recognizable.

[3] The following lines are from Hamlet: "to thine own self be true," "the play's the thing," and the suicidal "to be or not to be."

[4] Helicopter parents hover over their children.

a concerned mother and father to buy all manner of books and computer programs guaranteed to raise their child's IQ.[5] It has also driven much of the participation in such worthy activities as swimming lessons, music lessons, and sports teams, all with the goal to produce a very successful, but some would say hurried,[6] child.

For an individual, the decision about what to be when you grow up is an important one. For a country, these individual decisions are important as well. Countries are, after all, made up of many individuals. Once we know what the majority of a country's citizenry is doing, we can predict what that country will be known for when it comes to production. Why do some countries produce furniture[7] while other countries produce university[8] degrees? Let's take a look.

We have already looked at the benefits of free trade, but they are worth revisiting here. Anyone can be better off if he or she trades something from his or her own pile of goods for something in another's pile of goods if he or she happens to like the other item more. Trade assumes that the pile of goods is already accumulated. In our Halloween story a few chapters ago, the night's "trick or treating" was over before the trading began. On Halloween, the pile you have to trade with depends on how fast you move, luck, and finding a great neighbourhood in which to trick or treat. Sort of like life, don't you think?

So, what really determines the contents of the pile of goods sitting in front of you? To answer that, we need to back up a bit. Normally when economists talk about trade, they include the word *specialization* before the word *trade*. This pair of terms rolls off economists' lips like the names Rosencrantz and Guildenstern[9] do off the lips of a Shakespearean scholar. Most people produce specialized goods—a pile of goods that is limited in variety—and use those goods to trade for a wider variety of goods that they want or need. For example, a dairy farmer will sell milk to buy such items as pants, shirts, bread, and meat. Essentially, the farmer trades the milk he or she produced (actually, the cows did the producing) for food and clothing he or she didn't produce. Once an individual specializes in the production of one or a few items, he or she becomes dependent on others for what he or she wants but did not make—hence the need for trading partners.

SPECIALIZATION IS SPECIAL

One man cannot practice many arts with success.

Plato (427–347 bc), Greek philosopher

---

[5]   The term *IQ*, from the German *Intelligenzquotient*, was coined by German psychologist William Stern in 1912. The average IQ score is 100.

[6]   Elkind, David. (2001). *The Hurried Child: Growing Up Too Fast Too Soon*, 3rd ed. New York: Perseus Publishing.

[7]   From 1985 to 2006, China's furniture industry grew an average of 15 percent. China now ranks first in the world for furniture production. This sector employs approximately 13 million Chinese workers (China Building Decoration Association).

[8]   Of the top 10 universities in the world (by most rankings), the United States has six of them. The other four are in Britain.

[9]   Rosencrantz and Guildenstern are characters in William Shakespeare's *Hamlet*. Rosencrantz and Guildenstern were common Danish family names in the sixteenth century.

Why specialize? Why put yourself into the position of needing others? To be blunt, individuals who specialize can make more money[10] than those who do not. Economists think that the phrase *Jack of all trades but master of none* is true. We know that while many of you could do most things that you set your mind to, it is not possible with scarce resources to actually do everything your mind thinks about doing. You have to make choices, and those choices have opportunity costs. (This refrain might be starting to sound like a broken record, but it's important to be constantly reminded that all economic choices are based on scarce resources resulting in opportunity costs.) Everyone doing a little of everything will produce less *with the same resources* than everyone doing one thing and trading with others for what they did not make. Specialization allows us to do more with what we have. Here is the best part: More production leads to more consumption.

A Tale of Two Writers

I specialize in murders of quiet, domestic interest.

Agatha Mary Clarissa Christie (1890–1976), English crime author
Taken from *Life* magazine (May 14, 1956)

We can now think about who specializes in what. When you specialize, you are choosing to do something. The flip side is also true. You are choosing *not* to do something else. This choice is not random but based on a number of factors such as individual preferences, abilities, and opportunities.

To make things concrete, let's consider the writing histories of two people: Paul Krugman[11] and myself. As an economist, Krugman's career stands head and shoulders above my own. He has won a Nobel Prize in Economics and is very famous. I know who he is, but he has never heard of me. In addition to his academic publications as an economist, he is an accomplished writer, with a number of textbooks, popular books, and *New York Times* columns under his belt. I have never written a textbook or even penned a letter to the editor of a newspaper. So, what am I doing writing a book called *Cocktail Party Economics*? Why isn't Krugman writing this book if he is superior to me as both an economist and a writer? The answer to this question should bring hope to everyone. For you see, Krugman, like all of us, has only 24 hours in a day. He has to make choices like the rest of us about what to do with his time. He can spend his day enjoying various leisure activities, consulting, teaching courses, or writing. However, every time he chooses one activity, he cannot do another one. This fact presents him with a problem about what to do with his time.

Now, suppose that Krugman chooses to spend his time writing. There are still more choices to make. When he puts pen to paper (or should I say fingers to keyboard), the words that flow out of him must have a destination, and he has many great destinations

---

[10] I am reluctant to use the word *money*. Money isn't real but stands in for real things. Essentially, the specialist can make more money because he or she can make more outputs.

[11] Paul Robin Krugman (1953–) is an American economist, columnist, and author. He is a professor of economics and international affairs at Princeton University and a columnist for *The New York Times*. In 2008, Krugman won the Nobel Memorial Prize in Economic Sciences "for his analysis of trade patterns and location of economic activity."

to choose from. Let's see ... where can these words end up? A peer-reviewed journal, a *New York Times* column,[12] an economics textbook, or a popular economics book? Which should he choose? My guess is that since Krugman is a rational economist, he will go for the option that will give him the most satisfaction overall, which is probably connected to increasing his lifetime income as well. We know he hasn't written the kind of book you are holding (yet), and therefore he must feel that his words work harder for him in other places. Voila, he has left a book for me to write. Not to be overly modest, but I have been teaching introductory economics to young minds for more than 20 years. Helping people understand economic ideas is something I do rather well according to my student course evaluations. While I might be less talented than Krugman in many areas, in this one area we might (and I stress *might*) be pretty close. The moral of the story is this: Never feel that, because you are less talented than others, there is nothing for you to specialize in. You just have to find the right spot to fill.

Getting Technical

> *If Shakespeare had been in pro basketball he never would have had time to write his soliloquies. He would always have been on a plane between Phoenix and Kansas City.*
>
> Paul Westhead (1939–), American basketball coach
> Taken from *The 2548 Best Things Anybody Ever Said* (2001)

Economists would say that while Paul Krugman has an *absolute advantage* in all economic writing, I have a *comparative advantage* in writing a fun-filled, chatty-type economics book. Krugman has comparative advantage in the other types of economic writing (and he has written a lot!). Absolute advantage or overall talent will make you very rich because you are good at whatever you do. But absolute advantage will not indicate which activity made you rich. For that, we need to know what you have a comparative advantage in. So, what determines comparative advantage? To the general public, the answer that economists give sounds a bit like jargon but here goes: Whoever has the lowest opportunity cost in a particular activity has comparative advantage in that activity.

O, woe is you! Why are we back to opportunity costs? Well, the problem for very talented people is that everything they choose to do will incur a huge cost in terms of a forgone alternative. Given all of his writing options, it is very costly for Paul Krugman to write the kind of economics book you are holding, and to date he hasn't. I, on the other hand (now that my kids are older), gave up domestic chores to write this book ... a price I am willing to pay! My costs are definitely lower, and therefore I have the advantage for writing this type of book.

What matters is not what you excel at or what your competitor excels at. What matters is the relative difference. Paul Krugman is better than I am at all things economics, but he can't do everything. He is far better than I am at writing newspaper articles, but he may be only a little better than I am at writing a book of this type. Therefore, he focuses on what he is much better at doing and forgoes a book that is best written by me and only me. Hallelujah! While it is possible to have absolute advantage in everything, it is impossible to have comparative advantage in everything—unless, of course, you are God.

---

[12]   Many of Krugman's popular books are collections of essays or columns that he wrote for other sources.

Career Counselling

To all of you young people, here is my advice: Go after your comparative advantage dreams. If you happen to be the best at everything, then lucky you. Go for the career in which you clearly dominate. (I never really understood why Michael Jordan[13] switched from basketball to baseball. As an economist, I feel there must be more to this story. Fortunately, he returned to his real area of strength.) For the rest of you in the cheap seats who may not clearly dominate in any area, you don't have to be the best to enjoy a successful career. When you compare yourself to others, go for the close-second option. There is something significant for you to do. Having said this, I think it is also important to give you a reality check: Don't bang your head against a wall if there is no hope. If you are not even close to succeeding, try something else. For example, if you are 5 feet tall and want to be an athlete, you are unlikely to have a comparative advantage in basketball,[14] but other sports may fit the bill. You might consider gymnastics,[15] for example.

Pro Choice

Why in almost all societies have married women specialized in bearing and rearing children and in certain agricultural activities, whereas married men have done most of the fighting and market work?

Gary Becker (1930–2014), American economist and Nobel Prize winner
Taken from "The Economic Way of Looking at Life," Nobel lecture printed in *Economic Sciences* (1992)

Differences in comparative advantage also describe and predict how families function. Economic models based on the theory of comparative advantage take into account how men and women make free choices as they try to be as happy as possible given their circumstances. For many women, who due to biological[16] reasons have the comparative advantage in child rearing, the clear choice is to stay home to care for their children and households rather than to have a career. They do so because the opportunity cost of having a career is high. Often, the wages they would earn are not enough to justify the hassle and emotional cost inherent in the choice to get a job.

For many feminists,[17] basing the decision to stay home on the idea of opportunity costs does not sit well because they believe that traditional women's roles are a form of oppression or a social construction rather than the free choice of rational women. However, as a feminist myself, I consider research into the economic factors related to social structures as critical if social change is going to happen. It highlights the importance of the economic constraints that women face as they rationally make choices. For example, Patricia Apps and Ray Rees[18] found that the kind of help governments gave families

---

[13] Michael Jordan announced his retirement from the Chicago Bulls in 1993 but returned in 1995 and helped the Bulls make the playoffs.

[14] The shortest player in the NBA was Tyrone "Mugsy" Bogues at 5'3".

[15] The average height of a gymnast is less than 5'6".

[16] Recovery time needed from pregnancy and the ability to breastfeed.

[17] Betty Friedan's book *The Feminine Mystique* (1963) criticized the idea that women could find fulfillment only through child-bearing and homemaking. Friedan's obituary in *The New York Times* described *The Feminine Mystique* as one of the most influential non-fiction books of the twentieth century.

[18] Apps, Patricia, & Rees, Ray. (2004). Fertility, taxation and family policy. *The Scandinavian Journal of Economics, 106*(4), 745–763.

changed the degree to which women participated in the workforce. Governments that had individual taxation and publicly supported child care had more women in the labour force than those that had joint taxation (sometimes known as income splitting) and child payments. From a public policy point of view, if you change the opportunity costs, you change behaviour.

On a personal note, there are reasons why I have waited this long to write a book. When my children were small, I chose to spend my time on other activities. I confess that I was guilty of being a helicopter parent, and it took up a lot of my time. In my mind, the opportunity cost of writing a book was just too high. Fortunately, kids grow up. I'm happy that writing is not necessarily a young person's sport.

Gossip Column

David Ricardo (1772–1823) was born in London, England,[19] to a rich Jewish family, the third of 17 children. At 14, he began to work at his father's stock brokerage business. At 21, he eloped with Priscilla Anne Wilkinson, a Quaker, and together they raised three sons and five daughters. (Obviously not trying to keep up with his parents. Or maybe Ricardo limited the number of children because he heeded the warnings of his close friend the Reverend Thomas Robert Malthus [1766–1834] about the perils of overpopulation.[20])

Due to his non-Jewish marriage, he became estranged from his family and abandoned Judaism to become a Unitarian. Once disinherited, Ricardo set up his own business similar to that of his father. A very clever man, he made a fortune as a dealer of government securities, so much so that he retired at age 42 to Gatcombe Park[21] to pursue intellectual interests including economics.

Ricardo was the first to systematize economic theories and, in 1817, he published his ideas in *Principles of Political Economy and Taxation* (catchy title!). His most famous contribution is the theory of comparative advantage, where Ricardo argued that highly skilled and low-skilled labourers could benefit from trade with each other if they concentrated on the correct activity. He argued that the same thing could be applied to countries.

Ricardo pursued a career in politics, taking the easy way to Parliament. He was "elected" in 1819 as member of Parliament in Westminster for an Irish rotten borough[22] that had perhaps a dozen voters. He never visited it. However, his analysis of the world led him to argue for free trade and against the British Corn Laws, which probably would have been helpful to his electorate. The Corn Laws instituted tariffs that

---

[19]   I highly recommend the book *The Worldly Philosophers* by Robert L. Heilbroner if you wish to know more about Smith, Marx, Ricardo and Malthus as well as many other interesting if not unusual economists.

[20]   *An Essay on the Principle of Population*, through its six editions, was published from 1798 to 1826.

[21]   Gatcombe Park was bought by Queen Elizabeth II in 1976 and is the home of her daughter, Princess Anne.

[22]   A rotten borough was a parliamentary constituency in the United Kingdom that had a very few voters. It was an easy way for a rich person to get a seat and therefore achieve an unrepresentative influence in Parliament. The Reform Act 1832 disfranchised the 57 rotten boroughs that existed and redistributed representation in Parliament to more populated areas.

protected landowners-politicians from cheap foreign grain. This made bread very expensive for the poor workers. In an essay Ricardo published in the year the Corn Laws were instituted, he suggests that their abolition would put profits into the hands of the worker and industrial class and take it from the landowners. Despite being a landowner himself, he felt that would be a good thing.

Due to poor health, Ricardo retired from Parliament in 1823 and died in the same year. He was only 51. Much modern economic methodology dates from Ricardo. It's been said that Ricardo's greatest contribution to economics is the phrase *let us assume*.

THE BASIS OF COMPARATIVE ADVANTAGE

The raw fact is that every successful example of economic development this past century— every case of a poor nation that worked its way up to a more or less decent, or at least dramatically better, standard of living—has taken place via globalization, that is, by produc- ing for the world market rather than trying for self-sufficiency.

Paul Robin Krugman (1953–), American economist and Nobel Prize winner
Taken from *The Great Unraveling: Losing Our Way in the New Century* (2003)

The basis of comparative advantage goes beyond personal choices to national trade patterns. In fact, Paul Krugman was given the Nobel Prize for his work on trade models. Before him, David Ricardo had explained that trade between countries was due to the fundamental differences between those countries. For instance, it is easy to see how a country rich in natural resources will sell them to other countries that don't have those resources. In the same way, it is not hard to imagine that a country with a long growing season and fertile soil will produce food and sell it to countries that need it. Countries with very cheap labour have advantages in producing goods that are labour-intensive, whereas countries with highly educated populations have advantages in the knowledge economy. Each country, with its relative strengths, specializes in specific activities, and the direction of the flow of exports and imports is easy to guess. Ricardo provided the basic rationale for these trading relationships between countries that are very different from each other.

Same Difference

But what about the case of countries that are very similar to each other? History has shown that they still trade with each other. Take, for example, Sweden and Germany. Both of these European countries have educated, relatively well-paid labour forces and similar political systems. How does one explain the trading pattern between these countries given that there are no fundamental differences between them? To illustrate the point, let's look at cars. Sweden produces Volvos and Germany manufactures BMWs,[23] both of which sell in similar car markets. Both countries export their cars to the other country. Until Krugman looked at this issue, old trade theories had a tough time explaining why both countries produced similar products. Krugman combined two ideas that

---

[23] Volvo means "I roll" in Latin. BMW stands for Bavarian Motor Works.

became the basis of what is called New Trade Theory. First, he incorporated the concept of economies of scale. This means that as a company produces more and more of something, the average cost of producing that item goes down. It pays to be big. Second, Krugman added the idea that people prefer a variety of products of the same type. These two concepts, building on the basic idea of comparative advantage, predicted that both countries would continue to produce cars but different brands. Specialization is now at the brand level.

Bumper Sticker Protectionism

Out of work yet? Keep buying foreign.
Bumper sticker

When people oppose free trade, they tend to focus on the loss of specialized jobs to another country. The bad news is that, for some people (because of their age or aptitude), the ability to shift to another line of work is nearly impossible. They have personal reasons to be against free trade that make sense for them. Because of those personal reasons, these people will, of course, lobby for protectionism. However, in terms of the bigger picture, we need to answer an overarching question before we decide whether protectionism is warranted: How does protectionism in one sector affect the country as a whole?

But first, how does one protect? Essentially, protectionism tries to eliminate any comparative advantage of another country by "levelling the playing field." These policies might include

1. Tariffs (think taxes) on imported goods to make them more expensive to buy
2. Quotas that allow only a limited amount to enter the country
3. Rules and regulations that make it difficult for a foreign firm to sell its product in the importing country
4. Government subsidies and tax breaks (sometimes known as handouts) to firms who cannot compete with foreign companies

The problem with protectionism is that once we *level the playing field* (this phrase is uttered a lot by those who favour protectionism), there is no benefit to trade. In other words, if everyone's opportunity costs for identical items are the same, no one will ever trade with anyone else. There would be no point.

Let's explore protectionism further by looking at an example. I currently live in Canada, which does not normally grow oranges. I really like oranges and buy them regularly from the grocery store for what seems to be a reasonable price. They are transported by truck to Canada from Florida. I have a question for you: Why should my government block the flow of oranges from Florida to Canada just because someone has decided to produce expensive oranges in a Canadian greenhouse? Some may argue that these Canadian jobs at the greenhouse need to be protected at all costs. The employees at the greenhouse may not be able to find a job with as good a paycheque anywhere else. But let's pull back from the situation for a minute and think about this. By protecting the Canadian orange sector, we remove any advantage that the sunny Florida weather has in producing oranges inexpensively. If Canada restricts Florida oranges, the price of oranges will be driven up so that it is equivalent to its Canadian counterpart, and it is very costly to produce oranges in a Canadian greenhouse. Because oranges are now expensive, orange-loving consumers like me will reduce the number of oranges they purchase, although a good portion will now be made in Canada. Is this scenario worth it? I hope you are saying to yourself, "I don't think so."

Here is the big picture on protecting existing jobs: Domestic producers that compete with importing firms will gain from protectionism, but the consumer of those products will end up losing. I can't really prove to you here the relative sizes of the losses and gains. That would require more detailed analysis, which is beyond the scope of this book, but I *can* let you know the end of the story and hope that you believe me. Here is the scoop. When industries are protected in order to save jobs, the consumers lose more than the producers and workers gain. It is therefore not good for the entire country to protect any one industry just because it is in decline.

In our example, the protection of Canadian oranges[24] would generate a huge loss in terms of a drop in orange consumption. Oranges are, after all, good for you and valued by the consumer. The benefit to the Canadian producers of oranges in terms of jobs saved will never come close to the value of the losses of all consumers. In reality, it would be cheaper to pay the workers who cannot move to another position a pension than to protect their jobs to keep them from unemployment. Protectionism of this sort is a trap that decreases the overall value to all citizens as it tries to help a few of them.

This may sound bad, but it gets even worse. Protecting Canadian oranges causes scarce resources to stay in an uncompetitive industry and prevents them from naturally moving somewhere else in the economy. For example, the energy needed to keep the greenhouses warm could be used to heat homes. Furthermore, this affects our children, who grow up desiring and training for jobs in this industry because the wages are artificially high. Because they end up working in the Canadian orange industry, they don't do something that society really needs them to do. Protection has long-term consequences.

Dynamic Change

> *Instead of this absurd division into sexes, they ought to class people as static and dynamic.*
> Evelyn Arthur St. John Waugh (1903–1966), British writer
> Taken from *Decline and Fall* (1928)

Just to make life confusing (isn't that always the way?), protectionism for dynamic reasons might be the way to go, especially if you are a developing country. The criticism of protectionism above is based on a static model of economic production. In other words, comparative advantage is a given and isn't going to change. In our example, Canada will never be as warm as Florida, so it is unlikely to ever have comparative advantage in growing oranges. Protecting Canadian orange producers is a bad idea. But sometimes, for whatever reason, things can change.

---

[24] I do not believe that any oranges are produced in Canada for commercial reasons. This example is meant to be completely ridiculous, but the underlying principle is not. I chose this example because it focuses on the opportunity cost argument for free trade. I find that if I use a real-world example, the underlying idea gets lost in the heat of very real emotions.

For example, in the 1960s, the World Bank did a feasibility study for South Korea with respect to steel production and declared it a premature venture. This is a nice way of saying, "What a dumb idea!" It turns out that South Korea did not have the required raw materials and domestic market for the product. The country did not appear to have a possible comparative advantage in steel production. Nevertheless, in 1973, the South Korean government founded the Pohang Iron & Steel Co. Ltd. and provided the necessary funding to ensure its success. By 1985, the company was one of the lowest-cost producers of steel in the world (about two-thirds of the cost of steel in the United States). By 1988, the company was the eleventh largest steel company in the world. How did a country with absolutely no comparative advantage in steel production become a world leader in steel?

For some countries, temporary protectionism gives a reprieve from the winds of competition in order for them to get up to speed. These countries develop a comparative advantage where none existed, and this new comparative advantage becomes a source of wealth for those countries—thus the term *dynamic comparative advantage*. This reason for protectionism is called the *infant industry argument* because it supposes that the industry needs protection much like a child does in his or her early years. Economists get a little worried about using this argument to justify protectionism, because it is possible that the baby will never grow up. If protectionism remains permanent, we go back to our previous discussion. Then, it is basically a bad idea. Fortunately, for the Pohang Iron & Steel Co. Ltd, the South Korean government began the process of privatization in 1997, and the company was completely private by 2000. It continues to stand on its own feet and do well. In 2006, it was ranked the number two producer of steel in the world, just behind Arcelormittal.[25] Temporary protectionism actually produced a comparative advantage in this case. You've come a long way, baby.

National Sacrifice

You can't learn too soon that the most useful thing about a principle is that it can always be sacrificed to expediency.

William Somerset Maugham (1875–1965), English writer
Taken from *The Circle* (1925)

There is another argument for protectionism that makes good sense to many (even to some economists). This involves national security of some sort, whether it has to do with defence, food, water, or energy—the essentials of life. People who support protectionism for security reasons—whether it be food security, water security, or national defence—feel that the country should have production in these areas no matter what the cost. Unfortunately, the costs are great. The country will pay for that security with a lower standard of living overall, because it is not producing in the area of its comparative advantage.

Some people may be able to sleep better at night if they know that their country's defence system is in-house and that none of its fighter jets were imported. (In June 2009, IDG News Service reported that sensitive documents belonging to an American contractor were found on a hard drive in a market in Ghana. It seems that exported computer garbage may be more of a security problem than imported fighter jets.) At a more basic level, many

---

[25] Arcelormittal was formed in 2006 by the merger of Arcelor and Mittal Steel and has its headquarters in Luxembourg. It ranked ninety-first on the 2013 *Fortune* Global 500 list.

individuals favour some food or energy production in the event that all other countries stop selling them food or oil for some reason.[26] From an economist's perspective, as long as the price tag for this security is clear, a meaningful debate can occur about what level of security is essential. The security argument is kind of like the argument for insurance. Yes, those without fire insurance have a higher standard of living because they don't have premium payments, but what happens if their houses catch on fire? However, if you happen to live in a fireproof house, you may not need insurance. Maybe a basic insurance plan is good enough, rather than going for the deluxe coverage? In the same way that households need to analyze their home insurance needs, countries must figure out how risky their trading relationships are and then protect themselves accordingly.

UNDER THE INFLUENCE

If I have seen further it is only by standing on the shoulders of giants.

Sir Isaac Newton (1642–1727), English scientist and mathematician

The theory of comparative advantage, and all it implies, is one of the most influential economic theories affecting trade policy around the world. It turns out that David Ricardo, the father of free trade, became interested in economics at age 27 because he read a book while on vacation—not just any book, but *The Wealth of Nations* by the great economist Adam Smith. He did what Google Scholar tells its searchers to do: Stand on the shoulders of giants. Essentially, Ricardo's idea of comparative advantage predicts who will supply what in the market. The next chapter will explore one of the natural consequences of comparative advantage: supply (in the first of the Venti[27] chapters). If economics is known for anything, it is certainly known for the words *supply* and *demand*.[28]

---

[26] On October 17, 1973, Arab states placed an oil embargo on the United States (and later on Japan and the countries of Western Europe) as a punishment for its decision to supply Israel during the Yom Kippur War. The price of oil quadrupled by 1974. This control of a vital commodity became known as the "oil weapon."

[27] Recall that the Venti designation means that a little math is going to be thrown in. Don't despair. You can do this.

[28] The phrase *supply and demand* was first used by James Denham-Steuart in his *Inquiry into the Principles of Political Economy*, published in 1767. Adam Smith used the phrase in his 1776 book *The Wealth of Nations*, and David Ricardo titled a chapter of his 1817 work *Principles of Political Economy and Taxation* "On the Influence of Demand and Supply on Price."

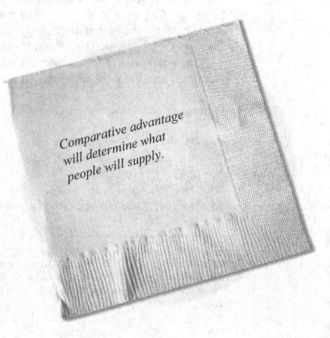

Comparative advantage will determine what people will supply.

CHAPTER 6

Supply Side (A Venti Chapter)

If you have great talents, industry will improve them; if you have but moderate abilities, industry will supply their deficiency.

Sir Joshua Reynolds (1723–1792), English painter

The sun has a warm glow as you look across the eighteenth hole to the fairway beyond. From your comfortable chair situated just outside the clubhouse, you have a tranquil view. Furthermore, the beer is cold and your muscles are relaxed as you stretch your legs out and cross them in front of you. The world feels like a great place at this moment. Laying your head back, you close your eyes.

From a nearby window—open to enjoy the late afternoon air—you hear bursts of laughter. From what you can tell, these folks have just finished a car rally and the winners are receiving their prize: a gift card for a free tank of gas.

"Let's go out on the patio and get a drink," says the winning driver.

"Great idea," the rest concur.

After rearranging tables to accommodate the group, the waiter takes their drink order. Easy conversation flows. It is the kind found among friends who have known each other for decades.

With mischief in her eyes, one of the women says, "So, what's this week's topic at the Old Boys' Club?"

A distinguished man with grey hair looks at her in mock horror. "The Retired Business Men's Association [said with emphasis] has an auto sector[1] analyst coming to talk about what is going on."

Another man with typical male-pattern baldness pipes up. "Good. Maybe the news will be better. All I know is that right now they're killing my pension income. I need it—especially because they are raising the green fees at the club."

The other men look shocked. "What?" they exclaim.

The man continues. "Yeah. I was talking to the manager. I guess the grounds crew all got raises, and the price of fertilizer is up. They have to raise the fees to cover the cost."

"Poor you," says a woman who appears to be his wife as she rolls her eyes and pats his arm.

A tall, athletic man gazes longingly at the golfers and asks, "So, who is in charge of organizing next month's activity? How about a golf tourney before the fees go up?"

"No. No. We agreed we would go the opera next month," asserts a woman with coiffed silver hair. The men all groan in a good-natured way.

---

[1] In 2008, the year the financial crisis took hold, U.S. auto sales dropped to 13.2 million units from 16.1 million units in 2007. According to data from Edmunds.com, the Detroit Three also lost 3.7 percent of market share over that year. Chrysler went from 12.9 percent in 2007 to 11 percent in 2008. GM went from 23.8 percent to 22.4 percent, and Ford went from 15.5 percent to 15.1 percent of the market.

SEPARATED BUT NOT DIVORCED: SUPPLY + DEMAND

I am like any other man. All I do is supply a demand.

Alphonse Gabriel "Al" Capone (1899–1947), American gangster

We will cover supply and demand much like the front nine and back nine of a golf course. In this chapter, we discuss supply and, in the next chapter, demand. In Chapter 8 we will bring them together and hopefully get a clearer picture of how the game of economics really gets played.

At first, some of the concepts we deal with will be challenging. Not only that, the media often oversimplify these ideas or confuse the concepts, which doesn't help matters. Getting back to the golf analogy, it may look easy to hit a little white ball into a little black hole, but a lot of physics and good technique are required to make sure your game goes well and you don't end up tossing your clubs into the pond on the seventh hole. Think of reading this chapter as if you are practising your putting on a green or hitting a bucket of balls at a driving range. There, you learn important fundamental skills, but it's still not the same as playing an actual game of golf. The road to understanding can seem tedious at times, but the tedious part lays down important building blocks for a good grasp of real-world events. So hang in there—you don't have to be a great economist to enjoy recreational economics, but the better you play, the more fun it is.

THE BASIC SWING OF THINGS

You have to learn the rules of the game. And then you have to play better than anyone else.

Albert Einstein (1879–1955), Nobel Prize–winning theoretical physicist

Before we start this training session, let's reiterate the key points made in the previous chapters.

1. People produce things with scarce resources.

2. Scarce resources mean there is an opportunity cost to use them.

3. The most efficient way to make a good[2] is to use the inputs or resources that have the lowest opportunity cost associated with them first.

4. The owners of low-cost inputs—whether labour, land, or capital—are said to have a comparative (or its synonym: competitive) advantage in the production of goods precisely because of their low opportunity costs.

These are pretty broad economic concepts, and so far I've been able to get away with using only words to talk about them. I hate to tell you this, but things are about to change as I get more precise. I'm going to use some graphs to explain things. While I was tempted to write a book without them, in the end I just couldn't do it. Here is why: Economists find that graphs effectively help us to tell the backstory that makes sense of the many comments and conversations about economics that often crop up at places like cocktail parties. Without these structured diagrams, economic words—which are rich in

---

[2] I know this might seem a bit weird, but economists refer to anything made that is a good thing as a "good." This is in contrast to something negative that gets produced (such as pollution), which we call a "bad." It might sound as if we're a bunch of 2-year-olds, but it works for us.

meaning—become jargon with no precise meaning at all. These visuals help us to picture the economic models thought to be running behind the scenes.[3] Without them, this book would be like golfing with a terrible stance, a bad grip, and the wrong clothes. Sad.

So, put on your thinking caps, because it is time to be a little more analytical[4] than we have been so far. If you get bogged down, don't worry about it. Stay with me and keep going. Try to get the gist of the entire chapter. You can always reread the tougher parts later—that is, if you want to. However, I won't be offended if want to mix a dry martini instead.

Gossip Column

Johann Heinrich von Thünen (1783–1850) was a German landowner-agriculturalist whose book *The Isolated State* (1826) was really the first to put forth an economic model that could be solved with mathematical tools. His model is the first example of marginal analysis (marginal cost is an example of marginal analysis), and while his book was devoid of graphs, it had many equations and tables that were even more daunting. *The Isolated State* was a serious treatment of spatial economics with predictions about land use around cities due to transportation problems and costs. Furthermore, von Thünen substantiated his ideas with empirical data, keeping meticulous records, thereby connecting theory with facts. This book is really the beginning of economic model building, which is the foundation of all modern economic thinking.

Alfred Marshall (see the Gossip Column in Making Introductions) said that von Thünen was one of his favourite historical economists. Paul Samuelson, the winner of the second Nobel Prize in Economics, declared von Thünen's work a "magnificent edifice of general equilibrium." This edifice is worshipped by location theorists, geographers, and Nobel Prize winners alike. Only ordinary economists have undervalued his contributions. This may be due to the fact that some of his ideas have not stood the test of time. For instance, von Thünen had some ideas about labour theory and was convinced that an important relationship was found in a particular wage equation. This equation was so important to him that he requested it be put on his tombstone. It reads $A = \sqrt{ap}$, where the natural wage, A, is the square root of ap, where p is the worker's product and a is the worker's subsistence requirements. This is an unfortunate use of tombstone space. The equation is really neither here nor there in economic theory, but von Thünen's location model is definitely on the academic map. More importantly, his way of thinking about theory was revolutionary. Unfortunately, spatial economics[5] is a specialized topic not found in most introductory economics texts and von Thünen's contributions to the discipline as a whole are often missed. Thankfully, Nobel Prize winners mention him from time to time.

---

[3] In Geoff Colvin's bestselling book *Talent Is Overrated*, Chapter 7 makes the point that elite performers in any field think in terms of models, not just facts.

[4] You will need to activate the left side of your brain in this chapter.

[5] For a clear lineage from Johann von Thünen to Paul Krugman, who was featured in the previous chapter, see Fujita, Masahisa. (2010). Evolution of spatial economics: From Thunen to the new economic geography. *Japanese Economic Review, 61*(1), 1–32.

WHO IS MAKING YOUR CAR?

Any customer can have a car painted any color that he wants so long as it is black.

Henry Ford (1863–1947), founder of the Ford Motor Company
Taken from *My Life and Work* (1922)

Essentially, economists picture the production of any good, whether a physical product or a service, as if it were one of many identical items in a line. For now, just imagine a line. Fortunately, I have one handy for you in Figure 6.1.

Let's take fuel-efficient cars—perfect for the afternoon car rally in the opening story—as an example. The line starts on the left with a point that represents the car that costs the least to make. Next in line, we picture another small fuel-efficient car that has the second-lowest cost of production. We continue this process until we place all cars of this particular type somewhere along the line in ascending order according to their opportunity costs.

FIGURE 6.1	Ordering of small fuel-efficient cars

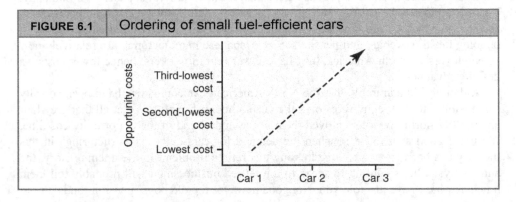

Visualizing a line (or lineup) of products like this helps us to keep our perspective straight when thinking about markets because it reveals what economists believe is the most important characteristic in the production of any good: opportunity costs. You see, economists sort companies by opportunity costs rather than by some other metric such as age or size, because ultimately only relative costs will determine which companies make the cars we drive. A business might be the "golden oldie" in the auto market, but if it spends more to make a car than the new company on the block, it gets sent to the end of the line or to the top right of the graph. This line is no "stairway to heaven." Car companies would actually prefer to be at the bottom end of this ascending cost line and will do whatever it takes to stay there. It appears that low costs are much like low golf scores. It's how you win the game.

Different Players, Same Game

There is one rule for the industrialist and that is: Make the best quality of goods possible at the lowest cost possible, paying the highest wages possible.

Henry Ford (1863–1947), founder of the Ford Motor Company

The big idea from this upward-sloping line of cars is that just because the cars are almost identical to each other, that doesn't mean their production costs are necessarily the same—and these differential costs matter. Just ask a representative from the Detroit Big Three about the impact of higher retiree[6] expenses on the price of their cars when compared to the Japanese Big Three.[7] Even though the cars produced by each of the companies may look equally attractive to the consumer, the underlying costs to make the cars may be radically different. This difference determines which company sells more cars and makes more profits in the auto sector irrespective of its long and glorious history.

Let's compare the costs incurred by foreign[8] and domestic car companies in North America. Both have similar hourly wage costs for their workers. So, that's not the difference. Aha, here it is: the cost for employee benefits! Until the most recent restructuring of the Detroit-based car manufacturers, the employee benefits gap sat somewhere between $25 and $30[9] per hour. This means that, in 2007, it cost approximately $2000 more for these companies to produce a car than it did for a rival Japanese car company. There is a price to be paid for having a long and storied history. Older companies such as General Motors, Ford, and Chrysler simply have many more retired employees with ongoing health coverage and pensions. Since Japanese manufacturers are relatively new as employers in North America, they have fewer retired workers, hence lower costs—a definite advantage.

Although it's admirable that the North American car companies have been socially responsible[10] to their employees over the years, the harsh reality is that all that grey hair among their former workers moved them to the higher end of the opportunity cost line. It's not a good spot to be in when the demand for cars tanks. "Restructuring" in this industry has been partly about addressing this retiree problem. In the opening story, the auto analyst who is coming to speak to the retired businessmen will probably tell them much of what I have just told you. Not good news for the old boys' pension funds.

Lining Up the Usual Suspects

I will not go so far as to say that to construct a history of thought without profound study of the mathematical ideas of successive epochs is like omitting Hamlet from the play which is named after him ... But it is certainly analogous to cutting out the part of Ophelia. This simile is singularly exact. For Ophelia is quite essential to the play, she is very charming—and a little mad.

Alfred North Whitehead (1861–1947), English mathematician and philosopher

---

[6] Toyota, with few retirees in the United States, spends less than $300 per vehicle on health care costs, compared to GM's more than $1600. Of course, the motor vehicle recalls that began in November 2009 and carried over into the next year raised costs significantly for Toyota.

[7] The Detroit Big Three are General Motors, Ford, and Chrysler. The Japanese Big Three—Toyota, Nissan, and Honda—all gained a higher percentage of smaller global sales. Thus, market share went up for them.

[8] The distinction between foreign and domestic has to do with head offices rather than the location of manufacturing or shareholders.

[9] White, Joseph B., Stoll, John D., & McCracken, Jeffrey. (2007, September 27). GM labor deal ushers in new era for auto industry." *The Wall Street Journal.*

[10] This probably has more to do with the negotiation skills of the United Auto Workers (UAW) union and the Canadian Auto Workers (CAW) union than with the kindness of the car companies.

Now, let's take that line of goods that we ordered according to opportunity costs and finally convert it to a typical economics graph. I can almost hear you saying, "Finally!" Remember that a picture is supposedly worth a thousand words. Well, I hope it's worth at least a few hundred to you, because the supply and demand framework is really the visual workhorse of depicting economic thought, so we are going to spend a bit of time on it. Hopefully it won't feel like I'm beating you over the head with a dead horse. (How do you like that for some mixed metaphors?) If you understand this way of thinking, you will be a long way down the yellow brick road.

If you talk to an economist about an economic problem, invariably he or she will pull out a pen and paper to graph what we call supply and demand curves. Economists do this over and over again. To the casual observer, it can feel like the movie *Groundhog Day*. However, these supply and demand curves are more than just pretty pictures; they tell stories. Now, don't be alarmed if you see a line rather than an actual curve. Economists call supply and demand illustrations "curves" even if they look like straight lines. Straight lines are easier to draw if you are artistically impaired ... and most economists are.

Let's first take a look at the supply curve in Figure 6.2. The supply curve captures, in a systematic way, the behaviour of all businesses as they react to a change in the price that is charged for their product. To illustrate, let's look at the behaviour of three car companies that at this point we'll call companies A, B, and C. In the graph, we will order all of the small cars they make according to their opportunity costs. To make the example easier to follow, I have shown all of the low-opportunity-cost cars as if they were produced only by company A on the left and all of the high-opportunity-cost cars as if they were produced only by company C on the right. In the real world, costs never separate out this neatly.

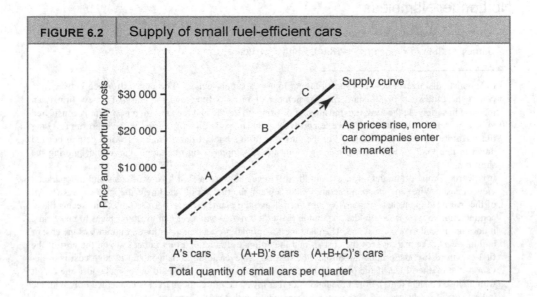

FIGURE 6.2   Supply of small fuel-efficient cars

If we replace the term *opportunity cost* with the term *price*, the line is called a long-run[11] supply curve and typically slopes upward from left to right. It slopes upward because usually prices start low and end high as more products are produced and sold in a market. Why is that? It's time to connect the dots between opportunity costs and prices.

Let's say that the price for a new fuel-efficient car is low—say, $10 000. According to the ordering of opportunity costs, we begin with Company A, because Company A and only Company A can cover its costs of production at that price. Since it is the only one that can survive by making cars at this price, only what it produces will be available to the marketplace, which means that the total number of cars on the market will be low. However, once people start buying more fuel-efficient vehicles, Company A becomes maxed out in its production capabilities. At that point, the cars have to come from another company and Company B is next in line, albeit with higher production costs. Higher costs mean that the price that Company B must charge needs to be higher as well.[12] Because all car prices are now higher, the executives at Company A think this is fantastic. They can now make more profit due to the difference between what it costs their company to make the cars and this new higher price—which, of course, they do charge! In contrast, Company B finds the price just high enough to get by on. Unfortunately for Company C, it needs a price of at least $30 000 to be a player in this market. It waits in the wings.

With a little extension of the logic, we can see that the price required to make a normal profit is the same as the opportunity cost of production. This shouldn't be surprising if you recall from Chapter 4 that economists assume that some level of profit is part of the cost of doing business. An important thing to keep in mind here is that the price of a car in the market is really a reflection of what it costs to make a car for the last company to enter the market. In our graph, $30 000 reflects Company C's costs of production, including the distribution of normal profits to shareholders.

No Longer Nameless

Experience teaches slowly and at the cost of mistakes.

James Anthony Froude (1818–1894), English writer

---

[11] Economists distinguish between short-run and long-run supply curves. The only difference between the two is the following: In the short run, the number of firms is fixed and the entry of a new firm is an increase in supply. In the long run, the number of firms is flexible and the entry of a new firm is considered to be a movement along a much more responsive supply curve. The supply curves in the short run and long run therefore have different slopes. For the purposes of this book, I don't think it's worth getting bogged down in this kind of detail. I am sticking to an upward-sloping long-run supply curve and ignoring the short run.

[12] It is worth taking a little detour to explain the difference between a firm's view of costs and the market's view of costs. When an auto manufacturer builds a plant, the first car off the line is the most expensive. All of the overhead is on that one car. As more cars leave the plant, the cost per car falls. This seems like a contradiction to what is said in the text, but in reality it is not. When a car manufacturer plans to make cars, it does not intend to make just one. The plant has an optimal production quantity that minimizes the cost of building cars. The market sees the cost around the optimal production point rather than on the cost of the first car. In reality, the production of only the first car is never going to happen and its high cost is irrelevant to the market. Even if the plant decided to decrease production, it would never make just one car. It would close up shop long before production got that low. Therefore, the market is concerned only with the lowest cost of producing cars for a particular manufacturer that really happens.

In our automobile example, the Japanese Big Three—Honda, Nissan, and Toyota—occupy the first three low-cost spots on the small car supply curve while the Detroit Big Three—Ford, GM, and Chrysler—are further along the curve at higher opportunity costs. (I think this was the correct order in 2007, but I wouldn't stake my life on it.) This ranking indicates a kind of "survival of the fittest" should the price for small fuel-efficient cars take a nosedive. Consequently, it was no surprise during the economic downturn of 2008–2009 that GM ended up in bankruptcy protection while Honda did not. Honda simply had the lower opportunity costs and could endure the lower prices better than GM. This is not to say that Honda's executives were happy about the lower prices, but the company was better able to absorb the brunt of the drop in car sales.

Picky Differences

The first day of spring is one thing, and the first spring day is another. The difference between them is sometimes as great as a month.

Henry van Dyke (1852–1933), American author, educator, and clergyman

When economists talk of supply, they usually are not referring to the particular number of units sold in the market. That number is called the quantity supplied, not supply. The idea of supply embodies much more than that. Sometimes people are confused by this distinction because *supply* and *quantity supplied* sound similar but are not the same thing. In Figure 6.2, supply basically *is* the line. On this supply line, we can have many *quantities supplied*, depending on the particular price point. Moving up and down the line changes the quantity supplied but it doesn't change the overall supply.

Maybe a golf[13] analogy will help to drive things home. There are a couple of ways to move a ball different distances down a fairway. One way is to use a particular club but change the force of the swing. The other way is to use the same force but change the club you use, because each club has a fundamentally different makeup. In our economic model, the distance the ball travels equates to the quantity produced and the force equates to the price. A change in force (price) changes the distance (quantity supplied), whereas changing the clubs—let's say using a pitching wedge instead of a 3-iron—represents a change in the overall supply. A change in supply happens only due to a fundamental change or shift in the way things are done—much like using a new club.

Failure to keep supply and quantity supplied distinct leads to incorrect conclusions when people discuss real-world markets, just as confusing a golf swing with golf clubs makes explaining a golf game difficult. In terms of market analysis, people most often get caught in vicious circles of logic. They say stuff like this: "An increase in demand leads to higher prices, which lead to an increase in supply only to see prices fall again, which leads to an increase in demand and prices are up again, which leads to an increase in supply …" Round and round she goes, and where she stops nobody knows.

This particular circle would have been broken long ago had the concept of movement along a curve (or change in quantity supplied) been used at least once. Instead, people litter their explanations with the *S* word and the *D* word and the conversation gets messy. Ultimately, you can't tell market stories that make sense without being careful

---

[13] The modern game of golf probably originated in Scotland around the twelfth century, with shepherds knocking stones into rabbit holes on the current site of the Royal and Ancient Golf Club of St. Andrews.

about supply/quantity supplied and its counterpart, demand/quantity demanded, any more than you can comment on a golf game without differentiating between the golfer's swing and his or her clubs. However, in economics you don't have to whisper.

How do you straighten out faulty economic statements? Well, we need to look closely at the role that price plays in the scenario. Does a price change motivate a change in the quantity supplied, or does some other change motivate a new price? The golfing commentator would ask the following question: Did the force change the distance the ball travelled, or did a change in golf clubs change how much force was needed? Once we sort out this confusion, we will also sort out whether it is a movement along a supply curve or a fundamental shift in supply.

Full Range of Movement

If I have done the public any service, it is due to my patient thought.

Sir Isaac Newton (1643–1727), English scientist and theologian

We begin with a movement along the curve or a change in quantity supplied. Essentially, this implies that if the price of a product goes either up or down, a company reacts to that price change by changing its production levels. It's like changing the force in your golf swing. Price and only price motivates the change. The arrows in Figure 6.3 indicate that the actual quantity supplied by a company changes when the price drops from $30 000 to $10 000 per car. In response to the price drop, companies drop the quantity they will make from 13 million cars to 9 million cars. Price changes motivate a change in the quantity supplied, but the fundamental supply stays put. (Just to keep this golf analogy going, the distance you hit the ball decreases if you use less force in your swing, but you are still using the same club.)

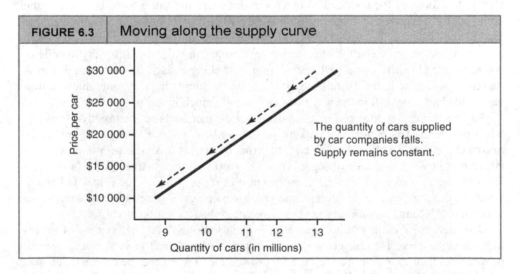

| FIGURE 6.3 | Moving along the supply curve |

The quantity of cars supplied by car companies falls. Supply remains constant.

The arrows on this graph just happen to show quantity decreasing rather than increasing because the example is about prices falling. However, if you flip the arrows around, you can show the quantity supplied increasing from 9 million cars to 13 million cars when prices rise from \$10 000 to \$30 000 per car. (However, the adage *what goes up must come down*[14] is not true in markets. Unlike for gravity, there is no law that says prices and quantities have to fall. It is entirely possible that they can keep going up and never come down.)

In the real world, when prices fall, companies that at one time produced their wares profitably cannot do so anymore (which probably stresses out the executives quite a bit). They now have to decrease the quantity they supply and have some options to accomplish this. For instance, they can downsize their workforce to get "leaner and meaner," thereby reducing opportunity costs. Or, they can simply go bankrupt and leave the market altogether. Either reaction is a response to lower prices in the market and from a long-run perspective is called a drop in the *quantity supplied* to the marketplace.

Another Cost by Any Other Name Is Still a Cost

> *We do not think good metaphors are anything very important, but I think that a good metaphor is something even the police should keep an eye on.*
>
> Georg Christoph Lichtenberg (1742–1799), German scientist and satirist

Next, we look at how we represent a business reaching—metaphorically speaking—for a new club. It is time for a shift or change in supply. This occurs when a business experiences fundamental changes to its costs that ultimately affect the price that must be charged for a product. In Figure 6.4 we see two different supply curves: one labelled *Initial supply* and the other labelled *New supply*. This figure is kind of like a before and after picture for the shift in supply.

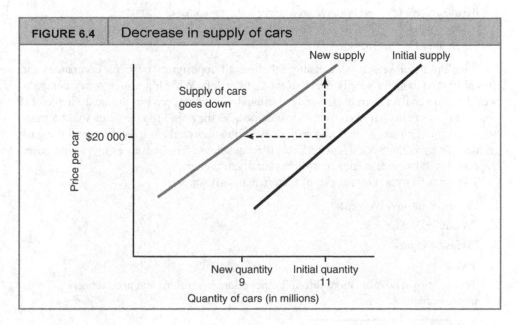

FIGURE 6.4	Decrease in supply of cars

Attributed to Sir Isaac Newton as a reference to the law of gravity.

On the initial supply curve, at a price per car of $20 000 the company could produce 11 million cars. When costs rise, there are two perfectly legitimate ways to explain what the company can do in response. The company could continue to make 11 million cars but it must charge more than $20 000 per car. Or, the company could accept the same price ($20 000) but produce fewer cars (9 million) at that price point. We visually represent the increased costs as a leftward shift of the supply curve along the X-axis. In this case, supply is said to have dropped because overall opportunity costs have risen. The car company is visually operating on a new supply curve and—yes, go ahead, you can say it—supply is down. Once it is on this new supply curve, the company can of course move up and down it to change the quantity supplied.

Essentially, supply and quantity supplied are all about opportunity costs. Therefore, companies care about anything that changes the cost of doing business. It doesn't matter if it is motivated by a movement along a supply curve or by a shift in one. When companies engage in cost-cutting they aren't usually being mean-spirited.[15] Often it's a matter of survival.

Furthermore, an analyst who digs into the inner workings of a company or investigates industry-wide trends before making market predictions in the media isn't just a Nosy Parker. He or she cannot predict anything without knowing the details of what happened to costs and why. The next section will dissect the possible reasons why supply curves shift one way or another—changes that will motivate new prices—and you will see that each scenario can be reduced to a change in the opportunity cost of doing business.

Business Fundamentals

We all, according as our business prospers or fails, are elated or cast down.

Publius Terentius Afer, known as Terence (195/185–159 BC), Roman playwright
Taken from *Hecyra* (165 BC)

Let's look more closely at what changes the overall opportunity costs for companies and thus shifts the industry supply curve to the right or left. What big issues worry company presidents other than market demand? (Demand will be covered in the next chapter.) If you end up at a cocktail party with business people, they tend to complain about a number of things: their employees, the rising cost of raw materials, the weather, and the government. Why is that? Well, each affects their businesses' bottom lines by raising costs. Economists illustrate this idea by shifting supply to the left.

There are five main categories of factors that shift supply:

1. Government involvement
2. Productivity changes
3. Prices of inputs
4. Weather
5. Technological advancement through innovation, invention, and production improvements

---

[15] In the 2005 film *Kinky Boots*, the owner, Charlie Price, describes the times he laid off workers as some of the worst of his life. To save the company he stops producing staid menswear and begins producing kinky boots for men. The supply of staid men's shoes decreased and the supply of kinky boots increased. Fortunately, this change in supply saved the company and the workers' jobs.

1. Government Involvement

A government that robs Peter to pay Paul can always depend on the support of Paul.

George Bernard Shaw (1856–1950), Irish writer and Nobel Prize winner in Literature

Since people love to complain about government, it gets the top spot. What are the major "sins" of governments? They tax and regulate businesses. (Sometimes, creating really complicated tax laws can feel like a combination of these!) Taxes take money out of the pockets of a company, and regulations force the company to jump through costly compliance hoops. Complicated tax laws require that companies hire expensive accountants in order to figure out legal ways to avoid paying the piper. Clearly, governments can increase the opportunity cost of doing business.

But governments giveth as well as taketh. They can do things like deregulate and subsidize, both of which benefit companies. Business leaders usually don't complain about these things at a cocktail party unless they occur in some sector other than their own. Then, you hear a lot of grumbling about how unfair the government is, which tends to put a negative spin on the party. May I suggest you introduce these folks to one of your lobbyist friends? If you don't think they can afford a lobbyist, how about buying them another cocktail and trying to redirect the conversation?

2. Productivity Changes

Jesus is coming. Look busy.

Bumper sticker and T-shirt slogan

How many times have you heard someone say that you can't get good help these days? Employers tend to complain a lot about the work habits of their staff. If an employee makes a lot of mistakes, arrives late, works slowly, leaves early, makes many personal calls during work hours, visits colleagues at the water cooler, searches the web all morning,[16] and takes twice as long to do something than anyone else does, then you can be sure that management is keenly aware that the cost figures are climbing along with their blood pressure. Low-productivity workers who happen to earn the same wage as high-productivity workers raise the cost of what is produced. They do "less with more"—that is, they produce less than they potentially could for the same cost. This reduction in productivity decreases or shifts supply to the left.

Remember, if you are ever at a cocktail party with employers who have "slackers" in their companies, don't get them started the topic of "good help." Believe me when I say the conversation can only go downhill. As an employee myself, I find it helpful to at least keep up the appearance of high productivity. That way, management stays happy with me. (By the way, if any of my employers happen to be reading this book, I hope you bought 10 copies—just kidding.)

3. Prices of Inputs

I can make more generals, but horses cost money.

Abraham Lincoln (1809–1865), American president

---

[16] Lim,Vivien K.G., Teo, Thompson S.H., & Loo, Geok Leng. (2002). How do I loaf here? Let me count the ways. *Communications of the ACM, 45*(1). These authors quote internet productivity losses between 30 and 40 percent.

Supply can decrease or increase if input prices go up or down. Labour is generally the most important input in the production process, so don't mention the dreaded word *union* to a manager during a cocktail party, especially if that manager is also the owner. You don't want to be responsible for a coronary. In a nutshell, unionization causes higher wages, salaries, and benefit packages—although, to be fair, it does tend to raise productivity as well—just not enough to cover the extra costs. On net, unions raise the cost of production and reduce supply.

The idea of scarcity also comes into play with labour because the scarcer particular types of employees are, the more employers will have to pay to hire and retain them, which can really "shift your curve." For some owners and managers, the old saying is really true: It is hard to get good help these days, at least at the desired price point.

In our modern technological world, labour usually works in tandem with physical capital. In the auto sector, some state-of-the-art factories cost more than a billion[17] dollars to build. As labour becomes more expensive (even non-unionized shops become expensive if they match wages to keep unions out), machines become a viable substitute for workers. In countries with cheap labour, there is less pressure to mechanize.

Next to labour and capital, oil is probably the third most important input for North American production. As oil prices rise, so do the costs to make most goods.[18] Most tangible goods are physically transported in some way or involve plastics of some sort. Furthermore, industrial machines need oil to keep them humming. Increases in the price of oil cause the supply curve of most products to shift to the left, indicating a decrease in supply.

4. Weather

Just for the record, the weather today is partly suspicious with chances of betrayal.

Charles Michael "Chuck" Palahniuk (1962–), American writer
Taken from *Diary* (2003)

Not all business people complain about the weather, but the ones who do probably rely on a particular kind of "good" weather. Ski resorts need it to be cold, road workers need it to be dry, and airlines need it to be safe. Farmers get the award for complaining the loudest about the weather. But we won't hold it against them since they depend a great deal on the vagaries of the weather. One bad drought, flood, summer hailstorm, or tornado can wreck a whole growing season, not to mention a farmer's day. Enough said.

5. Technological Advancement

A bore is a person who opens his mouth and puts his feats in it.

Henry Ford (1863–1947), founder of the Ford Motor Company

Bosses don't usually complain about the latest technology when they are at parties. If an employee invents some labour-saving device, the company can produce goods less expensively. It doesn't even have to be a monumental change. Simply tweaking (or the

---

[17] In 2008, Toyota opened a $1.1 billion assembly plant outside of Woodstock, Ontario, that employs about 1200 people.

[18] Oil-based products include such things as plastics, cosmetics, pharmaceuticals, and construction materials.

more sophisticated and substantive word *innovating*) existing processes can often increase productivity, which increases supply and makes management very happy.

Henry Ford is a good example of an innovator. He not only fathered the concept of the assembly line used to mass-produce his Ford Model Ts—an idea adopted by manufacturers around the world—but also developed the dealer franchise system. This allowed every city in the United States to have access to brand spanking new, yet relatively inexpensive, Ford Model Ts. Technology improvements and innovative business practices will increase or shift supply to the right, which contrasts with some of the more gloomy scenarios we have discussed so far.

CREATING LINKS[19]

One cannot be a good historian of the outward, visible world without giving some thought to the hidden, private world of ordinary people; and on the other hand one cannot be a good historian of this inner life without taking into account outward events where these are relevant. They are two orders of fact which reflect each other, which are always linked and which sometimes provoke each other.

Victor Hugo (1802–1885), French writer

Congratulations, you have finished the front nine of the course and (said with a Scottish brogue) it's time for a wee break. You deserve it. The inner workings of business aren't always obvious, but hopefully you have a better idea about the crucial role that costs play in determining a company's supply and quantity supplied. In the next chapter, we switch gears from supply to demand. Fortunately, since we are all consumers, you should be able to identify with the concept of demand (and quantity demanded) more easily, and you should find the next chapter a quicker read. Cheers!

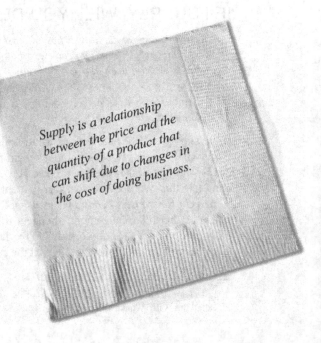

Supply is a relationship between the price and the quantity of a product that can shift due to changes in the cost of doing business.

---

[19]   A links is the oldest style of golf course.

CHAPTER 7

Demanding Clients
(A Venti Chapter)

The demand that I make of my reader is that he should devote his whole Life to reading my works.

James Joyce (1882–1941), Irish writer

There is a buzz in the air as you enter the foyer of the opera house. Can you believe it? The group of retired folks you saw at the golf course is here as well! You move closer to eavesdrop on their animated conversation. The women sparkle from the silver of their carefully coiffed hair to the gold of their shoes. All of them still wear their fur coats and they are sorting out what to do with them. Should they check their furs or keep them because of a chill in the foyer? For now, it looks like they're going to keep them on.

"*The Marriage of Figaro* is my favourite opera!" exclaims one woman.

"I am just glad it's a comedy. I don't really want to watch people die tonight," pipes in the balding man.

"Maybe you 'old boys' can pick up a few tips on how to keep your women. After all, for most of us it has been only 40 years," quips the woman with dancing eyes.

The men roll their eyes as they grin at each other. One of them smiles, wiggles his eyebrows like Groucho Marx, and says, "That's easy. Just keep her in expensive[1] chocolates."

As you watch these friends banter, you think to yourself: *Retirement looks like a lot of fun if I can stay as active as these people.* You remind yourself to buy some of those anti-aging vitamin supplements from a health food store that you recently saw advertised on TV.

IF I SUPPLY, WILL YOU DEMAND?

But the bounty of capitalism has at least one downside. It does not automatically produce what people really need; it produces what they think they need, and are willing to pay for ... if they are also willing to pay for snake oil, it will produce snake oil.

George Arthur Akerlof (1940–), American Nobel Prize–winning economist, and Robert James Shiller (1946–), American economist
Taken from *Animal Spirits* (2009)

If the supply side of markets has to do with opportunity costs, then the demand side is all about what buyers value—what gives them pleasure or happiness. Let's take a quick look at the psychology of the consumer. Have you ever been in a department store and heard something like this over the loudspeaker? "Attention, shoppers. Chocolates will be marked down 50 percent for the next 20 minutes in aisle 3!" If you have, you will notice that suddenly, with an almost herd-like movement, shoppers rush to buy the chocolates they may have previously passed over as "not worth it." Why did the mention of this price drop suddenly make those chocolates oh, so worth it? Was it the sultry voice of the announcer? I don't think so.

---

[1] Fritz Knipschildt is the mastermind behind the most expensive chocolate in the world and is sometimes called the Willy Wonka of Connecticut.

The explanation is all about marginal value. In Chapter 2, we discussed the concept of value in more detail, but here is a brief recap. Marginal value is the personal value to the consumer of an item when considered one item at a time. Here is the important idea: As the number of items purchased by the consumer increases, the value of each item in the psyche of the consumer tends to decrease. Think of it this way: The first chocolate goes in your mouth and gently melts. *Mmm* … fantastic! Better than sex, some would say.[2] You take a second chocolate. Again, you experience pleasure. However, it's never really as good as the first one. By the seventh chocolate you feel guilty (but who can resist the eighth!).

Economists think of the chocolates as items along a line where the first chocolate has the greatest marginal value and each successive one has a lower marginal value. It is possible to have so many chocolates that we wouldn't take another one even if it were free. In other words, the "good" has become a "bad" for you, and its marginal value has gone from a positive one to a negative one. Just because the individual chocolates look the same on the outside, they are not equal in value in the eyes of the consumer. It all depends on where that chocolate sits in the line in front of your lips … not to mention around your hips.

Looks the Same on the Outside

All animals are equal, but some animals are more equal than others.

Eric Arthur Blair, pen name George Orwell (1903–1950), English author
Taken from *Animal Farm* (1945)

Let's visualize this with—what else?—a line on a graph. In Figure 7.1, on the left side of the graph, we have higher marginal values that can be translated into dollars and cents. In this case, the price is $20 because of the low quantity (two) available. If we move from the left side down toward the right, the quantity available goes up. This means that we are willing to pay the most for the first item in the line because we value it the most. As we consume more chocolates (six now, instead of two per month), the price we are willing to pay falls from $20 to $5 because our marginal value for that chocolate—given that we have already had a few—drops.

Economists call the entire downward-sloping curve (all of the possible prices and quantities) the demand curve, or demand for short. This curve plots the customer's willingness to pay for different quantities of the same good. This curve also tells us how consumers behave when the price of chocolates changes. Again, as with the idea of supply, we need to hold constant everything else that could affect the consumer's desire for chocolates in order to sort out how price motivates consumption. All other relevant factors will be represented by shifts in the demand curve.

Just as we did with supply and quantity supplied, we need to keep the distinction between demand and quantity demanded crystal clear. To illustrate the idea of demand and quantity demanded, let's look at two ways to increase the quantity bought. The first way is for the consumer to experience a price drop. In this case, the demand curve remains the same but, due to a price decrease, the quantity demanded increases. The

---

[2] Salonia, A., et al. (2006). Chocolate and women's sexual health: An intriguing correlation. *The Journal of Sexual Medicine, 3,* 476–482. This study found that women who ate chocolate did have higher Female Sexual Function Index (FSFI) scores. However, younger women tend to eat more chocolate than older women, and once the data were adjusted for age the chocolate wasn't important anymore. Too bad.

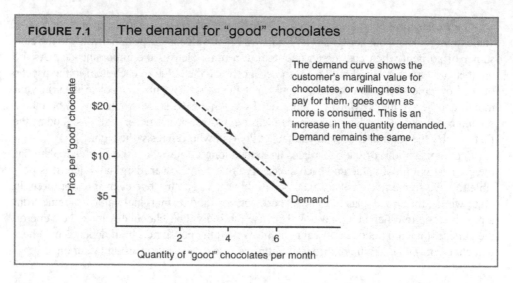

FIGURE 7.1   The demand for "good" chocolates

The demand curve shows the customer's marginal value for chocolates, or willingness to pay for them, goes down as more is consumed. This is an increase in the quantity demanded. Demand remains the same.

Price per "good" chocolate — $20, $10, $5 — *Demand*

Quantity of "good" chocolates per month — 2, 4, 6

second way is for something fundamental to occur that changes the consumer's values and willingness to pay for the item. These are shifts in demand and we will look at the big shifts later in the chapter.

Let's look at a change in quantity demanded first. Actually, we have already done most of this in the chocolate sale example. Basically, when prices change, buyers compare their marginal values (or willingness to pay) against what they have to pay to consume. Lower prices mean that marginal values can be lower, which only happens at higher quantities. Therefore, as prices fall, the quantity demanded increases.

When people hear about a special sale on chocolates in the department store, their brains (if they like chocolate, that is) may calculate that this new price is now below their internal "willingness to pay" value, which makes the chocolates worth purchasing when before they were not. Their brains also tell them to hustle over and buy some chocolate before it is all gone. As they buy more, their brains recalculate the new dropping marginal values of each successive package of chocolates until the last box's marginal value matches the sale price. The greater the drop in price, the more chocolates it takes to reach psychological equilibrium. The quantity demanded is up, but it is rare for a shopper to clear out a whole bin.

However, the consumption of chocolate can go up because of factors other than chocolates going on sale. For example, Halloween, Christmas, and Easter all seem to involve an unhealthy amount of chocolate. (I'm sure kids wish that back-to-school sales had chocolates as part of the tradition!) In Figure 7.2, we represent this kind of change in consumer behaviour with a shift in the demand curve. There are two stories that can make sense. One way to look at it is to say that, for the same price (say, $10), people are willing to buy more chocolates. In other words, their value for chocolates goes up during certain holidays. The quantity purchased at $10 goes up from the initial two to the new three chocolates per month. But another way to look at it is to say that people are willing to pay more to maintain current levels of chocolate consumption. Notice in the graph that, at two chocolates per month, people value chocolate at more than $10 per box. Either way, this scenario looks like a rightward shift of the demand curve, which is called an increase in demand.

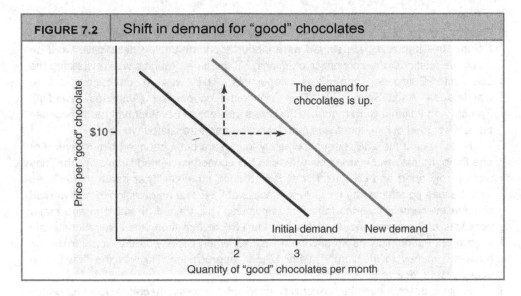

FIGURE 7.2   Shift in demand for "good" chocolates

The demand for chocolates is up.

Price per "good" chocolate

$10

Initial demand   New demand

2   3

Quantity of "good" chocolates per month

There are many more things that can change how consumers feel about chocolates. Here is an adult example: Suppose that a new study somehow proves that chocolate increases libido in women. I think most of us would predict an increase in the demand for boxes of chocolates. However, it is hard to say if women would buy the chocolates for themselves or if men would purchase the chocolates as an aphrodisiac … I mean gift.[3] In the end, it doesn't much matter to Charlie and his chocolate factory as long as things are looking up.

Gossip Column

Sir John R. Hicks (1904–1989) was the eldest son of a newspaperman and a nonconformist[4] minister's daughter. He won a mathematics scholarship to attend Balliol College, Oxford, but was not content with mathematics and after one year switched to the new Philosophy, Politics, and Economics (PPE) school, also at Oxford. Things did not go well, partly because he was "not well taught" in economics.[5] He finished with a second-class degree and no real qualifications in any of the three subjects,[6] even though it was evident to his fellow students and tutors that he was a very gifted person.

Hicks tried to follow in his father's footsteps as a journalist, but that didn't go well either. Fortunately (as he says in his own words during his acceptance speech for the Nobel Prize), economists were scarce, and he took a temporary lectureship at the

---

[3]   Valentine's Day week has the highest sales of boxed chocolates in the year.

[4]   A nonconformist is an English or Welsh Protestant of any non-Anglican denomination, chiefly advocating religious liberty.

[5]   See the *Oxford Dictionary of National Biography* by R.C.O. Matthews. This is the same college that Adam Smith expressed critical views about.

[6]   Hicks's autobiography for the The Sveriges Riksbank Prize in Economic Sciences in Memory of Alfred Nobel 1972.

London School of Economics (LSE) during the time of Lord Robbins (see Gossip Column in Chapter 1). He started as a labour economist doing descriptive work on industrial relations (the economics of unions). At the time, Robbins was revitalizing the LSE with European, non-British economists. This was in direct contrast to Cambridge's Anglo-Saxon feel. The Continental economists (Austrians, Swedish, French, and Italians) were formative in Hicks's intellectual development partly because he was so good at languages and could read their non-translated works.

Hicks was at the LSE for approximately four years but it changed him forever. For one thing, he met and married his wife, another economist named Ursula Webb. They were rarely apart and completely devoted to each other until her death in 1985. As well, he was so affected by his lack of success at PPE that he questioned and worked through everyone's theories from first principles. This trained his mind to see major concepts and connections. Furthermore, the LSE at that time was inspirational, with such great economists as Fredrich von Hayek.[7] When Hicks won the Nobel Prize, he gave the money to the library at the LSE in appreciation. He was the first British economist to receive the award.[8]

Hicks is described as the economist's economist, creating theoretical tools for others to use. His influence was transformative and felt in almost all branches of the economics discipline. It is difficult to narrow down what he should be known for. For the purposes of this book, I will tell you that most second-year economics students will recognize the terms *income* and *substitution* effects in the creation of demand curves. These are the basic tools taught in all economics programs. What most students wouldn't know is that Hicks developed these constructs ... and many others. (Unfortunately, textbooks don't usually name-drop and ideas appear as if they always existed. To counteract this problem, when Hicks taught a course he always made the students read the original papers.) Ultimately, Hicks received the Nobel Prize for his work[9] on general economic equilibrium theory (more on that in the next chapter) and welfare theory.

Hicks spent the last 35 years of his career as a Fellow of All Souls College, Oxford ... the place where he failed a fellowship examination many years earlier. At All Souls, Hicks was an active delegate of the Oxford University Press. Any early failures were completely forgiven and forgotten ... on both sides.

CONSUMER BEHAVIOUR

In opera, as with any performing art, to be in great demand and to command high fees you must be good of course, but you must also be famous. The two are different things.

Luciano Pavarotti (1935–2007), Italian opera singer
Taken from *My World* (1995)

In studying consumer behaviour, there are four main categories that can fundamentally shift consumer demand:

---

[7] Hayek (1899–1992) won the Nobel Prize two years after Hicks.
[8] This was partly because the Cambridge greats—Marshall and Keynes—had died. The Nobel Prize must be given to a living economist.
[9] The award was shared with another great economist, Kenneth Arrow.

1. Consumer preferences
2. Consumer income
3. Prices of related products
4. The number of buyers in the market

1. Consumer Preferences

In the affluent society, no sharp distinction can be made between luxuries and necessaries.

John Kenneth Galbraith (1908–2006),[10] Canadian-born economist
Taken from *The Affluent Society* (1958)

Tastes can and do change—sometimes voluntarily, sometimes with a little help from societal pressure. For instance, when I was a university student, I didn't dare wear fur on campus, even in the coldest weather, for fear that some animal rights activist would spray my fur with a hair removal product. As a meat eater, I didn't see the problem with wearing farm-raised mink (after all, they're not an endangered species and I really like the feel of fur, not to mention its warmth in the winter). However, back then, I succumbed to peer pressure and didn't buy a real fur coat. Alas, I've had a succession of fakes ever since. This type of societal pressure was very tough on the fur industry for a time. Fortunately for them, some famous hip-hop artists started to wear fur, which helped turn things around, especially among style-conscious younger men tuned in to that genre of music. Mink farms think that demand has now shifted in the right direction.

Retail clothiers make every effort to understand consumer preferences. They know that customers usually buy summer clothes before the summer starts and winter clothes before winter begins. There's a rhythm to many markets according to the ebb and flow of what customers want and when they want it. These preferences change not only with the annual seasons, but also with the seasons of life. North America has an aging population and many members of that population are fighting back, causing the anti-aging[11] market to grow steadily. I have tried an anti-wrinkle cream myself but unfortunately it "anti-aged" my skin so much that I got acne again.

Advertising powerfully taps into consumer preferences. Sometimes it's just a matter of informing customers about products they are unaware of or drawing attention to desirable features of the ones they do know about. Most of today's grocery stores abound with food labels that contain terms such as *no trans fats*, *light*, *organic*, *local*, and *fair trade*, precisely because today's consumers prefer or demand these kinds of products.

If you want to sell, say, a new line of clothing, it pays to let potential customers know that a member of the U.S. president's family wears your line. In addition to having great sway over teams of photographers, "First Families" seem to have great power to induce consumer demand. From Jackie Kennedy's simple suits, sleeveless A-line dresses, and pillbox hats to Malia and Sasha Obama's cute J. Crew inaugural dresses, inquiring minds want to know where these clothes or similar knock-offs can be purchased. Getting the word out can increase demand.

---

[10] Galbraith did his undergraduate studies at the University of Guelph, which is where Eveline Adomait works.

[11] The global market for anti-aging products was approximately US$122.3 billion in 2013.

Advertisers also seemingly create demand where none existed before. Theologians call this *ex nihilo*, or "out of nothing." It turns out that human demand is rooted in something—desires and wants—that marketing departments are trying to attach a product to. For instance, love and fidelity has a stone. It's called a diamond,[12] and we all know it's "forever." Why is that? Couldn't love just as easily be symbolized by a hunk of quartz? In the minds of most women, you can almost hear, "You've got to be kidding. Those days are over!" The marketing brilliance of the "diamond is forever" advertising campaign forever changed how young men propose to their prospective fiancées. Unfortunately for the men, a cubic zirconium simply will not do.

2. Consumer Income

A large income is the best recipe for happiness I ever heard of.
Jane Austen (1775–1817), English novelist
Taken from *Mansfield Park* (1814)

Everyone loves getting a raise. I once had my salary almost double overnight and I can't describe to you the euphoria I felt at the time. I know money isn't everything, but it sure is something. The reality is that most people do buy more stuff when their income increases. In my case, I no longer thought twice about the cost of a *caffe latte*. Economists call items that respond positively to an increase in income *normal goods*. Being normal sounds like a good thing. However, when you are in the middle of a recession, it's not that great to be "normal," as the auto manufacturers discovered. We would classify most cars, including SUVs, minivans, and luxury cars, as normal goods. When income is up, demand is up. However, the reverse is also true. When income goes down, demand goes down as well. The most recent global recession caused the demand for cars to go down in most parts of the world because normal goods simply go with the income flow.

We cannot classify all products as normal goods, however. Products like canned meat, macaroni and cheese, and rice and beans all do well when incomes fall because they are "belly-fillers." But these foods don't sell as well when incomes rise. Economists call these products *inferior goods*. (As you can tell, this term predates the era of political correctness.) You might be interested to know that in Birmingham, Alabama,[13] the ballet, the symphony, and the opera all experienced increased attendance during the 2008–2009 recession. I will let you make your own conclusions about how "normal" opera is!

Lastly, some products seem immune to income swings. We consider these kinds of products as necessities or the kinds of products you would buy only in limited quantities. These include such items as insulin, table salt, toilet paper, and cookies. I don't know too many diabetics who would go on an insulin spending spree after winning the lottery. Insulin purchases relate to a person's state of health rather than to his or her income level. Another example is ordinary table salt. I can assure you that the last time my income increased, I didn't go out and purchase copious amounts of salt. (Although, come to think of it ... margaritas, anyone?)

---

[12]   In 2000, *Advertising Age* named "A Diamond Is Forever" as the best advertising slogan of the twentieth century. "A Diamond Is Forever": How Four Words Changed an Industry. Voanews.com. March 22, 2007.

[13]   From the summer of 2008 to the summer of 2009, Alabama Ballet attendance grew 26 percent, while Opera Birmingham gained 21 percent and Alabama Symphony gained 13 percent.

3. Prices of Related Products

I sometimes wonder whether all pleasures are not substitutes for joy.

C.S. Lewis (1898–1963), British scholar and novelist
Taken from *Surprised by Joy* (1955)

A price change for one good can influence the demand for another. For example, when oil prices rise, drivers begin to search for more fuel-efficient vehicles. This means that oil prices directly increase small car sales and decrease the demand for gas guzzlers. Also, most North Americans borrow money to purchase or lease a vehicle. This means that the availability of credit also directly relates to the demand for cars, no matter what type. For reasons too complicated to outline in this book, Japanese car manufacturers enjoyed a comparative advantage in the small car market and focused production on them. In contrast, American car companies produced gas-guzzling SUVs and consequently took a substantial hit[14] when oil prices spiked above $100 a barrel. All car companies, however, experienced the collateral damage inflicted on the auto sector during the credit crunch. Both oil and credit are examples of products that go together with gas-guzzling cars and, to a lesser degree, fuel-efficient cars. They are called *complements in consumption*.

You can buy many products separately, but most people can easily see the pairings: hot dogs and buns, shampoo and conditioner (I always finish shampoo before the conditioner, which is annoying), peanut butter and jam. If the price of a complement goes up, the quantity that consumers buy of its paired product falls even though that product's price hasn't changed. Voila—a shift in the demand curve to the left on the graph.

Products also exist as substitutes for each other. Think about brands. If, for instance, one brand of toothpaste goes on sale and is available in a bin at the end of the aisle at a drugstore or grocery store, I guarantee that eventually you will find many tubes of the competing brands mixed in that bin as well, and someone's going to have to put them back in their rightful place.

Here's what happens: Customers walk through the aisles of their local store and pick up a higher-priced tube off the shelf because it's on their shopping list. However, as they get to the end of the aisle, they notice a bin with some other brand of toothpaste on sale. If they have no particular brand loyalty, they pick up the cheaper tube and leave the higher-priced one in the bin instead of returning it to where it belongs. Annoying, I know, especially if you take the wrong tube out of the bin only to find out it is not the brand on sale at checkout! To many people, the opportunity cost in terms of time to return the unwanted tube to its rightful place just isn't worth it. In the end, you have a bunch of competitors' products mixed together in the sale bin. This must irritate the store managers to no end. Now they have to restock the toothpaste. (Just so you know, I always make my kids return the higher-priced product to its rightful spot. I am not overly concerned about the opportunity cost of their time. However, I wish I was as successful at making them floss more regularly! That is a battle I don't always win.)

Consequently, if a company has a product priced slightly higher than its competitors, it must do everything in its power to demonstrate that its product is different in some meaningful way from the others on the shelves. It must be "new and improved" or have "magic crystals" with divine power to give you that "angelic smile" you need to impress

---

[14] *The Economist.* (2009, January 17). The big chill.

that special someone. It must set itself apart from the crowd because, if the consumer perceives that all products of a certain type have identical value, the low price wins. This means that as the price of a substitute goes down and customers decide to buy the cheaper product, the demand for all competing product lines takes a hit and goes down.

There also exists a particular type of substitute that, at first glance, doesn't really feel like a substitute to most people. It is the exact same product made by the same manufacturer but at a different point in time. I know this is kind of a *Back to the Future* idea, but a company can compete with itself. *What?* For instance, if you are a consumer in the market for a car and you know that a car will have a $4000 factory rebate starting next month, you will probably wait out the month and buy it later. The car today is a substitute for the same car one month from now. Today's market and next month's market[15] for the same car are actually different markets but very close substitutes. This means that when consumers expect prices to fall, they often defer their purchases. By the same token, if buyers expect prices to go up, they generally feel a sense of urgency to buy now. Businesses know this and don't want people to put off their purchases if they can help it. Therefore, businesses might mitigate customer concerns about future price drops by offering time-limited price guarantees. It could be something like "We will refund the difference if the price falls in the next 30 days." This guarantee helps to make a sale. Furthermore, stores know that the time cost to get the refund is often more than the price saving, and therefore many people can't be bothered to return to the store. Personally, I can never find the receipt to get the better price, even if I wanted to.

4. The Number of Buyers in the Market

Just because your friend decides to jump off a cliff doesn't mean you have to.

Margo Van Sligtenhorst (1939–), Eveline Adomait's mother

Simply put, if the number of buyers in a particular market goes up, the demand goes up as well. This might seem obvious but it's an important factor to consider when talking about demand. For example, baby boomers have made a huge impact on markets[16] in Canada and the United States, and they will continue to do so until they are gone. (Alas, I am one of these baby boomers.) For instance, as the first wave of baby boomers reaches retirement age,[17] economists expect the demand for health care services to increase. For some industries this will represent a huge opportunity, but for others it will be a challenge. Here's a hot tip for you: Many of these baby boomers will give up bungee jumping, so if you happen to own a bungee jumping company you might want to target the Echo generation in your advertising.

Sometimes, the number of buyers in one market can change due to circumstances or policies directed at other markets. For example, to deal with labour shortages over the

---

[15] Markets are always for a specific period of time, for example, the market for apples in a particular fall season.

[16] See *Boom, Bust & Echo* by David Foot.

[17] For a more fulsome analysis of the Canadian context, see the work of Professor Chris Regan in "Two Policy Implications Driven by Population Aging," *Policy Options*, October 2010, pages 72–79. He features a startling graph that shows that folks in their eighties spend four times more on health care than do those in their sixties.

years, both the Canadian and the U.S. governments have turned to immigration as a solution. New blood in the form of immigrants can radically change demand patterns for various products. For example, immigrants to North America from Northern Europe have generally been milk drinkers. In contrast, immigrants from Asia and Spanish-speaking countries have not been milk drinkers. As immigration from non-milk-drinking countries increased, the demand for milk turned sour. Furthermore, teenagers drink soft drinks and energy drinks rather than milk while on the go. Dairy producers would have been in real trouble if it weren't for two things that increased demand again: universal love for cheese and the celebrity-stacked "Got Milk?" advertising campaign.[18] Both of these factors made the low dairy-product consumers into higher dairy-product consumers, shifting demand to the right on the graph. Today, the fortunes of dairy farmers are looking up. Milk consumption is now a middle-class status symbol in emerging economies, which is driving up demand in countries such as China, India, and those in Latin America. Milk should continue to be like liquid gold as long as the melamine[19] stays out of it.

MEETING OF THE LINES

The meeting of two personalities is like the contact of two chemical substances; if there is any reaction, both are transformed.

Carl Gustav Jung (1895–1961), Swiss psychiatrist and psychologist

You may not have "got milk," but you do have the basic skills to put supply and demand together. Like golf—or marriage, for that matter—your technique will improve if you practise. Just remember that supply is represented by a curve that slopes upward and demand is represented by a curve that slopes downward. The next chapter will explore the meeting of sellers and buyers in markets. The game should be fun. Oh, by the way, good job on finishing the second Venti chapter!

Demand is a relationship between price and quantity that shifts due to changes in the consumer's world.

---

[18] "Got Milk?" is a campaign designed by the advertising agency Goodby, Silverstein & Partners for the California Milk Processor Board in 1993.

[19] Sanlu, the Chinese state-owned company, knew that its milk powder was contaminated with melamine, a chemical that causes kidney stones in young children. Babies who had ingested Sanlu's milk powder became ill with kidney problems in early 2007.

CHAPTER 8

Market Forces: A Beautiful Kind (Venti with an Extra Shot)

Order is not pressure which is imposed on society from without, but an equilibrium which is set up from within.

Jose Ortega y Gasset (1883–1955), Spanish philosopher

From centre stage, a female singer croons "Crazy." The thought, *She's no Patsy Cline but she's not bad*, flits through your mind. At that same moment, the double doors burst open, pushed by a group of rowdy college guys, shattering the melancholy mood. It's obvious that they're out for a night on the town. Each of them grabs a chair at the beat-up table near you, and they motion for the server to come to them. A beautiful young waitress makes her way over. After the requisite flirting and beer and food orders, she leaves the table and walks toward the kitchen. Their eyes track her steps. Once out of sight, the young men turn to survey the room. Their collective gaze lands on a group of 20-year-old women in the corner … who covertly return the favour.

You think, *This should be interesting.* Ludi incipiant[1]!

Holding court at a corner table is a beautiful blonde with four brunette girlfriends.

It's obvious from the conversation you can overhear that the young men are all attracted to the blonde and each would like to get her attention.

You think, *I hope they have watched the movie* A Beautiful Mind[2] *because they look as if they are about to make a fatal error by giving all of their attention to the same girl.* One of the young men mentions this fact, but he doesn't seem to be taken seriously.

Who knows how this game will eventually play itself out?

LOVE AT FIRST SIGHT

I had become interested in economics, an interest that was transformed into a lifetime dedication when I met with the mathematical theory of general economic equilibrium founded by Léon Walras …

Gerard Debreu (1921–2004), French mathematician and economist
Taken from Debreu's autobiography on the Nobel Prize website

---

[1] Latin for "Let the games begin."

[2] This example is not meant to be stereotypically sexist. Rather, it mirrors a pivotal scene found in the movie *A Beautiful Mind*. This movie features the life of the mathematician and economist John Forbes Nash, Jr. (1928–), who developed what is called the *Nash equilibrium* (NE). The NE states that a position is stable if there is no incentive to change one's strategy given that a player knows what everyone one else is doing. In the movie, the behaviour with respect to the blonde is not actually an NE. If one of the young men knows that all of his friends are going for the brunettes, then he should go for the blonde if she is really the prize. Therefore, everyone going for the brunettes is not an NE. It just goes to show that film producers never let a few facts get in the way of a good story. Nash received the Nobel Prize in Economics for this idea.

I know for many of you this is hard to believe, but some people actually love mathematics. I mean, really love it. They see the elegance of the language and can wax eloquent about it for hours. I work among these math-aholics in addition to being married to one. (Martin's other love—other than me—is chemistry. He routinely buys books with such riveting words as *volatile organic compounds*[3] in the titles, whereas my purchases are along the lines of *Men Are from Mars, Women Are from Venus.*[4]) At a recent department Christmas party, I found myself headed toward Martin and two colleagues engaged in an animated conversation. When I discovered that they were discussing the finer points of eigenvalues,[5] I veered toward the buffet table instead. While it is true that I avoided discussing mathematics that evening, it is virtually impossible to teach (or learn, for that matter) economics without using some math tools. This chapter will use the simplest of diagrams to show the mathematical concept of equilibrium. You will be happy to know that we will leave matrix algebra for another type of economics book!

SIMULTANEOUS EQUATIONS

I'm very well acquainted too with matters mathematical,
I understand equations, both the simple and quadratical,
About binomial theorem I'm teeming with a lot of news—
With many cheerful facts about the square of the hypotenuse.

Sir William Schwenck Gilbert (1836–1911), English librettist, and Sir Arthur Seymour Sullivan (1842–1900), English composer
Taken from *The Pirates of Penzance* (1879)

We captured the concepts of supply and demand in the last two chapters by visually representing them as two lines on a graph. Economists use the supply and demand framework to illustrate and make sense of how buyers and sellers play in the market. (Hopefully, they play nicely together.)

We saw in the demand chapter that price must fall to motivate additional purchases of an item. This is due to the fact that people drop the marginal value they place on something with each successive item available. In other words, the price people are willing to pay for something is dependent on how much is available. If we don't know how much of the product is available in the market, then we have no idea what consumers will pay (or what their marginal value is) and the whole demand curve is fair game.

On the supply side, we saw that as the quantity produced increases, the price the companies in a particular industry need to charge goes up as well. It must go up because the opportunity costs for the new entrants in the market are higher than the costs of the firms currently in production. Again, the price the industry as a whole needs to charge is uncertain until we know how much is needed and how many companies are active in the market.

This chapter takes the next step and nails down the price that will be charged and the final quantity that will be bought and sold in any particular market. All points on the

---

[3]   As it ages, all paper emits a complex mixture of organic compounds. This contributes to the familiar "smell of old books."
[4]   Written by John Gray and published in 1992.
[5]   Eigenvalues are often introduced in the context of linear algebra or matrix theory.

supply and demand curves are reduced to a single actuality in the marketplace when these curves get together. You might be thinking, *How can markets be about curves getting together?* Well, these curves, in a rather simple way, represent rational behaviour on the part of both companies and their customers. I know some people aren't too rational around curves, but rationality[6] seems to be a fairly good assumption to make about how people behave in markets.

How are the possible prices and quantities located on the individual supply and demand curves narrowed down to one actual price and one quantity? Take a look at Figure 8.1 and you will see that, mathematically, at some point these curves cross each other, and not in a Catholic sort of way.

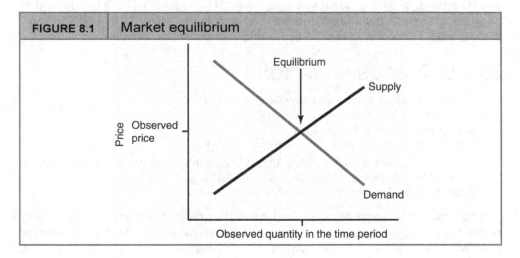

| FIGURE 8.1 | Market equilibrium |

This crossing point is called the *equilibrium intersection*. This means that one *and only one* price-quantity combination simultaneously satisfies both the buyer's curve and the seller's curve. (For all of you married folks, simultaneous satisfaction matters only in supply and demand interactions.) As long as the supplier's production possibilities overlap with the buyer's preferences, real exchange is possible and it can generate real numbers—actual figures that you have probably heard on business news networks or read in the financial section of the paper. This is no longer hypothetical supply and demand but real quantities supplied and real quantities demanded.

We will see in the next section that both sides of this market naturally gravitate to this equilibrium point. It is truly amazing that the amount that consumers want to buy is exactly the amount that producers make and there is no economic disagreement about the price. Sure, people on both sides of the transaction can complain about prices, but if they voluntarily exchange cash for the goods, then they are (as far as the economist is

---

[6]   Nobel Prize–winning economist Herbert Simon (1916–2001), in his book *Models of Man*, points out that most people are partly rational and partly irrational. This concept is known as *bounded rationality*. This irrationality can be due to the fact that individuals have limited information, limited time, and limited ability to make complex decisions. Most economists believe that, on average, rational models are predictive of reality. Others—behavioural economists, in particular—worry about the "bounded" part and make modifications to their models to incorporate this fact.

concerned, complaints or no complaints) agreeing with the prices. Adam Smith called this "the work of the invisible hand."

Observers of markets see only the equilibrium results—the final price and the volume of reported sales—and never get to see the underlying supply and demand curves. You can't go to consumers and companies and say, "Show me your curves." That information remains behind closed doors, deep in the psyches of consumers and the thinking of profit-minded owners and managers. Fortunately, knowing how the underlying model works means we don't need to mess with their minds to make sense of what is going on behind the scenes. Furthermore, if anything changes in their particular world, we can be armed and ready to make market predictions.

Getting Closer to Equilibrium

The faults of husbands are often caused by the excess virtues of their wives.

Sidonie-Gabrielle Colette (1873–1954), French novelist

In order to see why markets are driven to one magical price and quantity combination, let's first look at what happens when prices are above or below the equilibrium price. If the price isn't right, what forces the market into equilibrium and to a specific price and quantity combination that is stable?

To illustrate the concept of equilibrium, let's continue with our car[7] analogy from Chapter 6, only we will extend the analysis to all passenger vehicles, including light trucks. Figure 8.2 shows the starting point of vehicle prices that are too high. American consumers will not buy very many—only 9.8 million passenger vehicles. (I know this doesn't seem low, but for auto sales in the United States, it is.) On the other hand, at this price auto manufacturers would love to sell a lot of vehicles. They produce the large

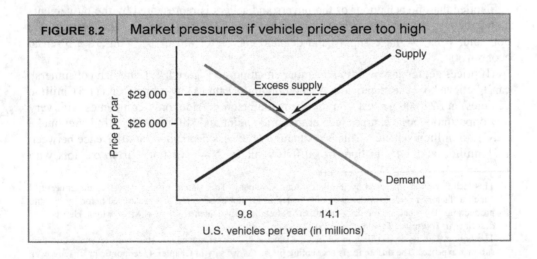

FIGURE 8.2	Market pressures if vehicle prices are too high

---

[7]   While the figures used in these examples are realistic for both the American and Canadian car markets, the use of them is not. Check out the report published by Scotiabank Group for the real story. It can be found at www.scotiacapital.com/English/bns_econ/bns_auto.pdf

amount of 14.1 million units. Hopefully, you can see that this is a problem. Auto manufacturers will actually make more vehicles than consumers want to buy. This is an
expensive mistake. These car companies now find themselves in a situation of excess
supply (the difference between 14.1 million and 9.8 million, which is 4.3 million vehicles), resulting in numerous car lots containing unsold stock.

Once management realizes what is happening, it usually calls an emergency meeting
of its high-level executives and quickly changes the company's plans. The company
doesn't want to have excess inventory piling up. (In fact, many car companies have
just-in-time[8] delivery to prevent big inventories of the parts used to make the vehicles as
well.) Unwanted inventories decrease the value of a company's bottom line.[9] Most
likely, the company will make the reasonable move to put its vehicles on sale and cut
further production. This action decreases the price and ultimately—due to the production
cuts—decreases the quantity available. In other words, the car manufacturer moves
downward along its supply curve toward the crossing point. Prices will be lower than the
original sticker price and the quantity of cars produced is no longer the overly optimistic
14.1 million vehicles.

As prices fall, consumers who previously didn't want a car at the higher price now
decide to buy at the lower "on sale, factory rebate, employee discount" price. Similar to
our chocolate analogy, the vehicle becomes more "worth it" and the consumer moves
along the demand curve to the crossing point. Prices are lower than the original price,
but the quantity of passenger vehicles bought is higher than 9.8 million units. Eventually, the quantity that consumers want to buy equals the quantity that dealers want to
sell, and the price stops dropping. Buyers and sellers meet at the intersection of supply
and demand. In other words, the market is in equilibrium with a price lower than the
original price of $29 000, and the number of cars bought and sold is somewhere between
9.8 million and 14.1 million units, the original quantity positions of the buyers and
sellers, respectively.

Notice that the behaviour of the buyers and sellers is represented by the movements
along their specific lines with a starting point and an ending point. Just connect the
dots and, voila, we have supply and demand curves for all to see. You are a forensic
economist!

If prices get too low, we find a similar situation. In Figure 8.3, Canadian consumers[10]
can't believe how cheap cars are. As a group, they want to buy a lot of cars (1.51 million
vehicles) at $24 000 per car. On the car manufacturers' side, only companies with very
low opportunity costs can produce at this price point and still make a profit. They make
only 1.45 million vehicles. This is a situation of excess demand—the difference between
1.51 million and 1.45 million, or 60 000 vehicles. Now we find barren car lots with

---

8   This technique was first used by the Ford Motor Company. This statement also describes the concept of
     "dock to factory floor," in which incoming materials are not even stored or warehoused before going into
     production. The concept requires an effective freight management system (FMS), which Henry Ford
     describes in *Today and Tomorrow* (1926).

9   The bottom line is the last line on an income statement. Income statements start with revenues and then
     subtract expenses. The difference is accounting profit. As we saw in Chapter 4, economic profits are even
     less, because some profits are needed to be in the business and are therefore a cost as far as economists are
     concerned. For example, if an entrepreneur gave up a job with an income of $40 000 per year to run a busi-
     ness, then accounting profits of $30 000 are really an economic loss of $10 000.

10   Canadian markets are usually one-tenth the U.S. markets. Passenger vehicles follow this trend.

lineups, waiting lists, rain checks, or whatever method best keeps track of unsatisfied customers. Whoever comes to a dealership after car number 1.45 million is sold will not be able buy one. Existing auto companies (or new ones waiting in the wings) realize that this is a profitable business opportunity and take the plunge to produce more vehicles, even if it costs more to do so. Thus, the quantity produced increases, but because of higher costs so do the price tags. The car industry moves along the supply curve toward the crossing point. The price rises above the original price of $24 000, and the quantity produced exceeds 1.45 million units.

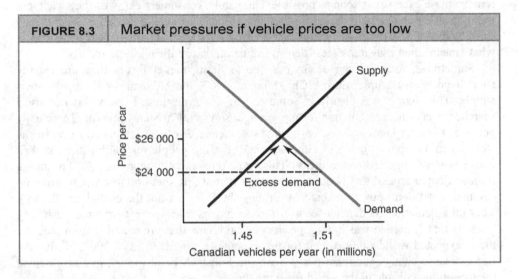

FIGURE 8.3	Market pressures if vehicle prices are too low

Consumers, however, now must pay more for vehicles, which causes some to decide not to purchase. People want to buy less because of the higher price. Therefore, consumers move along the demand curve toward the crossing point. As the disequilibrium disappears, prices rise higher than the original price, and the overall quantity that all consumers want to buy—although some were unable to buy—is lower than 1.51 million vehicles. Once we reach the crossing point, the market is in equilibrium. Therefore, if a market has an excess demand for cars, we can predict that car prices will be higher than the original price, and the actual number of vehicles bought and sold will be somewhere between 1.45 million and 1.51 million units after adjustments.

What Drives Equilibrium?

Drive thy business or it will drive thee.

Benjamin Franklin (1706–1790), American politician and polymath

When I told the story of reaching equilibrium in the car market, I hope you got the subtle message that, in either case, it is the car company who reacts to the consumer and solves the disequilibrium problem. These manufacturers, motivated by profits, change their production levels to strategically eliminate any excess supply or demand. (Of course, as a result of the manufacturer's responsive behaviour, the price that consumers must actually pay for the car changes as well.) We know that markets are in equilibrium when the quantity desired by buyers equals the quantity sellers want to sell. This matching of quantities happens at a common price point.

Profits are the force that drives markets and brings them into equilibrium. When organizations that produce things don't care about profits, such as with the communist central planning system under the former USSR, then it's quite possible to have a warehouse full of rotting vegetables that no one does anything about. Furthermore, without profits guiding production decisions, we can experience grocery stores with perpetual lineups, which can become a way of life. In a market economy, profit-minded entrepreneurs remove these excesses as soon as possible. Ultimately, consumers get what they want, but the motivation comes from the desire by business people to make the largest profits they can possibly make. If you have ever met a real go-getter entrepreneur, you would know what I mean when I say that excess demand situations excite them like no other.

Sometimes, excesses can occur, but due to these market forces they are usually short-lived. For example, during Christmas of 2007, the Nintendo Wii was in short supply. This market was clearly in some sort of disequilibrium. I know this because I searched everywhere to buy one for my younger son as a Christmas present. To actually get one, I had to know someone who knew someone else who happened to be in the store when a shipment came in. Stores weren't putting people on waiting lists, so Wii consoles were allocated to the lucky. This situation was very annoying. At the time, a rumour floated around that Nintendo had orchestrated this situation in order to drive up demand, but I don't buy it (actually, I did buy the Wii, just not the conspiracy theory). This miscalculation of demand cost Nintendo profits during the Christmas rush. My guess is that Nintendo was having production problems that prevented it from meeting the unexpected worldwide demand for this ingenious product.[11] As of 2008, production had increased enough such that the Wii was no longer difficult to buy, and it remained the top-selling console in the world for some time.

Gossip Column

The biggest influence in Léon Walras's (1834–1910) life was his dad. His father, a French economist, made his living as a school administrator because economics was not highly regarded as a separate profession in the French educational system. To please his parents, Walras applied to the École Polytechnique in Paris but failed the entrance exam twice due to his math skills. He then enrolled in a mining engineering school in Paris but didn't like it and spent his time having a really good time (some would say with a bohemian lifestyle) writing novels and critiquing art. His father convinced him to give this up to pursue economics, but because Walras did not have formal economics training (he was taught by his father or self-taught), he could not get a job as an academic.

Some of his father's socialist values and ideology must have sunk in because Walras then formed a cooperative bank with his friend Léon Say. In their opinion, the

---

[11]   According to NPD Group, the Wii sold more units in the United States in the first half of 2007 than the Xbox 360 and PlayStation 3 combined.

cooperative movement seemed preferable to revolution. They also published a journal espousing similar ideas to Walras's father about nationalizing land and tax policies. Unfortunately, approximately two years after inception, both the cooperative and the journal failed, but fortunately, Walras was offered the position of chair of political economy at the Academy of Lausanne in Switzerland. It was there that he combined his economic ideas with rigorous mathematics (whatever deficiencies he'd had earlier were eliminated) and wrote *Elements of Pure Economics*. This book took economics to new mathematic levels and he, along with William "Stanley" Jevons (1835–1882) and Carl Menger (1840–1921), are called the authors of the marginal revolution. Furthermore, Walras is often considered the father of general equilibrium theory, which was a new mathematical approach to establishing equilibriums in all markets at once. It appears that he is the founding father of much of modern mathematical economics.

Realizing that real-life markets might not solve themselves with nifty mathematical models, Walras developed a way for markets to clear called *tâtonnement,* which is French for "groping toward." Sounds interesting, but it's not what you think. Buyers and sellers call out prices and quantities. Most combinations lead to excesses, but the market will grope its way to equilibrium by decreasing subsequent excesses.[12]

At one point, Walras thought he was worthy of the Nobel Peace Prize (1906) and wrote his own nomination, which friends submitted. He felt his work in mathematical economics, which scientifically supported free trade, would lead to world peace if adopted. Unfortunately for Walras, Teddy Roosevelt won that year.

Walras wrote all of his works in French, and he was not recognized as an eminent economist until after his death, when William Jaffe (1898–1980) translated and published his works into English in 1954. This lack of academic recognition was very disappointing to Walras and he spent the last decade of his life frustrated, bitter, and sliding into senility and mental illness. It's too bad he never knew how famous his ideas would be among economists. Furthermore, he inspired great economists—specifically, John Hicks, Kenneth Arrow (new to us but important because he shared the Nobel Prize with Hicks), Gérard Debreu (who, along with Arrow, developed the modern-day general equilibrium theory), Piero Sraffa, and Wassily Leontief—to extend his ideas and make them usable. Sometimes fathers do not know they have children.

Curves Ahead

When producers want to know what the public wants, they graph it as curves. When they want to tell the public what to get, they say it in curves.

Herbert Marshall McLuhan (1911–1980), Canadian professor and media theorist
Taken from *Off-the-Wall Marketing Ideas*[13]

---

[12] Walras' Law states that when we are looking at the economy as a whole, all excesses over all markets sum to zero. Therefore, if one market goes into disequilibrium, it will force other markets—through spillovers and market linkages—to go into disequilibrium as well. This keeps the sum of the excesses equal to zero. Economists assume that if a particular market goes into disequilibrium, the individual players in that market react to remove it, thus all markets are also in equilibrium. Walras's general equilibrium theory is about both the sum of all markets and individual markets in equilibrium.

[13] *Off-the-Wall Marketing Ideas: Jumpstart Your Sales without Busting Your Budget,* by Nancy Michaels and Debbi J. Karpowicz.

When the market forces have done their work, disequilibrium (the state where the quantity demanded doesn't match the quantity supplied) gives way to equilibrium (the state where quantity demanded and supplied now match perfectly). The best way to find out whether markets are in equilibrium is to check inventory numbers. If the numbers are too high, the market has an excess supply; if they are too low, the market has an excess demand.

Once a market is in equilibrium, it can theoretically stay at this particular price and quantity combination forever, provided nothing causes either the supply curve or the demand curve to shift. But what are the odds of living in a world where nothing affects either the consumer or those who produce the goods? Basically, zero. Therefore, when a change occurs, we should to be able to predict what will happen in any particular market. We want to mind our Ps and Qs, or prices and quantities. What is the point of an economic framework if it can't predict anything useful when change happens?

SHIFTS HAPPEN

The network economy is founded on technology, but can only be built on relationships. It starts with chips and ends with trust.

Kevin Kelly (1952–), American editor and publisher
Taken from *New Rules for the New Economy: 10 Radical Strategies for a Connected World* (1999)

In the previous two chapters, we analyzed the supply curve and the demand curve separately. Specifically, we looked at the various stories that would shift supply and demand curves either to the right or to the left. Here is a quick review. A change in underlying production costs is represented by a shift in the supply curve. These include changes in productivity, input costs, or technology, which all impact the quantity businesses wish to produce at a particular price level. On the other hand, demand shifts represent changes in the consumer's experience. Changes in preferences, income, and expectations about future prices all change what people are willing to pay today and therefore can be illustrated by a shift in demand.

This chapter takes the next step to help you understand that these curves are not isolated from each other. If car buyers now prefer flashy cars, then car manufactures "experience" the increase in demand for flashy cars through market disequilibrium and will fix the problem. If steel costs suddenly rise, car manufacturers change the price of a vehicle and consumers "feel" the bad news and change how much they buy. In other words, we can represent these stories as one curve shifting and the other curve experiencing something moving along it. The supply and demand framework is very valuable in forecasting price and sales volume should something affect either the consumer or the producer of a product. Many real-world economic stories can be analyzed in this theoretical way.

Telling Stories That Make Sense

There are one-story intellects, two-story intellects, and three-story intellects with skylights. All fact collectors with no aim beyond their facts are one-story men. Two-story men compare reason and generalize, using labors of the fact collectors as well as their own. Three-story men idealize, imagine, and predict. Their best illuminations come from above through the skylight.

Oliver Wendell Holmes (1809–1894), American author and physician

Basically, there are only four stories that can happen if one curve shifts about. These stories have completely predictable consequences with respect to the ultimate price charged and the numbers of goods sold. We can picture them in the following four graphs. Let's keep it simple, shall we? Think of these as cheat sheets that we will use in the next section when we discuss ticket prices. You might want to keep your finger on this page as we proceed with the next section.

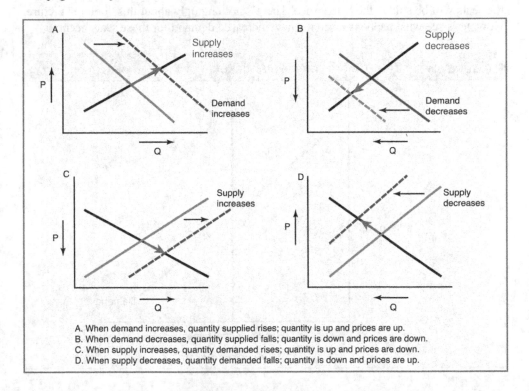

A. When demand increases, quantity supplied rises; quantity is up and prices are up.
B. When demand decreases, quantity supplied falls; quantity is down and prices are down.
C. When supply increases, quantity demanded rises; quantity is up and prices are down.
D. When supply decreases, quantity demanded falls; quantity is down and prices are up.

Now you can chat about economics like a pro at a social gathering. Maybe you should draw these graphs on a cocktail napkin and take them with you to your next party. Once you know the initial trigger for change, you can sort out which player's curve must shift and in what direction. Then you can confidently make your prediction on what will happen to prices and sales volumes in that particular market. Conversely, if you know what happened to price and quantity, then you know which shifting curve did the deed and which one got moved along. Once you know which curve shifted, you can look at the list of possible reasons for the shift and find the culprit. It is elementary, my dear Watson.

Irresistible Force

It was a marriage of love. He was sufficiently spoiled to be charming; she was ingenuous enough to be irresistible.

Francis Scott Key Fitzgerald (1896 –1940), American author
Taken from *Tales of the Jazz Age* (1922)

Suppose that we hear a story that the demand for some show in a big venue has gone up. It could be tickets to a sports team that miraculously starts to win games after a losing streak, or to some famous musician on a new concert tour. What can we predict will happen if nothing occurs to shift the supply of tickets at the same time as this increase in demand happens? To see what will happen, let's look at the state of the market before demand went up. In Figure 8.4, we see that if the ticket company gets it right, then all of the seats will be sold at the listed price. There's nothing ugly about this "before" picture. Now, let's see what happens when the new increased demand for those seats occurs.

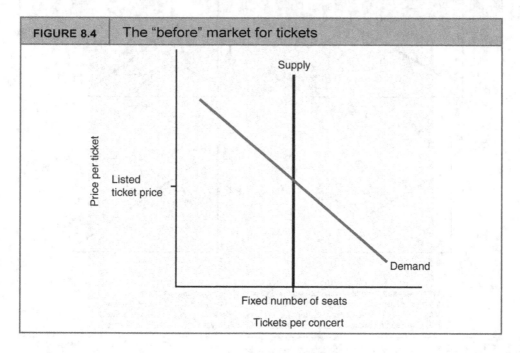

FIGURE 8.4	The "before" market for tickets

For starters, at current prices the demand is now higher and, for the particular price printed on the ticket, a company selling tickets for this venue will sell out of its stock in a matter of minutes. The market has an excess demand for tickets at that price point. Profit-minded individuals will try to correct this excess demand and some of the previously bought tickets will be resold for the true higher price in some other ticket resale market. Figure 8.5 illustrates this situation.

While a few consumers react to the higher price by angrily opting out of the market and complaining to their politicians, many customers are happy to buy a seat even at the elevated price. They would much rather get a ticket at a higher price than get nothing at all. This explains why people willingly pay scalpers more than the price printed on a ticket. Overall, if there is a fixed number of seats to be sold, an increase in demand will cause ticket prices to rise. Therefore, if you read a news story stating that an event now has higher ticket prices and that the performance has been sold out, you know that it must have been due to an increase in demand. You've solved the case! And another thing, just so you know, in the opinion of many economists the ticket resale market or the act of scalping shouldn't be a crime. It's just one more way in which the market corrects the initial disequilibrium problem.

FIGURE 8.5	Resale or "scalping" of tickets

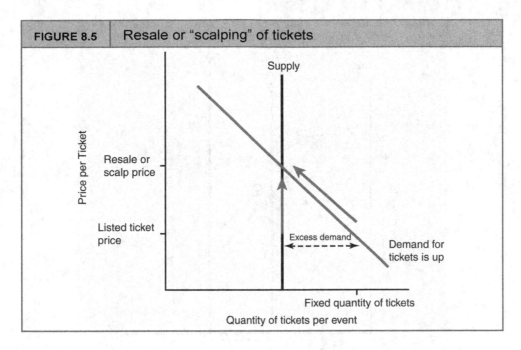

In contrast, suppose that the demand curve is the stable factor and supply shifts to the right. We get a different outcome, as illustrated in Figure 8.6. Recall that the usual reason the supply curve shifts to the right is because of a decrease in the cost of doing business. Suppose that the costs to put on a show fall because the rent for large venues is down—maybe due to real estate woes or to the building of another venue. As a result, the producers of these big shows decide to put on more shows and lower the price in hopes of expanding market share. After all, with lower rental costs, profit margins are now bigger. When the entertainment industry reacts to the lower rental costs by increasing the number of shows it wants to put on, the quantity of tickets available increases and the price per ticket falls. In essence, the decision to increase the number of available tickets shifts the supply curve to the right, which forces them to move along the existing demand curve for this particular live performance. More tickets on the market mean that many consumers value these tickets less. The only way that producers can actually sell these new tickets is to lower the price. In other words, an increase in supply leads to an increase in the quantity of tickets demanded. We know the story ends with ticket sales up and ticket prices down. Usually, no one complains about this situation to his or her legislators.

Home Inspection

An architect's most useful tools are an eraser at the drafting board, and a wrecking bar at the site.

Frank Lloyd Wright (1867–1959), American architect, interior designer, writer, and educator

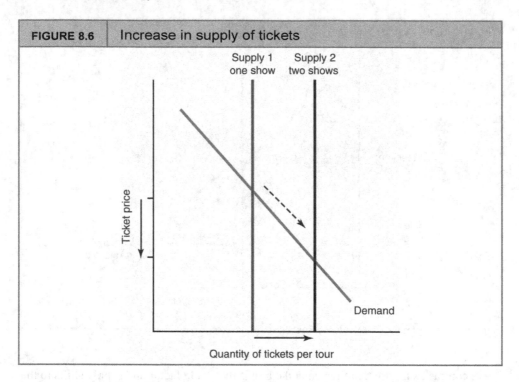

FIGURE 8.6 | Increase in supply of tickets

Most business articles give you a lot of facts and figures. The framework I have just used can help to explain how those figures come about. For example, in an article published in January 2009, the BBC reported that U.S. housing prices were down 15.3 percent in December 2008 when compared with prices in December 2007. Furthermore, the number of houses sold in 2008 was down 13.1 percent—the worst year in 10 years. What happened? The only story that predicts why both price and quantity were down is called a decrease in demand story. Demand must have shifted to the left. The article went on to explain that the credit crunch in the fall of 2008 made it difficult for borrowers to get mortgages to pay for new houses. (In Chapter 7 we saw that a change in the price of a complementary product can change demand. In this case, a mortgage is a product that is complementary[14] to houses because you usually need a mortgage to buy a house. When mortgage rates rise or mortgages become difficult to qualify for, this decreases the demand for houses.) Sure enough, this decreased the demand for U.S. houses in the fall of 2008. The economists quoted in the article were hopeful that dropping interest rates (the price of a mortgage) would cause demand to rebound.

Of course, predicting market results can get a little trickier if two shifts happen at once. Have no fear—just add the individual effects together. Suppose that we want to predict what will happen in the new housing market if interest rates go down at the same time that large tracts of timber are destroyed due to raging forest fires across North

---

[14] Recall that if the price or availability of one good changes the demand for another good, these goods are related to each other. They are either substitutes or complements. In this case, the availability of mortgages decreased, which decreased the demand for homes bought on credit. Since mortgages and houses are bought together, these goods are complements.

America. Lower interest rates should increase the affordability of building a new home and increase the demand for new houses. Given that lumber is a major component in new home construction, the new scarcity of lumber should increase the cost of building houses and cause the supply of new homes to go down. As shown in Figure 8.7, the interest rate change increases demand and the scarcity of lumber decreases supply. What happens to the price and quantity of new home construction?

FIGURE 8.7	The market for new housing construction

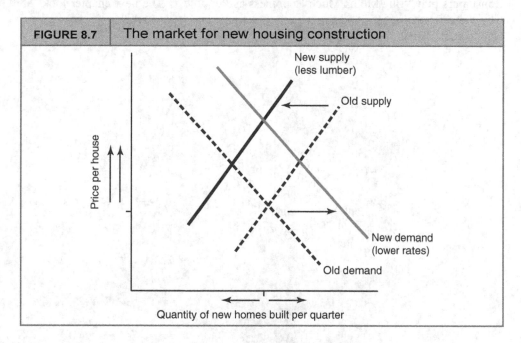

Using our cheat sheets, let see what happens.

- The increase in demand leads to higher prices and higher quantity.
- The decrease in supply leads to higher prices and lower quantity.

Overall, the price effects are additive, so prices are up but the quantity changes are moving in opposite directions. Therefore, we cannot predict what will happen to the number of new housing starts until we know which effect—supply or demand—is bigger.

Hopefully, I have given you a few tools to use when trying to understand business articles that can sometimes be intimidating or when listening to a business analyst drone on about what is happening in the stock, currency, car, housing, clothing, or whatever market they happen to be droning on about. The next time you are ensnared in a convoluted economic discussion, simply pull out pen and paper, cut though the clutter with a graph, and let the picture do the talking.

PLAYING GAMES

Economists try to predict outcomes of market interactions by modelling participants in markets, both buyers and sellers, as if they're playing a market game[15] under the assumption that each employs reasonable strategies to get what they want. The name of the game for those who produce the goods is called "How to Maximize Profits." Consumers play "Buy Me as Much Happiness as Possible."[16] The next chapter looks at why these strategies are good for society as a whole and how markets may be the best way to guarantee the most winners.

Profit-minded business owners cause markets to equilibrate. If supply or demand changes, then the market price and quantity also change.

---

[15] Many board games are based on economic principles. One such example is the game "Settlers of Catan" designed by Klaus Teuber. This game requires resource management due to scarcity and trading skills that give gains from trade. It was first published in 1995 in Germany by Franckh-Kosmos Verlag (Kosmos) under the name *Die Siedler von Catan*.

[16] Economists would say that consumers want to maximize their utility subject to a budget constraint, which sounds a bit strange to the general public. The word *utility* has its roots in the 1800s. According to utilitarians such as Jeremy Bentham (1748–1832) and John Stuart Mill (1806–1876), society should aim to maximize the total utility of individuals, aiming for "the greatest happiness for the greatest number." Society now uses the word *happiness* or *satisfaction* in place of the word *utility*.

CHAPTER 9

The Pursuit of Happiness: Efficiency and Equity (A Venti Chapter)

In this work I have attempted to treat economy as a calculus of pleasure and pain.

William Stanley Jevons (1835–1882), English economist
Taken from *The Theory of Political Economy*, 2nd edition (1879)

The great guacamole dip gets totally ignored in the last few minutes of a very close game. Everyone sits glued to the TV, holding their beers tightly as they wait for the final play. Even though this party is held at someone's home, each person is dressed in team colours and holds team paraphernalia. They've even painted their faces. These folks are true fans. They stayed with the team during the rebuilding years, rejoiced when strategic trades were made, and hoped it would all be worth it. The coach makes some mysterious signals to the quarterback, who nods back his acceptance. The players come out of the huddle and everyone in this home audience holds their collective breath. *Sssswhirlllll.* The ball is in the air and the pass is good. Pandemonium breaks out, and normally reticent men hug each other, shouting and pounding each other on the back. Hard-earned victory is sweet.

WE HOLD THESE TRUTHS TO BE ... UNDENIABLE

The truth is we are all caught in a great economic system, which is heartless.

Woodrow T. Wilson (1856–1924), American president

It has come to my attention—repeatedly, in fact—that many individuals think economists are not nice people. Somehow, our commitment to the concept of free markets has marked us as heartless souls who only live for the almighty dollar, euro, or yen. While I'll admit that there's probably the occasional jerk among us (which profession doesn't have at least a few?—although, come to mention it, I have never met a kindergarten teacher who wasn't a sweetheart), many of us are some of the nicest people you will ever meet. Really. We raise lovely families, volunteer in our communities, pay our taxes, and vote anywhere from the socialist left to the conservative right. Our conviction that self-interest[1] can be a good thing doesn't mean that we are necessarily more selfish than anyone else. Let me defend my profession and my colleagues[2] by explaining why we think the way we do about free and competitive markets and why that doesn't necessarily make us mercenary, capitalist pigs.

---

[1] The concept of self-interest comes from a quotation from the father of economics himself, Adam Smith: "It is not from the benevolence of the butcher, the brewer, or the baker that we expect our dinner, but from their regard to their own interest."

[2] See *Inside the Economist's Mind: Conversations with Eminent Economists*, edited by Paul Samuelson and William Barnett (Blackwell Publishing, 2007).

Be Seriously Happy: Optimizing Utility

I have arrived at the conviction that the neglect by economists to discuss seriously what is really the crucial problem of our time is due to a certain timidity about soiling their hands by going from purely scientific questions into value questions.

Friedrich August von Hayek (1899–1992), Austrian economist and philosopher
Published in *A Conversation with Fredrick A. von Hayek: Science and Socialism* (1979)

Up to this point, I have explained how markets work—the mechanics of the market, so to speak. Now I will explain why economists think markets are the way to go. Our support of free markets all boils down to how we think about cost, benefits, and the optimal allocation of resources in our society when faced with the scarcity problem. In truth, cost-benefit analysis gets at the heart of the matter as we look for the answer to the question, "How can people be as happy as possible given that we live in a world of scarce resources?"

We start by assuming that the benefit of anything to society comes from the happiness (or, in economist jargon, utility[3]) it brings to the individual enjoying it. A cool drink, a good game of football, or a great novel—all of these give people pleasure. That's enough for economists to say that these things have "value." Moreover, economists do not (when speaking as economists) generally make moral judgments about what makes people happy. As long as a person's activities don't spill over onto other people who have no choice in the matter,[4] we treat individual tastes and preferences as sacrosanct and as our starting point.

Basically, from an economist's perspective, if you want to read a killer thriller,[5] so be it. Who are we to censor your reading habits? If you want to watch a big-screen TV on game day, dress in oversized team jerseys, paint your face, and wave giant foam fingers … whatever turns your crank. However, if your reading or TV habits[6] cause you to stalk, kidnap, or hurt someone, then economists would say you should read less graphic material or watch less violent TV; your demand for certain types of entertainment has a negative spillover effect, and society cares—and should care—about what you are consuming. Chapter 11 will deal with this issue more thoroughly. For now, let's talk about markets where the social impact is limited to those who make the decision to consume or produce in the first place.

Once an economist knows that something will make people happy, we say there is a legitimate demand for this thing—whatever it is. Economists leave the establishment of

---

[3]   As we saw in the previous chapter, utilitarians such as Jeremy Bentham (1748–1832) and John Stuart Mill (1806–1876) believed that society should aim to maximize the total utility of individuals, aiming for "the greatest happiness for the greatest number." Another theory forwarded by John Rawls (1921–2002) would have society maximize the utility of the individual receiving the minimum amount of utility.

[4]   Chapter 11 will look at the cases of positive and negative spillovers in consumption or production. These are called externalities.

[5]   Stephen King has written a great book called *On Writing*, in which he questions the notion of writing only about "what you know." Given his genre of books, writing "what you know" would be a little scary. To be honest, this is the only book of his I could actually read.

[6]   In the *Annual Review of Public Health* (Vol. 27, pp. 393–415, April 2006), researchers L. Rowell Huesmann and Laramie D. Taylor found that fictional television and film violence contributes to an increase in aggression and violence in young viewers in both the short term and the long term. They consider violent TV, video games, and films to be a public health issue.

those tastes and preferences—in other words, what *ought* to make you happy—to the theologians,[7] moral philosophers,[8] and advertisers. This can seem like a bit of a cop-out, but in our professional lives economists avoid moralizing whenever possible. Our private lives are, of course, another matter. Once a group of economists has a few drinks, they can moralize with the best of them.

So, here is a common starting point for economists. Things can make people happy. Eating is better than starvation. Shelter is better than privation. A winning team is better than a losing one. But to what degree are these things better? And how do we compare happiness levels between people? You see, if we could quantify how much value a particular item has for different people, we could begin to answer the really important economic question of "If more people want something than is available, who in the group should get it and who should miss out?"

Pick Me, Pick Me!

Before we set our hearts too much upon anything, let us examine how happy those are who already possess it.

Francois de La Rochefoucauld (1613–1680), French author

Let's go back to the "stones story" I used in Chapter 1. Hopefully you remember that I showed up at a party with 10 stones that I was willing to distribute. Let's suppose that 20 people want the stones. Who should get them? It's time to get a little philosophical here and provide an overarching principle to which we can adhere.

Economists want the stones to go to the individuals who would appreciate or treasure them the most. I don't think this is unreasonable. Economists think there is a difference between a recipient tossing the stone in a jar on the kitchen counter when he or she gets home and someone wearing it as a necklace near his or her heart. Asking your mother for advice is different from getting unsolicited advice. Therefore, if we could somehow measure the happiness experienced by the 20 individuals due to the stones, we believe that society's happiness as a whole would be maximized if those individuals who value the stones most highly got them.

Wait a minute. Haven't we talked about value somewhere before? Guess what? The demand curve does that. It ranks items according to the marginal value each item gives—from high to low marginal values. It is the story of our chocolates in Chapter 7. The demand curve tells us something about what makes society (a collection of individuals) happy. We now have a tool to help us answer the first part of the question that was asked earlier in this chapter: "How can people be as happy as possible given that we live in a world of scarce resources?"

---

[7]   For example, the Reformation theologian John Calvin (1509–1564) wrote, "God wishes his gifts to be valued by us at their proper worth. The more precious they are, the baser is our ingratitude if they do not have their proper value for us."

[8]   To be fair, Adam Smith was primarily a moral philosopher and then a political economist. Most modern economists worry about two issues: equity and efficiency. Many might consider these very moral issues. For a terrific explanation of welfare economics, see *Economics as a Moral Science* by A.B. Atkinson. I am using *morals* in terms of individual behaviour rather than overall philosophy.

Productive Practices

The major incentive to productivity and efficiency are social and moral rather than financial.

Peter Ferdinand Drucker (1909–2005), Austrian-born writer
Taken from *The New Society* (1950)

Now, on to the part about scarce resources. Society cares, or should care, about how its scarce resources are used. We want to use our limited resources wisely and not waste them on producing the wrong thing. I'll illustrate this concept with an example. Suppose that I had 10 jobs that needed doing and 10 workers to do them. Who should get which job? I think it should make some sense to most people that I interview them to figure out how well they would be able to do the various jobs I need done. Economists would never want a neonatal brain surgeon to pick pecks of pickled peppers for a living. That would be a waste of scarce brain power. This, of course, is a very different philosophy from the communist system of Mao Zedong,[9] who intentionally assigned highly skilled people to low-skill jobs.

Because the most talented among us can to do many things, this means that if I put a talented person on one job, he or she is not available for another one. I need to consider this when I allocate workers to positions. "Wait another minute," you say. "This is sounding a lot like opportunity cost and comparative advantage again." Correct you are!

Essentially, companies with comparative advantage have the lowest opportunity costs. We saw that the supply curve conveniently orders producers according to their opportunity costs from low to high marginal costs. This was the message of Chapter 6. Therefore, supply tells us something about what it costs society to produce goods and services given that these resources are scarce. By producing goods as cheaply as possible, we ensure that resources aren't used on the wrong thing. The neonatal brain surgeon cuts heads, garment makers cut cloth, electricians cut wire, and poets have cutting wit.

Well, folks, we now have the tools to solve the question, "How can people be as happy as possible given that we live in a world of scarce resources?" Supply is about the wise use of scarce resources, and demand tells about our collective happiness. Let's get to work and use these tools to find the right answer.

There Are Limits

Maybe you have to know darkness before you can appreciate the light.

Madeleine L'Engle (1918–2007), American writer
Taken from *A Ring of Endless Light* (1980)

The dark side of the question "How can people be as happy as possible given that we live in a world with scarce resources?" implies the following reality: There is not enough to go around for everybody to be completely and utterly happy. Happiness has limits. Therefore, some tough questions will need answers and some difficult choices

---

[9]   Critics blame many of Mao's socio-political programs, such as the Great Leap Forward and the Cultural Revolution, for causing severe damage to the culture, society, economy, and foreign relations of China, as well as probable deaths in the tens of millions. Mao closed the schools in China, and the young intellectuals living in cities were ordered to the countryside. They were forced to manufacture weapons. It is only now that China is market oriented that it is truly taking a "great leap forward."

will need to be made. Some of the basic economic questions that must be answered by society are these:

1. Given that we can't make everything our hearts desire, what should society make?
2. Who should make the goods? How should they produce the goods, and what technology should they use? Where in the world should these companies locate?
3. Who should consume how much of these goods?

I'm sure you agree that these are pretty big questions whose answers have life-changing consequences for many individuals. The answers affect whether head-office executives locate in Singapore or San Francisco, whether the steel for an overpass comes from India or Italy, and whether your parents vacation in Florida or Fiji.

Fortunately, economists offer a method that helps to make good decisions—cost-benefit analysis, which is rooted in supply and demand analysis. In fact, these are the same thing. Demand tells us about the benefits to society of something and supply tells us what it will cost to make it. This approach helps to answer the questions of who, what, where, when, why, and how about any situation that involves choice.

FIGURE 9.1	Economic surplus

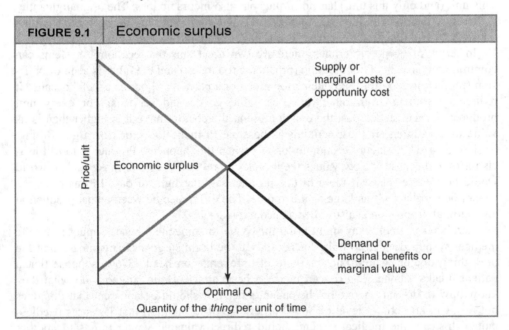

Another graph should help to clarify things. In Figure 9.1, we plot two lines. Demand is the marginal benefits side of the story and tells us about the relative happiness an item can give to those who consume it. On the demand curve, all individuals who highly value the *thing* (whether it is steel, vacations, or poems) occupy the front of the line on the demand curve (top left). Supply reflects the incremental or marginal costs of producing a product due to limited resources. All of the companies that can produce the *thing* cheaply sit at the front of the line on the supply curve (bottom left).

Drum roll, please! As long as the value of the *thing* to consumers exceeds the cost to make it on the production side of the economy, the *thing* should be made. Economists call the difference between the marginal benefit of the item and the marginal cost to produce it *economic surplus*. All items at the front of each line to the left of the crossing point generate surplus. Any items to the right of the crossing point do not generate economic surplus but rather put the economy into a loss position.

We now have a general principle for evaluating whether something should be made or not. If its marginal benefit exceeds the marginal cost, it should be made. If its marginal benefit does not exceed the marginal cost … don't bother. If each and every item is subject to the rigour of cost-benefit analysis, then the economic surplus is the greatest. Voila—the most happiness possible given scarce resources.

Getting It Right: Marginal Analysis

I knew once a very covetous, sordid fellow [perhaps William Lowndes[10]], who used to say, "Take care of the pence, for the pounds will take care of themselves."
Lord Chesterfield (1694–1773), British statesman

At optimal Q, or quantity, the cost to make that particular item is equal to its benefit. This unit (and only this unit) has no surplus but also incurs no loss. The optimal quantity is therefore the great divide that separates making too much from making too little. Like the story of Goldilocks and the three bears, only one quantity of anything is "just right."

In terms of economic crimes, there are two great sins that economic systems can commit. One is a sin of commission (producing too much) and the other is a sin of omission (producing too little). Producing too much of a particular good is a "sin" because it redirects resources from other, more valuable goods and services. For every unit produced and consumed past the crossing point, the cost to make it is higher than is its value to consumers. It most certainly is possible to make too much of a good thing. Society as a whole incurs economic losses[11] when this happens. Producing too little is also a "sin" because society values the product more than it cost to make it. The world would be a better place if more of this product saw the light of day. In this case, the economic surplus isn't as large as it could be. The difference between actual production and optimal production is also called an economic loss.

Here's an example that might bring this issue to someone's head. Suppose that the medical system decided to train doctors only to be brain surgeons. This means that the only thing doctors would know how to do is operate on heads. Now, suppose that a patient breaks a bone, gets cancer, or has a heart attack. Brain surgeons do what they know how to do and operate on the patient's head. It should be apparent that this does not result in an optimal level of brain surgeries (not to mention that it causes needless pain!). Instead, the medical system should redirect valuable young minds to another branch of medicine—maybe cardiology—that society values more highly. This example illustrates the concept that an overproduction of brain surgeries can lead to an underproduction of heart transplants. Think of it as simultaneous sinning!

---

[10] William Lowndes (1652–1724) was Secretary to the Treasury of Great Britain under King William III and Queen Anne. Lowndes was married four times and had children with each of his wives, 25 children in all. I wonder if he took care of his pence!

[11] Economists have a catchy name for this economic loss. We call it *deadweight loss*, probably due to some morbidity on our part.

A Kind Solution

When we risk no contradiction, It prompts the tongue to deal in fiction.
John Gay (1685–1732), English poet and playwright
Taken from *Fables* (1727)

One method of allocating goods would be a system in which a benevolent social planning department decides who should make an item and who should get it. All the planners would need to do is ask people to tell them their marginal values for the item and then rank individuals in descending order. I could have done the same thing with my stones, if I had quizzed the 20 people to try to ascertain who really, really wanted them.

On the production side, the planners could then ask firms what it would cost to produce these items and again rank them in order of ascending costs. Once marginal costs equal marginal benefits, production and consumption levels get set. The companies then produce the goods and hand the items over to the customers. Seems simple, right?

It's time for some reality. What do you think will happen if all that's required is for consumers and companies to reveal their relative values and relative costs, respectively? I hope you are thinking what I am thinking. I think a little lying would result ... okay, let's just say that *exaggeration* would occur. Consumers would be tempted to claim that they want something more than they really do in order to move up the line. They don't want to be past the cut-off point and lose out. As well, firms might understate their costs just to get the business. Only later will they surprise the planners (the government) with an extra bill to cover their extra costs.

Planners have no way to distinguish between those who really value something and those who don't and between those who can make something cheaply and those who use highly skilled resources on a low-skill job. Counting on an honour system to allocate scarce resources doesn't have much hope of working, given the incentives inherent in this kind of system to be less than honest. Is the optimal solution remotely possible? For the good news, keep reading.

Free Market System

A person who is gifted sees the essential point and leaves the rest as surplus.
Thomas Carlyle (1795–1881), Scottish writer

When those who produce and those who consume meet in the marketplace, the intersection of supply and demand generates something magical. It's called price. Prices are magical because, in most markets, they will guarantee that the optimal Q (quantity) will automatically happen. Markets force supply (marginal costs) to equal demand (marginal benefits) at the market price. This is why economists love free markets so much. We believe[12] that, in free markets, the right firms produce the right stuff, which finds its way into the right hands. It works better than most allocation systems to maximize the surplus and minimize the fuss.

So, why do market prices make society better off? In a free market, the equilibrium price that results when supply equals demand turns out to be a very important dividing

---

[12]   Given certain criteria that will be addressed in the next two chapters.

line. Notice in Figure 9.2 that the final market price of this *thing* equals optimal Q's marginal cost and benefit. Anyone who values this *thing* (it could be an apple, a hot tub, or a root canal) more than its market price is on the part of the demand curve before optimal Q and buys. The marginal benefit to these buyers exceeds the price they need to pay for it. (I know it seems hard to believe, but I willingly paid an unbelievable amount of money to have a root canal done.) However, anyone who doesn't value it as much as the price is to the right of optimal Q on the demand curve. These folks will not buy, because it isn't worth it to them. The price exceeds the personal benefits of consuming the *thing.* Markets force consumers to reveal the truth about their real values. There's no need for lie detectors. The right people get the goods.

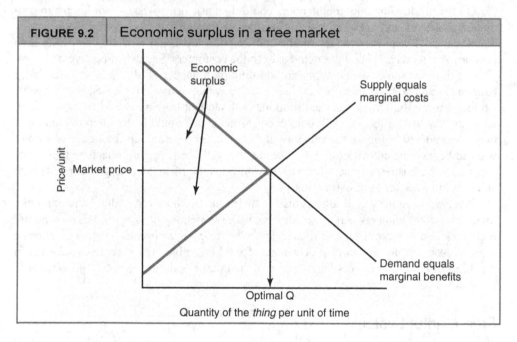

FIGURE 9.2	Economic surplus in a free market

There is a similar situation for supply. If a profit-minded company can sell the things they make for a price that is more than the marginal cost of making them, they go ahead and make them. These owners go to bed with visions of profit margins dancing in their heads. These companies produce the quantity on the left side of the supply curve up to optimal Q. If the marginal costs exceed the price, these firms don't enter into the market because to do so would generate losses for the owners. These are the companies on the right side of the supply line. Again, markets force businesses to face the truth about their costs, and the right companies end up making the goods.

Because market prices exist, each market participant automatically and intuitively performs a cost-benefit analysis for himself or herself. It turns out that this personal analysis produces the best results for society as a whole as well. Market price acts as a reference point to separate those who should from those who shouldn't.

Let me repeat this important result. When all is said and done, only people who value things more highly than the market price pay the price to buy the goods, and only companies that have low costs of production actually produce the goods to earn the market price. Markets can maximize the surplus fairly easily without the need for benevolence. Self-interest works to enhance the interests of society as a whole.

Message in a Price Tag

You know, Foley, I have only one eye—I have a right to be blind sometimes ... I really do not see the signal!

Vice Admiral Horatio Nelson, 1st Viscount Nelson (1758–1805), British naval officer

Prices also serve the important function of publicly announcing society's marginal costs and benefits. Economists say that prices act as accurate signals, communicating valuable information to the other market participants. For instance, when the price called "salaries" for particular jobs climbs, this informs young people that certain jobs are in demand by society. Depending on their individual preferences, these young people now have the opportunity to make intelligent career decisions based partly on the potential to make a good salary if that is important to them. If entrepreneurs see high prices for certain goods and services, they can take that information and start companies to provide those goods and services. Innovators invent products that provide value because of the profits they expect to make. They tend to use the prices of comparable products as signals in making their decision to go forward. Prices are a much more efficient way to transmit information to all of these players than any government commissioned report.

Gossip Column

Friedrich August von Hayek (1899–1992) was born in Vienna into a line of scholars and minor nobility. During World War I he was stationed on the Italian front, and this experience caused him to worry about the damage that political organizations could do. He vowed to make the world a better place and decided to become an academic. He thought and wrote about the role that socialism played in fascism and how collectivism (even when done in a voluntary way) usually leads to totalitarianism. (That's a lot of -isms.) During his life, he saw it all and came out in support of a laissez-faire (free and decentralized) system.

Von Hayek attended the University of Vienna, where he earned two doctorates, in law and political science, but he also studied philosophy, psychology, and economics. For a short time, he studied at the Institute of Brain Anatomy, which led him to think about economics systems in the same framework as neurological ones. He was truly a well-educated Renaissance man.

His influence on economists was extensive. He was one of the most important members of the Austrian School of Economics and was scooped by Lord Robbins to join the London School of Economics (LSE). He is the second most frequently cited economist (after Kenneth Arrow) by other Nobel Prize winners in economics when they give their Nobel lectures.

Von Hayek's impact hit the political streets when conservative politicians took his ideas and ran with them. Margaret Thatcher is said to have slammed Hayek's book

The Constitution of Liberty[13] onto a table during a party meeting,[14] saying, "This is what we believe." Students of von Hayek became part of Ronald Reagan's administration. (Maybe von Hayek sensed that he could be hijacked, because he wrote an essay titled "Why I Am Not a Conservative" found in the appendix of *The Constitution of Liberty*. Von Hayek identified his political stance as basically a classical liberal or libertarian one. For subtle reasons, he disliked using either term and preferred to be called a "Burkean Whig," which definitely clears up matters.)

Von Hayek became good friends with Karl Popper, one of the most influential philosophers of the twentieth century, also from Vienna and also a professor at the LSE. It is unclear who influenced whom, but each dedicated books to the other in appreciation of their respective influence.

Last but not least, Jimmy Wales, the founder of Wikipedia, credits Hayek's work on prices (as signals) and his thoughts on decentralized information in "The Use of Knowledge in Society" as central to Wales's thinking about how to manage the Wikipedia project.[15]

For a long time, von Hayek had more influence among political scientists than among economists, but lately there has been a bit of a revival of the ideas of the Austrian school with which he was associated.

He shared the Nobel Prize in 1974 with the Swedish socialist Gunnar Myrdal, who said that the fact that the prize was given to von Hayek and Milton Friedman showed that it should be abolished.

When one considers the impact of the man, it is worth quoting von Hayek's intellectual archrival, Lord John Maynard Keynes (1883–1946):

> *The ideas of economists and political philosophers, both when they are right and when they are wrong, are more powerful than is commonly understood. Indeed the world is ruled by little else. Practical men, who believe themselves to be quite exempt from any intellectual influence, are usually slaves of some defunct economist.*

EVEN STEVEN

There are two ways of being happy: We can either diminish our wants or augment our means—either may do—the result is the same and it is for each man to decide for himself and to do that which happens to be easier.

Benjamin Franklin (1706–1790), American statesman, philosopher, printer, writer, and inventor

It's time to pull back and think about why certain people consume more than others. How do economists deal with the issue of fairness? Much of what we think depends on the source of the differences in consumption. For starters, people are different and have different wants and wishes. Free markets work well in this case because they get stuff

---

[13] This book is number nine on the list of the 100 best non-fiction books of the century.

[14] Ranelagh, John. (1991). *Thatcher's People: An Insider's Account of the Politics, the Power, and the Personalities.* London: HarperCollins, p. ix.

[15] See the June 2007 issue of the libertarian magazine *Reason.*

into the hands of people who actually value the items and keep stuff out of the hands of people who don't value them. For example, one of my sons would never thank me if I made him Brussels sprouts, whereas my other son really likes them. If I dole out the sprouts equally to both of my sons, it would not be true to say that I have maximized their joint happiness. (However, it might make me feel like I'm a good mother if I force these little cabbages down my older son's throat. This is the idea of externalities, which we will look at in the next chapter.) This type of uneven consumption is not really a problem.

Well-functioning free markets typify the concept of freedom. Individuals have a free choice to go to the market and buy what they want. Firms have a free choice to produce and sell what they want with the available methods that work best for them. This freedom to buy and sell leads to economic efficiency. Scarce resources are allocated in such a way as to make the products that society wants with as few resources as possible. When free markets do this, it makes a lot of people really happy.

However, global differences in standard of living are about more than differences in people's wish lists. Willingness to pay also embodies the idea of ability to pay. Obviously, there are many people in the world who, through no fault of their own, have little to bring to the table. They could be children, elderly, disabled, uneducated, or politically oppressed. They have little ability to pay, which also makes their willingness to pay less. The hard, cruel facts are that markets are about exchange, and you have to sell something to buy something. For most people, the most important thing they have to sell is their labour. However, some people just can't work. Others work hard, but their work doesn't pay enough. There is a fundamental difference between people who choose to work less and therefore make less money and those who work very hard but whose type of labour is relatively abundant. Abundant labour is typically of low value, which leads to low remuneration. Consumption can be down for either reason—diminished income or diminished wants. One is a problem of fairness and the other is not.

Differences in consumption can also be due to systemic unfairness. Some folks are just lucky. They may be lucky enough to have inherited wealth, which is the reward of an ancestor's labour. These idle rich can conspicuously consume.[16] Others may have won the genetic jackpot and are more talented, beautiful, or intelligent, which increases their odds of bringing something to the market table.

A more common good-luck story would be that children are born into a middle-class family that has resources and chooses to invest them in these children. This increases what these lucky kids bring to the table in acquired human capital. Their parents endow upon them all manner of lessons, skills, and good health, which benefits them (and which they hopefully appreciate once they are older). This is not true for most children in the developing world. These children inherit wars, displacement and refugee camps, dysfunctional despotic governments, and all manner of diseases. Certain rights are inalienable, but to be lucky isn't one of them.

---

16 The term *conspicuous consumption* was introduced by economist and sociologist Thorstein Veblen in his 1899 book *The Theory of the Leisure Class*. Veblen used the term to depict a specific behavioural characteristic of the *nouveau riche*, a class emerging in the nineteenth century as a result of the accumulation of wealth during the Second Industrial Revolution.

Ignorance Is Bliss

All you need is ignorance and confidence and the success is sure.

Samuel Langhorne Clemens, pen name Mark Twain (1835–1910), American author and humorist

The unfairness of it all has philosophers and economists alike thinking about how to set up a fair or just system of distribution. The famous and influential philosopher John Rawls, in his book *A Theory of Justice*, argued that systems should be set up as if they were designed under a veil of ignorance. In other words, imagine what a system should look like if you get to pick a system to live in but you know nothing about your final place within it. Most of us, for reasons of self-interest, would then care about how low the bottom of the totem pole is and want it raised.

Nobel Prize–winning economist Amartya Sen thinks about equity issues in terms of an individual's capability to be and do what he or she wants to be or do. His argument is that it is not enough that an individual has the right to do something. The individual must also have the capability of exercising that right. He calls this *effective freedom* and advocates policies aimed at removing obstacles (economic or otherwise) and giving individuals the capability of achieving their human potential and dignity. For example, a woman may have the right to own a business but if she, for cultural reasons, never qualifies for a loan, then this prevents her from exercising that right. This capability approach is very much behind using something like the Human Development Index rather than a poverty line to measure poverty.

In developed countries, governments (and their armies of economists) have taken on greater roles in achieving equity between their citizens. Normally, this involves taxes and spending programs. With equity as the backdrop, economists favour methods of redistribution of resources that do not change the incentives to behave efficiently. Let me illustrate the problem. Suppose that someone has decided she likes leisure more than goods, and she is willing to consume fewer goods to have more free time. Suppose that another individual wants to have a higher standard of living in goods and works long hours to achieve this. Then, suppose that a government decides that this is not fair with respect to consumption (it does not believe that anyone would actually value leisure and instead believes that the first individual is unable to find work). The government then taxes the hard-working person and redistributes the income to the leisure-loving person, who will of course take the money. It shouldn't take much to see that there is little incentive to be a hard-working person.[17] Overall, consumption and happiness will go down. This is viewed by economists as an economically inefficient outcome because individual behaviour is changed or distorted by the government's tax policy to equalize what is, in this case, a free choice in consumption.

---

[17] From the hard-working person's vantage, it doesn't matter if the recipient didn't want to work or couldn't work. Taxing hard-working people reduces their incentive to work and therefore leads to economic inefficiency. The reasons why the recipient isn't working only matter from the vantage of equity.

eTrade-offs

... the conflict between equity and economic efficiency is inescapable. In that sense, capitalism and democracy are really a most improbable mixture. Maybe that is why they need each other—to put some rationality into equity and some humanity into efficiency.

Arthur Okun (1928–1980), American economist
Taken from *Equity and Efficiency: The Big Tradeoff* (1975)

Equity and efficiency issues are in tension. Efficiency tries to create as big a cake as possible, and equity tries to keep the pieces of the cake to a similar size. The problem is that once everyone knows how you are going to cut the cake, it changes how big that cake is actually made. Economists think of equity and efficiency in terms of trade-offs.[18] This is especially true for government "tax and spend" programs. It is virtually impossible to find one of these programs that doesn't affect incentives and lead to economic inefficiency. All public servants can do is try to minimize the damage of going one way or another. Here, you get many differences and much debate between economists about what is the best thing to do and about which side—fairness or efficiency—is the better one on which to err.

Death and Taxes

"If they would rather die," said Scrooge, "they had better do it and decrease the surplus population."

Charles Dickens (1812–1870), English writer
Taken from *A Christmas Carol* (1843)

I just can't resist belabouring the point of how hard it is for governments to get economic policy right. Here's a complicated example that illustrates the point. At first blush, an economic policy that appears less distorting is death taxes (a.k.a. inheritance taxes or estate taxes). After all, this type of tax shouldn't change your ability to work hard and enjoy the fruits of your labour during your lifetime, because it only happens once you are dead. It also equalizes wealth to the next generation, reducing the dynastic buildup of wealth into a few hands (more on this in the next chapter). However, once people know that this is the policy, they can change their behaviour. They can spend every dime of their wealth before they die, leaving little savings, or financial capital, to the next generation. This could lessen the productive capacity of the economy and possibly reduce everyone's consumption—not exactly what the government wants to happen. Others employ very expensive accountants to look for ways around the death taxes. This is a waste of good brains on a non-productive activity. Finally, it is possible to buy such a big life insurance policy that you effectively pass on the wealth anyway. When it comes to not paying taxes, the adage *if there is a will, there is a way* could never be more true.

---

[18] My esteemed colleague Atsu Amagashie has pointed out that I am a bit "old school" in my thinking here. While this trade-off is true for industrialized countries, it may not be true for countries with large disparities between the rich and the poor. In that case, it is possible to make a change in equalizing standards of living and actually see production (efficiency) go up. The problem with big disparities between the rich and the poor is that the odds that the poor will revolt rises. Civil unrest cuts down on production as well as on rich people's heads.

What if governments try to equalize things by spending on public education? This partially evens out the human capital across rich and poor families, which enables poor children to get ahead. However, public funding of education never fully levels the playing field because rich families can invest more in their children's education by buying into neighbourhoods with better schools or better extracurricular activities. In practice, no public policy is perfect, and sometimes you are just plain lucky to be born into a well-off family in a great country; other times you hope your luck changes, and you become a slumdog millionaire.

Capitalist Tools

> *The meaning of economic freedom is this: that the individual is in a position to choose the way in which he wants to integrate himself into the totality of society.*

Ludwig Heinrich Edler von Mises (1881–1973), Austrian economist
Taken from *Economic Policy: Thoughts for Today and Tomorrow* (1979, based on lectures given in 1959)

Free and competitive markets are often called efficient markets and usually work well to make a big cake or an economic surplus. Creating equity involves losses in efficiency, but economists (to varying degrees) see that as being worth it. This does not mean we abandon markets. *Au contraire*, we usually support policies that enter the market to fix the problem rather that those that do not.

The next two chapters explore the times when free markets do not work. There are many and sundry reasons why markets produce inefficient—never mind inequitable—results. Economists call these situations *market failures*. It is not precise to say that markets aren't working. It is more correct to say that they aren't working correctly. Knowing where the problems are can lead to solutions, often market-based ones.

Markets allocate goods efficiently, although not always equitably.

CHAPTER 10

The Name of the Game
(A Skinny Venti Chapter)

When a man tells you that he got rich through hard work, ask him: Whose?

Donald Robert Perry Marquis (1878–1937), American writer

The stag and doe[1] is in full swing when you arrive. With the wedding a mere three weeks away, you have heard rumours that tensions are running high in the family. In the corner of the room, the groom (egged on by the groomsmen, of course) downs shots in quick succession. He seems quite willing to let any problems go for the night. You wonder if the bride is able to do the same.

Sure enough, you discover that the bride is not having as much fun as her husband-to-be. Near the back door, the maid of honour wipes the bride's mascara-stained cheeks and comforts her with these words: "Don't worry. I'm sure your family's department store will be fine. You know those big-box stores can't give service the way a small family-owned business can."

The bride responds: "All I know is that Dad and Mom have been walking around as if someone has died since they found out the town gave the approvals. Lately, every time a bill comes in for the wedding, they look worried. I wish I wasn't having such an expensive wedding. If I had known this was going to happen, I would have gone simpler."

"Listen there is nothing you can do now but really enjoy your wedding. It won't make your parents happy to see you miserable. It will make paying for the wedding feel worse. Who knows, maybe you can use some of the money raised tonight toward the cost. Let's get out of this drafty hall and have some fun."

"Okay, I guess you're right."

As they walk toward the party room, with the maid of honour's arm firmly around the bride's shoulder, you think, *That's what friends are for.*

COMPLICATING THE PROBLEM

In short, competition has to shoulder the responsibility of explaining all the meaningless ideas of the economists, whereas it should rather be the economists who explain competition.

Karl Heinrich Marx (1818–1883), German political philosopher, political economist, and social theorist
Taken from *Das Kapital*, Volume III (1894)

Congratulations, you have done most of the heavy lifting in this book! There are a few more ideas that require a little graphing and grappling, but they build on what you have already learned. Hopefully, they won't seem too complicated.

Let's briefly summarize the basic concepts of a free market before we add another complicating layer. We know that, in markets,[2] sellers and buyers meet to voluntarily

---

[1]   A stag (male) and doe (female) is a party given before a couple gets married.

[2]   These markets could be garage sales, bazaars, auctions, eBay, online orders, the classified ads in newspapers, or stores. Any forum that connects buyers with sellers is a market.

exchange something—it could be a good, service, or resource. When markets are in equilibrium, these buyers and sellers agree to buy and sell a particular amount of a thing for a particular price per unit. In equilibrium, that price is equal to the marginal cost and benefits of the last unit made. Should either the buyer's or the seller's situation change, then demand and supply analysis helps us to predict how the price of the item and the quantity changing hands will change as a result of the new economic scenario. The new equilibrium prices and quantities are simply the logical consequences of the underlying costs of production and consumer preferences. This means that prices can't be too high, too low, outrageous, exorbitant, gouging, a pittance, or whatever other emotional, morality-laden word people like to throw around. Prices are simply the fallout of what people want and the underlying opportunity costs to provide for those wants. Furthermore, these prices act as signals that help the system to maximum economic surplus. The market price is right … except when it's not.

What Can Possibly Be Wrong?

In economic life competition is never completely lacking, but hardly ever is it perfect.

Joseph Alois Schumpeter (1883–1950), Austrian economist
Taken from *Capitalism, Socialism and Democracy* (1942)

As I said, I'm going to add a complicating factor, one that directly affects the young bride in our story and the reason for the tears. This chapter will look at the role that the number of buyers and sellers plays in setting prices and determining the quantity of goods bought and sold. It turns out that a decrease in the number of players in the market can change the quantity available from economically right to socially wrong. Chapter 9 explained what economists mean by the concept of the socially optimal amount. We found that anything that alters the quantity changing hands from the optimal quantity to one that is either too high or too low decreases the economic surplus and is, in a socio-economic sense, wrong. This chapter will look at the situation where the quantity of something in the marketplace is consistently "incorrect" or just plain "wrong" economically due to the ability of one player to "corner a market." We will compare that "incorrect" quantity with what would occur if there were a multitude of independent buyers and sellers.

A Numbers Game

What is the greatest number? Number one.

David Hume (1711–1776), Scottish historian and philosopher[3]

Let's look at the first extreme. The lowest number of buyers or sellers possible in a market is one. It turns out that if you are the only buyer or seller in a market, you are in a very powerful position. We have names for each of these players and they all start with the prefix *mono-* (which sounds like a disease—however, the economic type of mono I would love to catch!). We call a single seller of anything a *monopoly* and a single buyer in a market a *monopsony*. The "anything" in question here can be a good or a service on

---

[3]   Adam Smith and David Hume (who was a decade older than Smith) were friends and collaborators.

the output side or a resource on the input side. So, what is the power of being the one and only? Well, basically, you get to see the other player's curve and pick where you want to be on it. In other words, monopolies can choose their optimal price–quantity combination on their customer's demand curve and monopsonies can cherry-pick their optimal spot on the seller's curve.

Getting a Clue

We must recognize that as the dominant power in the world we have a special responsibility.
George Soros (1930–), Hungarian-born businessman
Taken from *The Age of Fallibility: The Consequences of the War on Terror* (2006)

Let's begin with the monopolist. If you are the only seller in a market, then every price–quantity combination on the entire demand curve is yours—all yours—to choose from. Economists would say that the monopolist is a price setter. Once it sets a price, only one quantity on the demand curve matches that price, so essentially it is a quantity setter as well—but economists never call a monopolist that. Setting the price is a very important decision for a company to make, both for itself and for society as a whole. The company determines the quantity produced and consumed of something, which we know has social ramifications. Unfortunately, it makes more sense for monopolists to pick a price that maximizes their own profits than worry about picking one that maximizes the economic welfare of society.

In contrast, a competitive firm is one among many firms selling in a crowded market. Any one company in a particular sector that sells basically the same thing as everyone else doesn't really have the ability to change the overall market price. Rather, a competitive company looks at the price that everyone else charges and charges the same. A competitive business has no reason to do otherwise. After all, if it sells something at a slightly higher price than its competitors, customers can simply buy from the competition. If it slightly underprices the competition, it will get a lot of business but cut into its profit margins and not make enough income to cover its opportunity costs. More to the point, it doesn't need to charge a lower price to get all of the customers it wants. Thus, competitive companies tend to charge what everyone else charges, and economists call them *price takers*. As we saw in the previous chapter, the price they "take" maximizes the economic surplus in the system.

In the real world, very few perfectly competitive markets exist. This category of market requires the existence of identical—not just similar—products with many sellers in play. Commodities would be the best example of such a market. After all, a tonne of wheat from one farm looks a lot like a tonne of wheat[4] from another. Therefore, when wheat farmers sell their identical wheat on commodity exchanges, they get identical prices to each other during a given round of trading. Individual farmers can't manipulate the price of wheat on the big electronic board by changing how much they decide to sell because they just aren't big enough to make a difference. For these competitive sellers, the reaction to the posted price is really a case of "take it or leave it."

---

[4] Wheat is a grass that originated in the Fertile Crescent region of the Near East. It is one of the top three cereals produced worldwide. The other two are corn and rice.

For this reason, the markets for commodities such as wheat, oil, milk, and poultry are also the markets where producers try to organize in order to get a higher-than-competitive price. These organizations are usually called marketing boards and their purpose is to act as monopolies and get monopoly prices for their members. While examples of perfect competition are going the way of the dodo bird, many products are similar enough and the number of sellers in those particular markets is big enough that the markets exhibit qualities close enough for us to consider them relatively competitive markets. Economic models don't have to be perfect to be close enough for economists to find them useful.

Analyze This

Concern for man and his fate must always form the chief interest of all technical endeavours. Never forget this in the midst of your diagrams and equations.

Albert Einstein (1879–1955), German Nobel Prize winner in Physics

In order to see what price monopolists will set, let's review what a demand curve looks like and sort out what this shape means for revenues. Recall that market demand curves slope downward. The monopolist pretty well owns the whole curve and sees every part of it. (Believe me, the big monopolies have entire departments that try to figure out exactly what their demand curve looks like. This process is called forecasting and can be done by economics units if the company is really big[5] or by marketing departments.)

A couple of things would be clear to anyone analyzing the market data: In order to induce consumers to buy more, the monopolist would need to lower prices. Furthermore, the revenues generated by a sale are the combination of the price of the product multiplied by how many items were actually sold. In this case, both the price and the quantity change as the monopolist moves down the demand curve. Therefore, for the monopolist, this means that revenue has two opposing forces. By lowering prices to sell more units, the monopolist decreases the amount of potential revenue on the units at the front of the line. However, by selling more product, they can make more revenue on the additional units even if the price is lower. In other words, making more output has revenue trade-offs that monopolists need to consider. They lose potential revenue on the price drop but gain revenue on the quantity increase. Monopolists take these trade-off considerations seriously when they make production decisions.

The owners of competitive companies face no such trade-offs. For a given market, demand, and underlying costs, these owners don't really change prices. Recall from earlier chapters that if these companies decide to raise the price, they will end up losing customers. Conversely, they don't need to lower the price to keep their customers. Prices are set by the overall market activity, where everyone basically charges the same amount. Competitive companies can't increase revenue by changing the market price because they are too small to make any real impact, but they can increase their revenues by selling more products.

This is not to say that prices never change in competitive markets. They change if everyone's costs change or if the market demand changes. This would happen on a

---

[5]   For example, Hal Varian (1947–) is the chief economist for Google.

market-wide scale and would have an impact on everyone in a sector. While market prices can change when everyone independently acts in the same way, they do not change because one competitive owner wakes up one morning and decides to change the price. No one player has that kind of power, and sometimes the market prices can appear very random to the business owners involved.

Okay, so let's say that you own a monopoly. What price–quantity combination is optimal? We can safely say that it is probably not the quantity of zero (unless, of course, costs are so high that it isn't worth it to produce the product at all. In that case, who cares if you have a monopoly over your product? You are not in the market. This explains why a monopoly over eight-track cartridges isn't worth much today. You still need demand to make monopoly power meaningful.) As we travel down the demand curve (see Figure 10.1), we start with high prices and low quantities and end with high quantities and low prices.

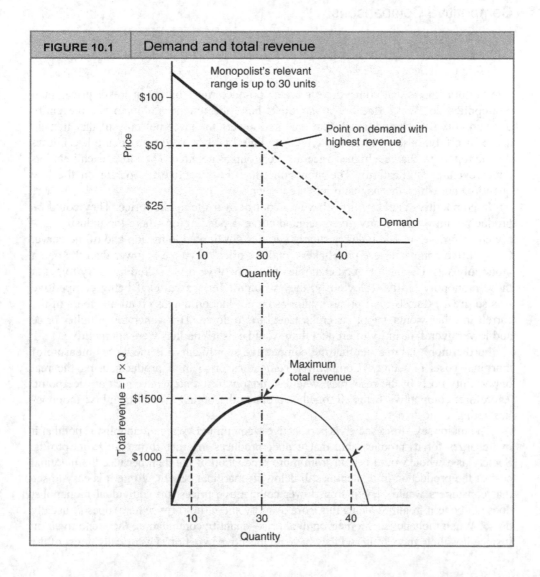

FIGURE 10.1 | Demand and total revenue

Revenue is calculated by multiplying the price of the product and the quantity sold. It turns out that revenues first rise, reach a maximum, and then fall as quantity increases.

Notice that at quantities 10 and 40 units, the revenue for this firm is the same at $1000. At the lower quantity (10 units) the price is higher ($100), and at the higher quantity (40 units) the price is lower ($25). When these different prices and quantities are multiplied together, we get the same total revenue ($1000). However, because the higher-quantity production level will cost more to make, 10 units is preferred to 40 units in the monopolist's mind. From Figure 10.1, it should be obvious that no right-thinking monopolist wants to produce more once its revenue starts to fall—ever. Therefore, production beyond 30 units is out of the question. To the monopolist, only the top half or higher-priced part of the demand curve is relevant.

Competitive Comparisons

Less is more.

Robert Browning (1812–1889), English poet and husband of Elizabeth Barrett Browning
Taken from *Andrea del Sarto*

The bottom line is that competitive markets produce more output at lower prices than monopolies do. Why? Because monopolists have the unique ability to see the entire demand curve. Each additional item they sell lowers the price not only of that item in and of itself, but also of all items before it in line. In other words, producing less allows the monopoly to charge a higher price for the group as a whole. Therefore, each item has huge revenue ramifications. The monopolist has the incentive to operate on the low quantity end, which means that prices are higher.

In competitive markets, firms have no control over the market price. They could be producing anywhere on any given demand curve depending on where the industry supply curve crosses it. The industry supply curve is not limited to the top end of the curve. Competitive companies are price takers, and the price they take is lower than the one a monopoly sets. Cartels are good examples of competitive firms colluding to try to get at these monopoly profits. (Obviously, they wouldn't form a cartel if being competitive was so great.) Cartels raise prices by imposing production quotas on all members of the cartel; in other words, supply is orchestrated to go down. This generates a higher price and lower overall quantity of product than would exist if markets were competitive.

Furthermore, it turns out that the competitive supply curve is the "true" measure of marginal costs to society. Competitive companies price their products using the real opportunity costs of the resources, whereas monopolies strategically pick a price point. Therefore, competitive firms all together produce the optimal social quantity; monopolies acting alone do not.

The major sin—from society's perspective—committed by the monopolist is not that it overcharges for its products, but that it underproduces in order to maximize its profits. Society as a whole would benefit from more production of the item because the marginal cost of the production of an item is still below its marginal benefit. While it is easy to see that consumers would benefit from lower competitive prices, the individual monopolist does not benefit from producing this extra quantity and it (no surprise here) doesn't usually do so. When monopolists hit their optimal price–quantity combination, they tend to sit on it since it is their gravy train and they have no incentive to get off. Historically, most of the richest people in the world had some sort of monopoly power. Needless to say, the ride for them was first class. In the case of monopoly production levels, it is justified for society to act through its governments to trade off the interests of the monopoly in favour of the interests of the society. In other words, governments try to maximize the overall economic surplus. This will probably mean taking away some of the monopoly's power.

Monopoly Money

It's possible, you can never know, that the universe exists only for me. If so, it's sure going well for me, I must admit.

William Henry "Bill" Gates III (1955–), American business magnate, philanthropist, and author

Taken from *Time* magazine (January 13, 1997)

The source of monopoly power can take various forms. Looking at the all-time richest self-made men[6] in North America, we can see a variety of sources to choose from. For instance, John D. Rockefeller (1839–1937), the all-time richest self-made man, bought up the competition until his company, Standard Oil, gained control over the North American oil market. To a lesser extent, Andrew Carnegie (1835–1919), the second richest self-made man, did the same thing in steel. Sam Walton (1918–1992), ranked in the top 10 richest self-made men, went into small-town America, which had room for only one discount store, effectively gaining a monopoly in those towns. By the time the other discount stores realized the benefit of Walmart's strategy, they were behind the eight ball. It then became a race to see who could open a discount store in the next small town first. Cornelius Vanderbilt (1792–1877), ranked in the top five, was philosophically opposed to the government-formed monopoly in the New York steamship industry and competed with it anyway. By undercutting prices, he made a hefty duopoly profit.[7] He then went on to form 13 railroad lines, with monopoly control over those routes. (It just goes to show that what you say and what you do can be very different.) Fredrick Weyerhaeuser (1834–1914) bought up huge tracts of timberland, gaining control over this natural resource. He is also in the top 10. In the top five, John Jacob Astor (1763–1848) created the first business trust[8] in the United States, from which he operated his fur, real estate, and opium businesses. He also benefited from protectionist trade policies, which prevented outside competition in the fur trade. Marshall Field's (1834–1906) wholesale[9] business (where he made his big money) provided goods to other merchants in the central and midwest United States. Chicago's rail and shipping hub made this (and his place in the top 10) possible. Bill Gates, through Microsoft, owns valuable patents. This puts him in the top five[10] all-time richest self-made men in North America.

---

[6] Unfortunately, there aren't any women in the top echelons of self-made money. Hopefully that will change in the future.

[7] This market structure has two firms. The chapter's Gossip Column economist, Antoine Cournot, showed that the quantity produced in the market by two firms is less than competition and more than monopoly. The profits are in-between as well.

[8] Trusts were set up with the intention of creating monopolies, restraining trade, and fixing prices. Antitrust laws came into effect to combat these businesses. Standard Oil was also a trust.

[9] His retail store was the precursor to Macy's.

[10] This rank can change depending on the value of his stocks.

Anything that keeps the competition out effectively gives monopoly power to a company, along with the associated profits. Right now, the music industry is lobbying for tougher rules on illegal music downloads precisely because unenforced monopoly power is no power at all. Currently, Disney's[11] patents on cartoon characters maintain monopoly profits for Disney.

> *Mickey Mouse is, to me, a symbol of independence. He was a means to an end.*
>
> Walter Elias "Walt" Disney (1901–1966), co-founder of Walt Disney Productions
> Taken from *Organisation and Complexity: Using Complexity Science to Theorise Organizational Aliveness* (2004)[12]

While enforcement of creative rights can look like a simple case of theft prevention, we saw in Chapter 4 that society may want a statute of limitations on licences, copyrights, and patents. Society benefits when songs become part of the public domain and can be used to create something new or just enjoyed because they are old. However, society also benefits from the creation of intellectual property in the first place. Furthermore, the incentive to create may be connected to the creator's ability to extract monopoly profits. In other words, the creator supplies something that didn't exist before, but only if he or she has monopoly control over it. This implies trade-offs. Society cares about both sides of the market and tries to reach a compromise.

Recent requirements administered by the World Trade Organization mean that a copyright extends for a minimum of 50 years after the death of the author, which seems quite long enough to extract monopoly profits for the creator and his or her descendants while guaranteeing that the creation will at some point become part of the public domain.

Gossip Column

Antoine Augustin Cournot (1801–1877) was born in the small town of Gray, now part of France. He was educated in local schools until age 15 and then worked as a clerk in a lawyer's office for four years. He studied law and philosophy on his own, reading such works as those of the famous mathematician Pierre-Simon Laplace. He realized that he needed more schooling to do what he wanted to do and enrolled in a math prep school. He then won entry to a school in Paris when he was 20 years old. Two years later, the school was shut down due to political reasons and he transferred to La Sorbonne, obtaining a licentiate[13] in mathematics. He then got a job as an adviser to Marshal Gouvoin Saint-Cyr and as a private tutor to his son. This job gave Cournot a lot of time to pursue his studies. He would work for Gouvoin Saint-Cyr for 10 years. (I guess the son finally grew up.) At age 28 he earned a doctorate in sciences, focusing on mechanics and astronomy.

---

[11] The Copyright Term Extension Act (CTEA) of 1998 extended copyright terms in the United States by 20 years. This law is known as the Sonny Bono Copyright Term Extension Act, the Sonny Bono Act, or the Mickey Mouse Protection Act.

[12] By Jacco Van Uden, page 43. You have to admit, the book has a memorable title.

[13] Licentiate (from the Latin *licentia docendi,* meaning "permission/right to teach") is the title of a person who holds an academic degree called a licence.

Cournot's thesis caught the attention of the mathematician Simeon-Denis Poisson, who would prove to be a faithful mentor and friend to him as he managed his way through the halls of academia. Poisson helped Cournot, then aged 33, find a permanent appointment as professor of analysis and mechanics in Lyon. A year later, Poisson found him a rectorship at the Academy of Grenoble. At age 37, Cournot was called to Paris as Inspecteur Général des Études because of the behind-the-scenes workings of Poisson. It was in this year that he published his economic masterpiece, *Recherches* (1838). This work was largely ignored by economists because it was so mathematical to read. He rewrote it twice to make it more palatable to readers, but it was never a success in his lifetime. (I really hope that doesn't happen to me.)

Cournot was the first to mathematize economics and should be looked at as the godfather of mathematical economics, predating Léon Walras[14] and Stanley Jevons by one generation. In fact, Cournot attended school with Walras's father, and Walras credits Cournot as inspiration for his work. (Much later, John Forbes Nash would rework from first principles the duopoly [two firms] solution that Cournot had developed decades earlier in *Recherches*. Nash did not know of it at the time. The equilibrium would become known as the Cournot-Nash equilibrium.) Much of Cournot's economic work was dismissed by the academics of his time, leaving Cournot crushed. On a brighter note, his philosophical writings were highly regarded in that community of French scholars. He did live long enough to see his economics work vindicated by Walras and Jevons and was very grateful when Walras went to the Institute de France and accused the economic academics of injustice toward Cournot. Cournot died later that year.[15]

Unions and Other Professional Associations

If I went to work in a factory, the first thing I'd do is join a union.

Franklin D. Roosevelt (1882–1945), American president

When labour acts with 'one voice, it becomes the only legal seller of labour to a company. This ability requires legislative power to maintain. Employers have incentive to try to break a union because unions fundamentally raise production costs. Unions act as agents for workers in negotiations with management and usually bargain for higher wages, better benefits, and increased health and safety requirements; as well, they institutionalize in the workers' collective agreement practices such as featherbedding.[16] All of these factors increase the cost of doing business for the company. The early history of the labour movement is filled with companies so intent on preventing a union from forming or on destroying an existing union that workers were actually killed. (There is no fury like management under the threat of unionization.) Therefore, governments must

---

[14] The subject of Chapter 8's Gossip Column.

[15] See www.newworldencyclopedia.org/entry/Antoine_Augustin_Cournot and www.economyprofessor.com/ theorists/antoineaugustincournot.php for more on his life and work.

[16] Featherbedding is the requirement of more workers per job than would normally be necessary. For example, the requirement of a minimum of three firefighters on a fire truck would be featherbedding. This requires a minimum of three workers on every truck when two could do the job.

create laws to prevent companies from engaging in violent[17] (and not-so-violent) union-busting practices, which hopefully prevents tempers from flaring and things from getting out of control. In general, once a union forms, it will most certainly use its new-found monopoly power. This increases the cost of production, which in turn ends up decreasing the number of workers the company hires. I hope you recall from Chapters 6 and 9 that this means that the supply of output and the economic surplus are both down.

Join the union, girls, and together say Equal Pay for Equal Work.
Susan Brownell Anthony (1820–1906), American civil rights and women's rights leader

Professional associations (medical, accounting, law, and engineering groups) and non-professional organizations (technicians and trades) exist as another form of labour monopoly, particularly when they restrict entry into their organizations through unnecessarily tough educational requirements. Non-professional licensing for individuals, such as cab drivers or buskers, also controls who can legally offer services.

The law acts as the enforcer, maintaining monopoly power by requiring a certain designation or licence in order to practise or operate a service. Workers inside an organization make it hard for outsiders to get in, usually by hiding behind the guise of needing to keep standards up. This practice is not necessarily in the public's interest. If these licences or designations truly limit entry into these markets (in contrast to handing out licences to anyone who applies), then society will enjoy fewer health care services, cab rides, and juggled balls than what society deems optimal. Again, supply and economic surplus are both down.

Cartels and Collusion

The strong equilibrium point f just described is one of "unrelenting ferocity" against offenders. It exhibits a zeal for meting out justice that is entirely oblivious to the sometimes dire consequences to oneself or to the other faithful—i.e., those who have not deviated.
Robert John Aumann (1930–), Israeli-American Nobel Prize-winning mathematician
Taken from "Acceptable Points in General Cooperative n-Person Games" (1959)[18]

Cartels are groups of producers that agree to not exceed certain production quotas in order to keep market prices up. They are essentially co-operating with each other to meet a common goal of making more profits. Individually, each member must voluntarily restrict its individual supply, which decreases the overall supply. The Organization of the Petroleum Exporting Countries, more commonly known as OPEC, represents a good example of a cartel. Each member country has a limit it can sell on the world oil market. However, cartels like OPEC have unstable monopoly power because of an individual member's incentive to say it is keeping to its quota while in reality it is sneaking more output onto the market through the back door in order to make more profits. (OPEC has big problems with members cheating on quotas, precisely because detecting and

---

[17] Baldwin-Felts Detective Agency was known for violently attacking labour union members in such mining areas as Ludlow, Colorado, and Matewan, West Virginia, on behalf of employers. The Ludlow Massacre involved three coal mining companies, one of which was owned by the Rockefellers.

[18] In *Contributions to The Theory of Games IV*, Annals of Mathematics Study 40, edited by A.W. Tucker and R.D. Luce.

punishing a cheating OPEC member is virtually impossible. Oil looks like oil and isn't distinguishable by member state.) Once many countries cheat, the world price of oil drops to competitive prices. (That is how all other members know someone is cheating. They just can't prove who.) This on-again, off-again quota system helps to partially explain the wild gyrations in oil prices as they swing between monopoly and competitive levels.

Other examples of cartels are the milk and poultry marketing boards[19] found in Canada. These farm cartels continue to exist because the government imposes trade restrictions on these particular foodstuffs and enforces strict food safety laws. Let's take the dairy market as an example. It is very difficult for Canadian milk producers to cheat on their quotas when it is clear which dairy farm shipped the milk to the milk processing plant. Any producer that ships more than its quota is fined. Furthermore, it is illegal to sell unpasteurized milk (and any farmer caught doing this is charged), thereby removing any alternative markets to sell in. Not only that, but there are stiff tariffs on imported milk, and foreigners don't really sell in the milk market except for specialty products like cheese. As a result, the dairy cartel is very stable and profitable. This is good for dairy farmers but not so good for society. Milk production and economic surplus are down.

Both OPEC and quota-enforcing marketing boards are examples of legal cartels. Usually, cartels are illegal precisely because they decrease production and lower economic surplus. Therefore, most countries have laws against colluding behaviours such as price fixing or bid rigging. In Canada, everything from driver education schools to waste disposal companies has seen criminal convictions for illegal monopolistic activities. As you can see, the role that government plays in terms of competition policy can seem a bit two-faced. Sometimes governments support monopolies and other times they nail them.

For example, Bill Gates has spent many years fighting various U.S. governments over the issue of monopoly power. The many plaintiffs alleged that Microsoft abused its monopoly power when it bundled Internet Explorer with Microsoft Windows, preventing real competition from other firms. In 2001, the U.S. Department of Justice reached a settlement with Microsoft that, in part, required Microsoft to share its application programming interfaces with other companies who could then use them to compete in similar markets. I'm sure that the thought of being forced to break Microsoft into many little companies as a worst-case scenario kept Bill Gates up at night and that the final settlement brought him some relief.

MONOPSONY

People will buy anything that is "one to a customer."
Sinclair Lewis (1885–1951), American writer

We have seen that, if you are the only seller in a world with many buyers, you are a monopoly. In contrast, if you are the only buyer in a world with many sellers, then the buying power is in your hands. You have what is called a monopsony. In this case, you get to see the entire supply curve, and you decide how much you want to pay when

---

[19] Not all marketing boards restrict production. In order to be a cartel, production restrictions must be in place.

you buy. So, what is the rationale behind the process of picking the monopsonist's preferred price? Because supply curves usually slope upward as the monopsonist buys more of the seller's product, it has to pay more for the entire lot. This means not only that every additional purchase costs more in and of itself, but also that all previous units will now be priced higher. Stopping at a lower quantity enables the monopsonist to suppress the price per unit on all units purchased. Big buyers, therefore, stop buying at lower quantities than would be bought if there were many buyers in a competitive market. Because less is bought, the price paid to suppliers is lower.

Trouble

Two wrongs don't make a right, but they make a good excuse.

Thomas Stephen Szasz (1920–2012), Hungarian psychiatrist and academic
Taken from *The Second Sin* (1973)

Our opening story showed a young woman worried about her parents' retail business. A big-box store is moving in and her parents are stressed out about it. Do they need to be? Maybe. One feature of big-box stores is that they are big buyers of merchandise. They pay less for their products than small buyers, which allows them to underprice smaller stores. In addition, large players can access suppliers who are further away at lower costs than a small firm can. We already saw in Chapter 3 that Walmart is a big buyer of Chinese goods. Economists call the cost savings of buying in bulk *economies of scale*. For any store that imports heavily from developing countries, its monopsony buying power along with economies of scale are usually what gives it monopoly power on the home front. This is all very bad news before a wedding. It is quite possible that the bride's parents will be driven out of business.

Labour markets also have big buyers. Small towns with one major employer often experience low wages and employment levels. Because of this, these employers are ripe for unionization. Most of the early history of unions appears to have occurred in this kind of situation,[20] whether it is a mining company or one major manufacturer in a small town. From the vantage of the public interest, unions together with monopsonies can be a good thing. Not only are working conditions more humane, but employment can actually go up. (Proving this point is beyond the scope of this book, but I couldn't help but mention it. It appears that two wrongs *can* make a right.)

Sports Channels

A sportsman is a man who, every now and then, simply has to go out and kill something.

Stephen Butler Leacock (1869–1944), Canadian economist and writer

Professional sports are also full of these monopsony–union combos. The owners (acting as one) have monopsony power over whoever plays in their league. If a hockey,

---

[20] Most miners also lived in company towns, where everything was owned by the company and the workers were paid in company money called *scrip*. This became a very oppressive environment. Colorado's legislature passed laws to outlaw scrip as well as mandate other improvements to life in these mining towns, but these laws were poorly enforced. To get a picture of life in these towns, I recommend watching the movies *October Sky* and *Matewan*.

baseball, soccer, football, or basketball player wants to play professionally, there are very few places to do so, and for many young men it is a dream come true to play and get paid at the same time. Therefore, the owners have an incentive (given the monopsonist's ability to see the entire supply curve) to keep salaries low and the league small. Once a union comes in, salaries go up. Depending on how much incomes are raised, it is actually possible for employment in the league to go up.

This was certainly true of the National Hockey League. In 1967, the NHL Players' Association formed. Salaries increased, but not to the levels seen in other sports. That year, the league expanded from the original six[21] teams to twelve teams. Over time, the league has grown to 30 teams. (Note: Some players tried to unionize in 1957–1958 but the union was busted when the owners either traded the problem players or sent them back to the minors. The union was able to form only because of the role played by the Ministry of Labour in Ontario and the commitment by the union's first president, Bob Pulford, to not go on strike in the first contract.) This example illustrates the point that, when a monopsony's labour force is unionized, not only wages but also employment goes up. Society and my brothers-in-law are better off because they get to watch more hockey.

Creative Destruction[22]

As a matter of fact, capitalistic economy is not and cannot be stationary. Nor is it expanding in a steady manner. It is incessantly being revolutionized from within by new enterprise.

Joseph Alois Schumpeter (1883–1950)
Taken from *Capitalism, Socialism and Democracy* (1942)

Most industries live between the extremes of pure competition and monopoly. Think of it as a continuum with relative firm power changing over time. Let's look at the auto sector to illustrate this point. The Detroit Big Three had significant market control until the advent of free trade. They were closer to the monopoly end of the spectrum. Because these firms were so profitable, unions had something to fight over. (Monopolies tend to find each other.)[23] Add together the impact of oligopolistic[24] car companies, which on their own raise prices together with unions that further raise prices, and it is safe to say that cars were priced on the higher end. Furthermore, government-enforced trade barriers kept cheaper cars out of the market. Once Japanese firms decided to locate in North America to get around these protectionist practices, the Detroit Big Three were in trouble. More firms were competing with each other, moving the North American car

---

[21] These six teams (Montreal Canadiens, Toronto Maple Leafs, Detroit Red Wings, Chicago Blackhawks, Boston Bruins, and New York Rangers) are collectively known as the Original Six.

[22] Joseph Alois Schumpeter (1883–1950) was an economist and political scientist born in Moravia, now the Czech Republic. He popularized the term *creative destruction* in economics. The basic idea is that monopoly profits aren't so bad because they create an incentive for companies to come up with some other way to provide a similar product, thus destroying the monopoly power of the original company.

[23] Walmart is a big seller in small-town America and a big buyer of product from various Chinese firms and has managed to stave off unions. On the other hand, the Liquor Control Board of Ontario (LCBO) is a big buyer of alcohol from around the world and a big seller in the province. It is both a monopsony and a monopoly. By the way, its employees are also unionized.

[24] A few companies. Not quite a monopoly, but not competitive either.

manufacturers further away from the monopoly end toward competition. Their ability to raise car prices was diminishing. Furthermore, these new foreign car companies weren't unionized, which gave them cost advantages.

The Detroit car manufacturers made monopoly-type profits for a long time. Whenever there is a lot of money on the table, some bright person is going to figure out some way to get his or her hands on it. It doesn't require a degree in rocket science to see why foreign companies found ways to get around this little trade problem. The moral of the story is this: If there are monopoly profits[25] to be had, people are going to go for them. It is only a matter of time.

LOOKING FOR THE RIGHT ANSWERS

Right or wrong, the customer is always right.

Marshall Field (1834–1906), American businessman and philanthropist[26]

Monopolies (unions are an example of a labour monopoly) charge more and sell less than competitive suppliers. Monopsonies buy less and pay less then competitive buyers. Both of these *mono*s decrease economic surplus because they underproduce and are therefore free market failures. The next chapter will look more carefully at all kinds of market failures, with a view to providing solutions to these problems.

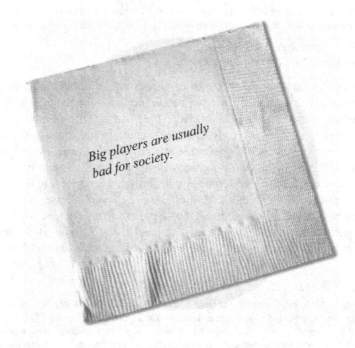

Big players are usually bad for society.

---

[25] You can't stop innovation if there is money to be made. When phone companies had monopoly power, in came the cellphone.

[26] The University of Chicago was founded by both Field and New York's John D. Rockefeller to rival nearby Evanston's Northwestern University. Field is number seven on the list of all-time richest self-made men. Rich people are usually friends with each other.

Getting an F: A Look at Market Failures

We have forty million reasons for failure, but not a single excuse.

Rudyard Kipling (1865–1936), British author born in India

The weather this afternoon is perfect. Friends and family arrive en masse bearing gifts, and make their way to the festively decorated backyard. After years of childlessness, the happy couple has finally adopted a little one. The bailiff served the court papers this very week. From beginning to end, what felt like an endless process took a little over three years. The star of the show—a little boy—sits on the ground surrounded by young would-be mothers, all trying to get his attention. He starts to cry, and his mom picks him up and soothes him. Everyone smiles.

As if on cue, the hired wait staff bring out trays holding flutes of champagne for the adults and sparkling juice for the younger guests. The boy's dad, looking a little emotional, raises his glass to propose a toast. At that moment, the quiet is shattered by the sound of a chainsaw next door. It seems that the neighbour who borders on the back of the property has chosen this moment to cut down an old maple tree to make way for a swimming pool. The noise is deafening. Awkwardly, the dad walks to the fence and asks for a reprieve. Unfortunately, due to scheduling issues, the man is unwilling to change his plans and the noise will continue. There is no choice but to herd everyone indoors.

MODEL OF PERFECTION

Trifles go to make perfection and perfection is no trifle.

Michelangelo di Lodovico Buonarroti Simoni, commonly known as Michelangelo (1475–1564), Italian Renaissance artist

The story we just read illustrates a kind of market failure. (Sometimes, when a tree falls,[2] everyone hears it!) Each individual clearly wanted something specific from the day, but at least one party walked away unsatisfied with the way things worked out. Economists today often grapple with the issues of market failures. This means that markets do not serve society well because they fail to bring about the desired result. While things don't always work out neatly in markets, fixing the problem can be complicated. Sometimes buyers and sellers can solve their own problems, but other times markets are going to need a little help, particularly from governments, to make them work well. This chapter will travel into the darkness of failures but, like most economists, I always wear my miner's light to look for free market solutions if they are remotely possible.

---

[1] Chapter 11 is a chapter of the United States Bankruptcy Code, which permits reorganization under the bankruptcy laws of the United States. When a company fails, that does not mean the market does. In the spirit of Chapter 11, any market failure should be restructured in order to succeed.

[2] *If a tree falls in a forest and no one is around to hear it, does it make a sound?* can be viewed as either a philosophical riddle about reality (posed by philosopher George Berkeley in 1710) or a scientific observation about the nature of sound (in *Physics* [1910] by Charles Riborg Mann and George Ransom Twiss).

Before starting in on the depressing stuff, let's begin on a positive note. Generally, markets work well. They almost effortlessly coordinate large groups of people to either produce or consume goods and services, creating this wonderful thing called economic surplus. This connecting of buyers and sellers can seem so smooth that it may feel as if some invisible hand is directing human activity to do the right thing. We know now that the coordinating function of markets works because of the role that prices play, as opposed to some big hand in the sky. We saw that prices signal to the various players in the market useful information about the marginal costs of producing and the marginal benefits of consuming. The market players then make choices based on that information. When the informational content of prices accurately reflects the true value of the product, the final quantity produced and consumed is socially correct. Furthermore, this quantity is made by the right companies and consumed by the right customers. Markets can get a lot of things right, and economists label the ones that get it right *efficient markets*.

But what if, for some reason, the information the price conveys is wrong and doesn't accurately reflect the true marginal benefits of the product or the marginal cost to make it? Now is the time for the rest of the story.

Terms and Conditions

Digressions, objections, delight in mockery, carefree mistrust are signs of health; everything unconditional belongs in pathology.

Friedrich Nietzsche (1844–1900), German philosopher and philologist[3]

What I am about to tell you does not negate everything I have said thus far about the efficiency of unfettered free markets. In fact, a competitive free market is normally the gold standard test[4] against which all market activity should be measured. Of course, we don't live in a perfect world and so we want to look at why markets fail to live up to this ideal or why the test itself may sometimes be flawed. Prepare yourself for a longer than normal chapter, because failure often takes longer to explain than success. You might want to pour yourself a stiff drink.

Here are the five general categories of problems that lead to market failures:

1. The market doesn't have enough players in it.
2. Market activity produces either positive or negative spillover effects not taken into account by the decision makers.
3. Property rights are either unclear or unenforceable.
4. Governments change the price or quantity of something.
5. Some market participants know more than others about what is really going on.

1. MARKET POWER: MADE FROM CONCENTRATE

People of the same trade seldom meet together, even for merriment and diversion, but the conversation ends in a conspiracy against the public, or in some contrivance to raise prices.

Adam Smith (1723–1790), Scottish moral philosopher and political economist

---

[3]   Philology considers both form and meaning in linguistic expression, combining linguistics and literary studies.
[4]   In medicine, *gold standard test* refers to a diagnostic test or benchmark that is regarded as definitive.

In the last chapter we looked in detail at markets with only a few players. To recap, if any buyer or seller has some control over market share and chooses to exercise that control by limiting quantity, then from society's perspective that market will not make enough goods or services. These concentrated markets simply fail to allocate scarce resources properly. The concentration ratio is often defined at the percentage of the market serviced by the biggest four firms. The bigger the percentage, the higher the concentration. In extreme cases, only one player—a monopoly, monopsony, or union—is in control. In each of these cases, what is controlled is very different, but the results are the same. Each market will result in not enough final output made.

In Chapter 9 we learned that, from society's perspective, the socially optimal quantity of a product occurs when the marginal benefit of that item equals the marginal cost to make it. Moreover, in Chapter 10 we also learned that due to private self-interest, big businesses[5] have no incentive to provide enough goods in the marketplace. It is more profitable to restrict output directly, as does the monopolist, or indirectly, as do monopsonies and unions.[6] Large players stop producing when society's marginal benefit of the output still exceeds the output's marginal cost. This presents society with a problem.

Monopoly Power

Power tends to corrupt; absolute power corrupts absolutely.

Sir John Emerich Edward Dalberg Acton (1834–1902), English historian

Any form of concentrated market power can be a problem; however, society tends to focus mostly on monopolies. There are a number of approaches that can take the teeth out of a monopolist's bite, and they all involve the government. The government can do any of the following:

A. Create laws that encourage competitive markets

B. Regulate the monopoly

C. Own the monopoly

A. Create Laws That Encourage Competitive Markets

As a preventative measure, society tries to solve the monopoly problem by passing laws that prevent markets from concentrating in the first place. These laws have such winning names as *anti-combine laws*, *anti-competition laws*, or *antitrust laws*, depending on the country. These laws usually have provisions that prevent collusion between competitors or practices that force competitors out of business, Governments also have rules about how mergers and acquisitions can be done legally.[7] The goal of such legislation is to

---

[5] Note that a union is a business just like a monopoly and monopsony.

[6] In 1992, the Canadian Radio-television and Telecommunications Commission ended the monopoly of long-distance phone service by Bell Canada and the provincial counterparts. It used to be quite common for people to end conversations by saying, "Better get off the phone, this is long distance." Now, with cheap phone plans, people don't mention cost anymore.

[7] The banking sector in Canada has seen mergers between types of financial institutions. (For example, TD Canada Trust is a merged company made from a bank and a trust company. This merger happened in 2000.) However when TD and CIBC applied to merge, the request was denied by the Finance Minister Paul Martin on December 14, 1998, due to concerns of anti-competition in the Canadian banking sector.

make it easier for small players to participate in the market, thereby keeping the numbers of firms up. For example, most developed countries have laws against predatory pricing. These laws forbid existing companies from temporarily dropping their prices to prevent another player from making a profit, thereby driving it out of business or preventing it from entering the market in the first place. For example, the European Commission fined French internet service provider Wanadoo millions of euros after finding it guilty of inhibiting competition in the market for high-speed internet access by charging below-cost prices. The commission claimed that Wanadoo's behaviour restricted the entry of competitors and the potential for competitors to develop. The concern is that once the competition is wiped out, the prices increase again to monopoly levels.

B. Regulate the Monopoly

Sometimes there just isn't enough demand to support more than a few companies. Furthermore, the economic benefits of size (yes, size does matter) can make some firms a natural monopoly. Governments, in this case, regulate their behaviour in the market. For example, utilities such as cable companies must petition their particular public utilities commission before they can change their rates. These companies may be big, but the government doesn't want them throwing their weight around.

C. Own the Monopoly

> *The theory of Communism may be summed up in one sentence: Abolish all private property.*
> Karl Marx (1818–1883), German author of *The Communist Manifesto* (1948)

Finally, governments sometimes just decide to own a company or nationalize it. For example, in Canada, provincial governments own most of the electric power utilities, usually with the word *hydro* somewhere in their names.[8] Government ownership in Canadian Crown corporations[9] included Air Canada, Canadian National Railway,[10] and Potash Corporation of Saskatchewan until these companies were privatized. Privatization is the act of selling publicly owned companies to the private sector.

Each of these solutions—laws, regulations, and state ownership—addresses the issue of market power. The efficacy of these approaches is not the topic of this book, but in terms of pecking order, free market types prefer laws to regulatory agencies and prefer regulators to state ownership. Those suspicious of free markets prefer the reverse order.

2. EXTERNAL RELATIONS: SPILLOVERS

> *Truth in philosophy means that concept and external reality correspond.*
> Georg Wilhelm Friedrich Hegel (1770–1831), German philosopher

---

[8]   Hydro-Québec, BC Hydro, and Ontario's Hydro One are good examples of this. Canada is the world's second largest producer of hydroelectricity in the world (after China) and one of a few countries to generate the majority of its electricity in this way.

[9]   The terms *Crown corporations* and *Crown entities* are used by Commonwealth countries to indicate government-owned corporations.

[10]   The Canadian National Railway is now a public company with 24 000 employees and market capitalization of $64 billion in 2015.

Usually, market prices help people to make good personal decisions because the price accurately reflects the true costs and benefits of something to society. In this case, the personal decision to buy and sell matches what society would like to see happen. But the costs and benefits of the decision maker are only socially correct if they are private. What do I mean by private? There can be no spillover effects; in other words, whatever a person does should not have an effect on individuals who have no say in the matter. If spillovers occur, then the market price is no longer an accurate signal of the true overall societal costs and benefits. Economists say that these markets have *externalities*.

Let's look at our opening story. Because these neighbours live side by side, the action of one neighbour imposes a cost on the other. The tree-cutting neighbour wants a pool and has hired someone to take out his tree. The other neighbours want to have a party to celebrate a significant event in their family. They would like it to be outside in their backyard and meaningfully quiet. They end up being disappointed by the outcome. However, the result is not just a personal disappointment, it is inefficient. The tree-cutting, pool-loving man did not take into account the negative costs of his actions on his neighbours. With a little coordination, another suitable date could have been arranged for either the celebration or the chainsaw massacre. Markets are supposed to efficiently coordinate people's activities. Not so in this case. All that the markets accomplished on this day was to provide the champagne and take out a tree. Markets didn't address the crucial point of optimal timing for the day's events and therefore, as an effective coordination mechanism, the markets get an F.

Unfortunately, from a market economist's perspective, the production and consumption of many products spill over in either a positive or a negative way onto innocent bystanders. This causes the production levels in the market to be socially wrong. In the case of negative externalities, more output than is socially optimal happens. In the case of a positive externality, not enough output occurs.

Let's start with a positive externality. Professional gardeners often talk of "borrowing" from the neighbour's property when landscaping. This means that you take into account the next-door hedge, gardens, and other attractive features when developing your own property. I happen to live on a street populated by retired people who love to garden. With every additional nearby rose garden, my property value goes up, and I did not have to pay for it. I am enjoying the view as well as a positive externality. However, it wasn't always this way. I once lived on a street where a man did oil changes in his front yard. Needless to say, I didn't enjoy this view and complained bitterly with the rest of the neighbourhood about the negative effects his yard was having on our property values.

The existence of externalities explains why neighbours care so much about what private citizens do to their front yards. The front yard isn't private. My examples may seem trivial but, as town councils that try to revitalize their downtown cores realize, what the neighbours do affects both property values and business prospects.[11] This point was brought home to me when my son took driver's education. I admit that it gave me pause as I dropped him off for his first lesson to realize that a massage parlour was in the back of the building. A worried mom, I of course talked to the owner of the driving school.

---

[11] A new mall always tries to sort out the anchor stores—the large stores that make the mall worth going to—first before it attracts renters for the rest of the space. Small stores care who the big stores are, as it affects the pedestrian traffic between them.

He assured me that the two groups of customers never crossed paths. I hope so, because I really didn't want to think about this particular externality. More importantly, I didn't want my son thinking about it.

To solve the externality problem, we need to address the two issues of property rights and transaction costs. The next section in this chapter will explore property rights more generally, but it is worth mentioning how property rights play out with respect to externalities. So, I ask you, who do you think should have had the right to get their way in our opening story: the tree-clearing neighbour or the celebrating family in the backyard? Once we know who has the right, it is possible for markets to sort themselves out. Nobel Prize–winning economist Ronald Coase showed that well-defined property rights could eliminate externality problems without further government involvement. The parties would simply negotiate a price with each other to get to a solution because it's clear who should do the paying. Without property rights, there are two problems to solve: who should pay who and how much? Two questions are harder to get answers to than one—especially when emotions are running high.

Gossip Column

Ronald Harry Coase (1910–2013) was the only child in a working-class British family.[12] His life story reads like a series of serendipitous events that finally let him to a Nobel Prize in Economics.

As a young boy, Coase suffered from a weakness in his legs that required him to wear leg irons. This weakness landed him in a school with other children who had both physical and mental disabilities, and he took courses in such riveting topics as basket weaving. Fortunately, he was a reader. For some reason he can't recall, he missed taking the entrance exams for the local secondary school, which should have happened when he was 11. His parents lobbied, and he was allowed to write the exams when he was 12. Fortunately, he was then awarded a scholarship to a good school. Once at school, Coase wrote the matriculation exam and passed with distinction in history and chemistry but, because of the loss of one year from age 11 to 12, he did not take Latin. Who cares, you say. Well, this ruled out a further degree in history, which would have been his first inclination. He was left with chemistry, but the required mathematics proved not to his liking. Finally, he switched to commerce.

Coase took mostly business and accounting courses until his final year, when he happened to take an economics course from Arnold Plant, who had just arrived at the London School of Economics. Plant introduced Coase to Adam Smith's *invisible hand* and changed the focus of his life. His intention to this point had been to go into law. Because of Plant's recommendation, the University of London awarded Coase a travelling scholarship, which took him to the industrial heartland of the United States to study how firms operate. His studies allowed him to ask businessmen why they did things in-house rather than through contractors, and the answers he got indicated that it came down to transaction costs. If it was cheaper to do something in-house, a

---

[12] Again, the *Oxford Dictionary of National Biography* is a great source for information about this British economist.

company did it in-house. Otherwise, it subcontracted. Coase published an article on this idea in 1937 called "The Nature of the Firm." This is the first of two papers that would win him the Nobel Prize. He was only 27 years old.

At age 50, he wrote the other Nobel paper, which looked at property rights and externalities—the Coase theorem, if you will. The groundwork was done during the intervening years as Coase studied natural monopolies, especially those in communication. He did more thinking about the role that property rights could play in allocating the radio frequency spectrum and wrote about it in an article. This first published work outlining the Coase theorem had the exciting title of "The Federal Communications Commission." Economists at the time read his conclusions, and many wondered how such a good economist could get it so wrong. If he was right, the implications would be quite profound in that the role of government in correcting these types of markets was much less than previously thought. Government simply needed to assign property rights, and the market would sort itself out.

George Stigler invited Coase to a workshop in Chicago. During this visit, a number of big-name economists who thought his ideas were in error invited Coase to expound on his views. The group took a vote before Coase began and only 1 out of 21 thought he was correct. After the conversation, everyone thought he was right and encouraged him to write another paper, which has the better title "The Problem of Social Cost." When Coase gave his speech accepting the Nobel Prize, he said that if these economists had not encouraged him to write the article, he would not have done so. That would have been a great loss, because at the time of the Nobel speech it was the most cited paper in modern economics.

Coase, without mathematics, revolutionized how economists thought about the role of government and law in economics, and it all happened almost by accident.

Who Could or Should Pay to Solve the Problem?

The physician can bury his mistakes, but the architect can only advise his client to plant vines—so they should go as far as possible from home to build their first buildings.

Frank Lloyd Wright (1869–1959), American architect

Many of the modern solutions to pollution—a major negative externality caused by businesses producing goods—are based on the principle of polluter pays. In other words, society at large retains the right to a clean environment and, in general, holds polluters responsible for fixing the problem. However, it doesn't necessarily have to be this way. We could just as easily make the party experiencing the negative effects of the pollution responsible for fixing the negative externality they are experiencing. Now, I realize this may go against your instincts of justice, and you may say, "What? Make the victim pay? That just isn't right." You are correct in saying that this becomes a problem of justice, but justice isn't an economic problem. It is an ethical, political, and moral problem. The big economic problem here is that too much pollution is happening. To solve that problem, we don't necessarily need the polluter-pays principle.

Let me give you an example of a market-based solution where the victim pays to correct a market failure. It is reported that because he was short, impresario (what a cool word) Billy Rose made it a practice to buy four tickets when he went to the theatre. Two of the tickets were for himself and his escort. The other two were for the seats directly in front of him; he would leave these seats empty so he could have an unobstructed view of the play. Instead of complaining to the theatre or asking the person in front of him to move his or her head, Billy Rose solved his externality problem himself by paying the price to avoid the problem altogether. For Billy, this expense was worth it.

Rose's solution also demonstrates the issue of relative transaction costs when it comes to externality problems. When transaction costs are low, individuals can find a solution for themselves. It turns out that Rose could easily solve his problem when he purchased the two extra seats. This simple transaction involved only him and the box office. How much longer does it take to say, "Four tickets, please" instead of "two tickets"? The time and money cost of solving this problem are relatively low. I know many of you might be thinking that theatre tickets are expensive, but this solution is cheap when compared to going to court or fighting city hall to solve problems. People solve their own externality problems all the time when they live in expensive gated communities, plant trees on the property line, or put up three-metre fences.

Let's look at a more complicated case that entails huge transaction costs. What if manure (yuck) from numerous farms located upstream from a town leaches into a river and enters the water supply downstream? The number of people involved makes it virtually impossible for each party to negotiate individually with the others to actually solve the problem. While a solution would highly benefit the entire group of townsfolk, the cost for any one person to solve the problem would be very high and some would say prohibitive. The townsfolk need to act together to make the cost worth it. To solve this problem, some level of government would usually need to take on the issue, but sometimes it can be handled by a concerned citizens group.[13] Now the cost of negotiation is lower because of economies of scale, which means that the cost incurred by the government to represent one citizen isn't much different from the cost to represent thousands. The cost per citizen, however, goes way down.

Once governments decide to act to reduce the sewage (externality) in the city's water supply, there is more than one way they can accomplish this goal. The first two solutions I am going to provide are market based, because they put a price on pollution. The third solution is outside the market system. Each policy has administration costs associated with it. If the costs to run any program exceed the benefits of it, the government should try another plan.

The basic solutions are these:

A. Tax bad behaviour or subsidize good behaviour

B. Cap and trade, which caps the level of pollution by selling pollution permits. Allow these permits to be traded in an open market.

C. Regulate to reduce bad behaviour

A. Paying for Sins or Providing Rewards for Virtues

You can't trust water: Even a straight stick turns crooked in it.

W.C. Fields (1880–1946), American comedian and actor

---

[13] In 1978, Lois Gibbs, a local mother and president of the Love Canal Homeowners' Association, began to investigate why there were many health problems in the area. Gibbs discovered that her neighbourhood sat on top of 21 000 tons of buried chemical waste.

To economists, it doesn't matter if the environmental program is a carrot or a stick type of program. (A horse can be convinced to move by either a carrot in the front or a stick in the rear.) Economists think either approach can work. This is really another way of addressing who will pay for the problem. For example, on one hand, the government could charge a pollution tax on the farmers who are polluting. Farmers can avoid the tax (a stick) by spending money on some system that prevents manure from going into the river or they can let the manure flow and accept a higher tax bill. Either way, the polluter is "paying to pollute." Because it now costs the farmers to pollute, this policy raises the cost of farming and the supply of animals goes down. Less animals mean less manure, and no one has to raise a stink.

On the other hand, the government could have a mechanism in place whereby the victims affected by the pollution pay the polluter through their tax dollars (a carrot) to pollute less. In this case, the farmers are motivated to reduce their supply of animals in order to get the government funds. Again, the result is fewer animals making poop. Each of these approaches ensures that less fecal material makes its way into the water supply of local homes, although who ends up paying the bill is different. The nature of the program can be either a carrot or a stick type to get the polluter to co-operate.

B. Permitting Pollution

Another way in which the government can handle this problem is to limit the quantity of pollution it will tolerate by limiting the number of pollution permits it issues. If the number of permits is less than the number farmers need, permits are now scarce and they become valuable pieces of paper that can be bought and sold. The right to pollute will now cost something. There are a couple of ways to "pay," depending on who owns the permits.

On one hand, existing farmers may be "grandfathered" the automatic right to some of these pollution permits. They still pay to use a permit because it could be sold to some other farmer. The permit has an opportunity cost. On the other hand, the government may require every polluter to buy a permit. Then, all farmers pay out of pocket. Again, permits that have a positive market value raise the cost of production and the supply of farm animals shifts to the left. To be sure, the grandfathered farmers will be richer than those who must pay out-of-pocket, but that's not what is relevant. The reduction in pollution is the real goal. Either payment plan will achieve this.

Carbon trading[14] is an example of a permit-type system whereas a carbon tax is … well, a tax. Economists like these approaches because they put the true social cost of polluting in front of company accountants, who now see pollution as a costly activity due to either the value of the permits or the cost of the taxes they need to pay. The costs of production are now higher and, as we saw in Chapter 6, higher costs shift the supply curve downward to a lower quantity. In the end, a reduction in output means less pollution.

C. The Regs

Finally, governments establish laws that regulate spillovers between citizens without any direct transfers of monies. In terms of pollution, the government may require manufacturers' pollution emissions to be under certain numbers. I am pretty familiar

---

[14]   This is sometimes called a cap and trade system.

with this world because my husband is an environmental engineer who works in consulting. Most of his clients hire him to test their air pollution levels to make sure they are in compliance with government regulations. It turns out that if you are under the legal levels by a smidgen, you are fine. If you are over by a smidgen, you are not fine and might even get fined—and will probably pay more than a smidgen. Of all the methods used to control pollution, economists like this one the least. Regulations do not take into account the fact that the cost to comply can be financially painful for some companies but be relatively inexpensive for others. Economists would like to see the overall level of pollution go down but we would prefer to reduce pollution using the least amount of scarce resources possible. Some companies spend a fortune to get their numbers down only a smidgen, which doesn't really help to reduce pollution much at all. Economists prefer tax and permit type solutions to regulations.

Often at the neighbourhood level, however, market-based solutions don't seem to work. The multitude of municipal bylaws speaks to this reality. For example, most urban centres require citizens to maintain their properties to some degree. This standard may be as simple as having to mow your lawn once it gets to a certain height, shovel the snow within a certain amount of time after a snowfall, or stop playing loud music after a certain time of day. Some municipalities go even further and legislate the colours you are allowed to paint your heritage house or forbid a clothesline in your backyard or pesticide use on your front yard. City hall has established these laws in response to some externality. With regard to the opening story, an applicable bylaw could be established to ensure that neighbours are entitled to two weeks' notice before a tree comes down in their area. Many communities even have laws in place that make it illegal for people to cut down a healthy mature tree without permission. All of these types of bylaws serve as non-market approaches to the externality problem.

Good Neighbours Make Good Fences

The Bible tells us to love our neighbours, and also to love our enemies; probably because they are generally the same people.

Gilbert Keith Chesterton (1874–1936), English writer

The unfortunate externality of the tree clearing in the opening story is similar to something that happened to me, only it was a hedge rather than a tree. (I must tell you that I was very ticked off at my neighbour for doing what he did.) Ironically, it all happened on Good Friday, 2009. I can only imagine my neighbour's conversation with his wife on that fateful morning. Maybe it was something like, "Hey, honey, today I think I'm going to cut down a hedge! What better way for the neighbours to experience the true meaning of Easter?"[15] Somehow, he was able to borrow a truck and trailer from another neighbour down the street who happened to be gone for the weekend. (It's so nice to know that my other neighbours—friends of my backyard neighbours—knew what was going to happen in my backyard before I did!) I came home from church only to have him knock on my door and explain that he wanted to take out the hedge … as soon as he could back up the truck.

---

[15] Christians mark Good Friday as the day of Jesus' crucifixion. This Friday is called "Good" because Jesus' sacrifice was to pay for the sins of the world. Easter Sunday marks His resurrection and the beginning of new life.

The hedge is on his property, so many of you will say, "Tough luck, but it is his hedge. You should be thankful he told you at all." You are correct, but this hedge lies outside his chain-link fence and is not accessible from his yard. (Initially, he built the fence in front of his hedge because of his Rottweiler, but now he also has a pool.) Furthermore, our property extends beyond his yard to another neighbour who was not taking out the rest of the hedge. Once the chainsaw stopped, our backyard looked like someone had given the hedge a bad haircut. A third of the hedge was cut to the ground and the rest was three metres tall. To add insult to injury, he asked my husband to move his truck and trailer so the remains of the hedge could be removed (much more conveniently) through our yard and driveway. When the assault was over, we were left with an eyesore and no privacy. I quickly made some calls about putting up a wooden fence.

Here is my opinion on the matter, and you can take it for what it is worth. When in an exchange between neighbours it's clear that markets don't work well, I think a little common courtesy goes a long way in maintaining good relations. I should have been given at least two weeks' notice about the hedge coming down. In the end, the only good thing I got out of the experience was a perfect example of externalities for my book. Once I realized that, I did smile about the whole thing.

3. PROPERTY LINES

Portia: This bond doth give thee here no jot of blood; The words expressly are "a pound of flesh."

William Shakespeare (1564–1616), English writer
Taken from *The Merchant of Venice*

My story nicely segues to the problem of property rights that are impossible to establish or enforce. On Good Friday, my neighbour essentially behaved as if he had all of the property rights even though, in my mind, the issue wasn't so clear-cut. According to Ronald Coase, if the property rights are absolutely clear, then I was not without options. If my neighbour had the right to do what he did and I didn't like it, I could have kept the hedge if I was willing to pay him more not to cut it down than the amount he valued it gone. Unfortunately, the events happened quickly and it was a civic holiday, which meant I couldn't make any inquiries into what my rights actually were. If I had wanted him to be on a sticky wicket,[16] I could have said, "Go ahead and take out the hedge but don't step one foot on my land," but that seemed a little too high drama for me. In the end, I blinked and let him have his way.

Public Property

What happens when property rights are functionally irrelevant? Two pertinent examples are what economists call *public goods* and *common property*. To be a pure public good, an item must have two salient characteristics: It must be non-rivalrous and non-excludable in consumption. *Huh?* Let me explain. Non-rivalrous means that my consumption of a good does not result in less of it for you to consume, and

---

[16]   The phrase *sticky wicket* comes from the game of cricket. The pitch becomes hardened due to drying rain, which makes batting difficult.

non-excludable means that my consumption cannot exclude you from consuming the item. It may be easier to understand if I give you an example. Suppose that I drive up and down my street looking for a wireless internet connection for my laptop. When I find one (and I will), I'll be able to use the connection without the homeowners knowing that we are all online at the same time. My internet use does not rival theirs (one extra user shouldn't do much to slow things down) and they have not excluded me from their property. In this situation, the internet connection is acting as a public good. To exclude non-payers, the internet customer has to install a firewall. The act of my connecting to an account I am not paying for is called free riding.

Internet service providers have figured out how to get rid of this free rider problem, but other goods are not so easy in terms of excluding people. If my neighbour decides to plow our street after a snowstorm, he cannot stop others from driving down the plowed road. If one shipping company decides to build a lighthouse,[17] it cannot stop other ships from using the light to guide their way. Without government funding, not enough public goods would be provided, because they are costly to produce and difficult to extract revenues for. This is why governments in developed countries are in charge of such things as roads, national defence, and policing. These are public goods, not because they serve the public but because they are non-excludable yet have a huge value to all who use them. They are worth publicly funding.

Public Health and Education

Health and education have both a private and a public component to them. Certainly, the private return on education is high for people, and that is why families scrimp and save to send their little ones to university or college. But on top of the private benefits, there is also a public good component to education. The more educated a population, the greater the engagement in civic duties such as voting and support of free speech, and the lower the crime rates. Furthermore, fundamental non-commercial research done by universities and colleges serves the public good. There is nothing to patent and only a very rich philanthropist or government could pay for it otherwise. Think of what the world would be like without the foundational work of Max Planck[18] or Albert Einstein!

Public spending on health is another example of a private–public combination. Immunization programs reduce the number and effects of debilitating diseases. While immunization benefits the recipient, the negative spillover of infectious diseases warrants government funding of immunization programs for those who would not pay for it. A healthier population is a more productive population.

---

[17]   Ronald Coase showed that lighthouses in nineteenth-century Britain were privately provided and that ships were charged for their use when they came into port. Markets seemed to be working for this public good. Upon further analysis, the truly free market lighthouses didn't survive long. Only those that the government granted the right to collect a "light due" for did so. Eventually the government bought up the lighthouses because the private lighthouses started to act as monopolists.

[18]   Planck was appointed dean of Berlin University, after which it was possible for him to call Einstein to Berlin and establish a new professorship for him (1914). The two scientists became close friends and met frequently to play music together. Planck is the founder of quantum theory and won the Nobel Prize for Physics in 1918.

Law and Order

If you're in the Chicago area anytime soon and you see a red-haired girl driving around—in the words of Elmer Fudd—be vewy vewy careful.

John Ortberg (1957–), American minister and author
Taken from *Everybody's Normal Till You Get To Know Them* (2003)

One public good that is vital if markets are to function properly is a well-defined justice system. What is the point of working hard if your work is stolen or your employer refuses to pay you and you have no recourse? What value do property rights have if they are not binding? Citizens need to know what the rules are and be confident that they are enforced. These rules should seem fair to most people. This averts revolutions or strikes[19] that can shut down economies completely.

Think of justice as rules of the road. If everyone drives close to the speed limit, drives on the correct side of the road, and gives the right of way when they should, traffic keeps moving. Traffic cops help to enforce these rules, which would surely be broken if it were not for their existence. While a cop on every corner would be excessive, not to mention expensive, we do want a few of them around here and there. But even with a decent traffic system, accidents sometimes happen, and markets are no different. If we notice that a particular intersection has more accidents than "normal," it might be worth increasing surveillance of that corner. The same can be said for markets. If one market fails badly for whatever reason, a small change in government intervention could fix it. The entire market system doesn't need to be changed.

The Tragic Commons Revisited

In Chapter 4, I mentioned that the big problem with the environment is ownership. This is especially true with transnational issues such as global warming or overfishing in the oceans. In this case, the environment is rivalrous or depletable but not excludable. In fact, almost every country in the world emits carbon dioxide into the atmosphere, which depletes environmental quality, and many countries send out fishing trawlers, which depletes the fish stocks. Without some sort of global property rights system, we are in big trouble.

4. GOVERNMENT INTERFERENCE

I make a fortune from criticizing the policy of the government, and then hand it over to the government in taxes to keep it going.

George Bernard Shaw (1856–1950), Irish playwright

So far, I have been extolling the virtues of government intervention in fixing market failures. I must now switch hats to look at market failures caused by government programs. Frankly, when governments intervene in a market to change the price or the

---

[19]   The largest general strike that ever stopped the economy of an advanced industrial country—and the first general wildcat strike in history—occurred in May 1968 in France. The prolonged strike involved 11 million workers for two consecutive weeks, and its impact was such that it almost caused the collapse of Charles de Gaulle's government.

quantity for reasons other than externalities or public goods, they mess with the perfection of the free market. Usually the government has the best of intentions, but that doesn't mean that what it does is right. The government gets it wrong not because it is evil but because when it disconnects itself from free markets it loses valuable information about what people value or a firm's opportunity costs. Government policy is a bit like doing brain surgery while blindfolded. It is really tough to get right.

For instance, the government might think that the rents poor people pay are too high and decide to legislate rent controls. This has the very bad result of driving owners of rental housing out of business, reducing the number of rental properties, decreasing rental quality, and creating a housing crisis. Left-wing Nobel Prize–winning economist Gunnar Myrdal criticized governments who used rent controls to solve the problem of affordable housing, characterizing them as bad planners without vision or courage.[20] Ouch!

When a government intervenes to change price or quantity to a number other than the efficient free market amount, economists say that the government is distorting the market. The price no longer conveys the correct information and distorts the decisions of the consumers or producers in the market. In the case of rent controls, the landlord sees low rents and decides to get out of the rental housing market, even though there are lineups outside the apartment building of people looking for the low-priced housing. The price no longer reflects the true demand for the apartment and ceases to influence the landlord appropriately. Swedish economist Assar Lindbeck went on to say that rent controls were the most efficient way to destroy a city other than to just bomb it!

While governments have the best of intentions, almost everything they do to change the market price—whether it be to raise wages with minimum wage legislation, protect domestic jobs with tariffs, tax or subsidize consumer products, or pay farmers more with agricultural price supports—distorts the market and misallocates scarce resources.

In a civilized society, it is virtually impossible to get rid of taxes, so what can be done to deal with life's inevitable distortions and failures? Economists Richard Lipsey and Kevin Lancaster showed that, given an unavoidable failure in one market, it might be worth it to have a distortion in another market. This is called the theory of the second best. For example, if a mining company is badly polluting, it might be optimal to let the company become a monopoly. A monopoly (usually a bad thing) would reduce production, which is good for the pollution numbers. Or, suppose that a monopsony hires too few workers and pays its workforce too little. Then, adding a union could increase not only wages but also the level of employment. In both stories, two wrongs *can* make a right. This means that the simple laissez-faire shoe doesn't fit all feet. A little analysis might be necessary.

5. I KNOW SOMETHING YOU DON'T KNOW

It is a very sad thing that nowadays there is so little useless information.

Oscar Fingal O'Flahertie Wills Wilde (1954–1900), Irish writer

---

[20] Myrdal, Gunnar. (1965, August 25). Opening address to the Council of International Building Research in Copenhagen. *Dagens Nyheter*, p. 12; cited in Rydenfelt, Sven. (1981). The rise, fall and revival of Swedish rent control. In Block, Walter, & Olsen, Edgar (eds.), *Rent control: Myths and realities*, p. 224. Vancouver: The Fraser Institute.

Markets work well when everyone has access to the same relatively accurate information, but once one person knows more than others do, we have asymmetric information and this can lead to market inefficiencies or, more bluntly, to market failure. In broad strokes, asymmetric information causes problems because people use the information strategically while others cannot. When people are strategic, they improve their personal lot in life, and that may mean they keep some things quiet. Economically, when different players know different things, it is hard to get those who know more to behave appropriately with respect to either risk or effort. Usually, this scenario leads to too much risk and not enough effort.

Essentially, the economic crisis of 2007–2009 had its roots in asymmetric information, and the buzzwords of this type of problem were thrown around the media as pundits tried to explain to the public what on earth was happening. The next chapter will look at the issues of the economic crisis more closely as they relate to financial markets in particular.

Risky Business

As a general rule the most successful man in life is the man who has the best information.
Benjamin Disraeli (1804–1881), British prime minister and novelist

The risk of any decision, when it is accurately known by everyone involved, is not a problem even if the risk is very high. Risk is not a market failure. Fully informed consenting adults can freely consent. Problems occur when one party either hides the truth or changes its behaviour, which essentially changes the truth. Economists have great names for these situations, which make it all sound more formal. Concealing the truth is called *adverse selection*; changing behaviour is called *moral hazard*.

The classic academic paper on adverse selection is George Akerlof's "The Market for 'Lemons'." This paper, for which he won the Nobel Prize,[21] set forth the idea that the person who knows more—the seller of the car—has an incentive to hide the fact that the car is a lemon from the buyer who knows less about the car. Buying a used car is therefore a tricky venture. If the market price turned out to be the average between good cars and lemons, then lemons make a killing and good cars sell below their true value. Given that the owners of good cars don't want to sell their vehicles for less than they think they are worth, only lemons exist in the second-hand market and the price reflects that fact. This is a bad thing because owners of good cars also want to sell their vehicles, and buyers would be willing to pay the price if they knew the cars were good. Essentially, the market for good cars disappears because of asymmetric information.

Participants in markets can solve this problem. The owner of the car could signal the worth of the vehicle by offering warranties, guarantees, or endorsements by famous people. The buyer of the vehicle could screen the car for quality by taking it to a mechanic for a look under the hood, reading consumer reports, or buying only from a friend or relative. Screening and signalling are expensive, but these methods keep the market for good used cars alive. As long as the benefit of the solution exceeds the cost of solving this problem, the world is better for it.

---

[21]   Writing "The Market for 'Lemons'": A Personal and Interpretive Essay, http://nobelprize.org/nobel_prizes/economics/laureates/2001/akerlof-article.html

The insurance industry worries more about risk than any other industry. Life insurance companies want to insure healthy people who are likely to live longer lives. Adverse selection problems are rife, but insurance companies try to get an accurate risk picture by asking for medical and lifestyle information during the application process. In other words, they screen. Once they agree to insure you, the risk isn't over. Moral hazard problems arise when people change their behaviour after the policy is issued. Suppose that a policyholder suddenly decides to take up skydiving or mountain climbing. He might buy a hot little sports car and drive like a maniac. She might start smoking or drink more heavily. If the insurance company had known what the policyholder was going to do, the rates would have been higher to reflect the true risk of this person. The only thing insurance companies can do is put caveats in the contract that make the policy null and void under certain conditions. For example, most life insurance policies will not pay out if the person commits suicide within the first two years. I guess they figure that people who plan to commit suicide and are thoughtful enough to buy a life insurance policy to leave money for those left behind will probably change their minds after two years.

E for Effort

> *Quality is never an accident; it is always the result of intelligent effort.*
> John Ruskin (1819–1900), English art critic

Adverse selection and moral hazard can also apply to effort. In adverse selection, workers misrepresent their abilities or skills to get hired. Moral hazard happens if an employee shirks his or her duties once hired. In these cases, the workers know more about themselves than the employers do, hence there is an asymmetric information situation and, more importantly, a market problem.

Employers try to solve the adverse selection problem through rigorous hiring processes. Again, this is screening. They scrutinize cover letters and resumés for any relevant work experience, education, or typos. This is why recommendations are so important to the employer and why "who you know" might be more important than "what you know" in terms of landing a job.

Often, potential employees try to signal their quality to employers. Showing up to the interview with appropriate attire, a reputable degree, or fantastic letters of reference signals to the employer that you are not a lemon of an employee.

Once a worker is hired, there is still the problem of moral hazard. Employers can't monitor their employees all day long. As the saying goes, *When the cat's away, the mice will play*. The market has developed payment schemes to try to solve mediocre performances, whether it be through shirking or playing too safe. These are called incentive-compatible compensation schemes. If you can say that without stumbling, you're hired! This could include piece rates, bonuses, commissions, and requirements for billable hours. You earn more if you produce more. If you become a senior executive, your pay will include stock options. In other words, you make more income if the company's stock does well.

Firms might do as Henry Ford did. He paid higher than market wages, known as efficiency wages. This removes any desire by a worker to lose a particular job. The benefit of shirking or absenteeism goes down, and morale goes up. Ford's chief of labour relations estimated that productivity rose 51 percent after Ford instituted these higher wages. More importantly, from 1914 to 1919 profits doubled.

These are all market-based solutions to solve the moral hazard problem. They align incentives with desired results from the employer's perspective. One thing is certain: Anything that can get relevant information to the party that needs it is a good thing. However, none of these complicated, costly compensation schemes would be necessary if people were fully informed to begin with.

CASING THE POINT

A thinker sees his own actions as experiments and questions—as attempts to find out something. Success and failure are for him answers above all.

Friedrich Wilhelm Nietzsche (1844–1900), German philosopher

Congratulations, you have finished reading everything you ever wanted to know about markets but were afraid to ask! The next chapter will look at financial markets as a case study. Essentially, everything in this book finds examples in the fascinating world of finance.

Markets can fail for various reasons. Governments can help, but they have to be careful not to make things worse.

CHAPTER 12

Numb€rs: Financial Markets

There is no safety in numbers, or in anything else.

James Grover Thurber (1894–1961), American writer and cartoonist
Taken from "The Fairly Intelligent Fly" in the *New Yorker* (February 4, 1939)

As you walk into the ballroom of the luxury hotel, the first thing that hits you is the sea of dark suits—black, navy, grey—on both men and women. The only break in the dark palette comes from the white shirts and red bowties of the wait staff milling around with trays of canapés and wine. You are here to celebrate the merger of the accounting firm[1] that does your company's books with another major player in the industry. Along with entrepreneurs and industrialists, the guest list looks like a who's who in the financial sector. Bankers, bond traders, stockbrokers, and hedge fund managers chat as they enjoy a drink on the accounting firm's dime. The atmosphere is rife with power, importance, and money, and you hope you don't say anything that seems remotely stupid[2] to anyone. From a passing tray, you scoop up a glass of Château Margaux[3] and look for a group to join.

ACCOUNTING FOR THE FINANCIALS

The ease of mathematical manipulation may lead to a neglect of those issues that are hard to formalize or, equally dangerous, to a distortion in the way we look at those problems ...

Peter Skott, economist
Taken from *Mythical Ages and Methodological Strictures: Joan Robinson's Contributions to the Theory of Economics Growth* (2004)

Before we start looking at the financial sector, I think it would be good if I told you what is not going to happen in this chapter, just so that those of you who are skipping ahead to read about financial matters won't be disappointed. I am not going to explain what happened in the financial crisis of 2007–2009 in excruciating detail. That has been done—with great finesse, I might add—by economist Robert Shiller,[4] who has the comparative advantage in this topic. I am also *not* going to outline every conceivable financial product known to man. I can't think of anything more unbearable.

Rather, I am going to describe the economics underlying the financial markets. This will enable you to understand many details described by other sources, whether they be books, magazines, newspapers, or Wikipedia. I admit that I picked one of the most

---

[1]   The Big Four accounting firms worldwide are PricewaterhouseCoopers, Deloitte Touche Tohmatsu, Ernst & Young, and KPMG. This group was known as the Big Eight until 1987, and was reduced to the Big Five through a series of mergers by 1998. The Big Five became the Big Four as Arthur Anderson suffered irreparable damage following the 2002 Enron scandal. The Big Four "accounted" for close to US$127.7 billion in revenues in 2015. This group is thought to be an oligopoly.

[2]   The first book in English on stupidity was *A Short Introduction to the History of Stupidity* by Walter B. Pitkin (1932).

[3]   "Investment wines" are considered by some to be Veblen goods after economist Thorstein Veblen, who coined the phrase *conspicuous consumption*. The uninformed (like me) should watch out for scams in this market. It is highly unlikely that this wine is available at this gathering.

[4]   *The Subprime Solution: How Today's Global Financial Crisis Happened, and What to Do about It* (2008).

complicated of all market systems as an application, but I think it is particularly important that you understand some of this since it truly affects everyone in the world. I should warn you that the plethora of names for available financial securities can be mind-boggling. For some reason, finance types love to make relatively simple things more complicated than is necessary. Perhaps it's because this field is dominated by men who may feel they need to compensate for something.

Cadastral Survey[5]

Power is the great aphrodisiac.

Henry Alfred Kissinger (1923–), German-born political scientist, diplomat, and winner of the Nobel Peace Prize
Taken from The *New York Times* (January 19, 1971)

Recall from Chapter 4 that the financing behind buying a machine or piece of property is called financial capital because it is the paper trail recording the acquisition of the real capital. For example, a factory matches up with the corresponding mortgage used to buy that building or with the shares belonging to the owners of the building. The factory or real asset is paperized.[6] However, finance has evolved since the early days. With all of the exotic names for these paper financial instruments, it can appear that finance is now utterly divorced from the real economy that produces goods and services—but it isn't. You just have to look a bit harder.

There are many ways to slice and dice financial instruments, and I have chosen to put things into the broadest categories possible. Think of it as sorting the laundry. While they are all clothes, the darks go in a different pile than the whites or permanent press. Fundamentally, every financial asset (even those I don't mention in this book) can fit into one of the following five categories: money, debt, equity, derivatives, or some grouping of the first four.

Each of these categories could literally fill a book. In fact, each of them has. My summary of each type of of asset will be quick and dirty—which probably doesn't fit well with the laundry analogy.

1. Money

Money is the safe haven for individuals and companies when the real economy looks scary, because in low inflationary times money keeps its value. In fact, financial investors[7] often hold money if they think the other categories are going to tank. Nassim Taleb,[8] the author of the bestselling book *The Black Swan: The Impact of the Highly Improbable* and one of the few voices to predict the financial crisis of 2007–2009, was

---

5   Cadastral surveys are used to document the boundaries of land ownership.

6   This is one of the big problems in developing countries. They have either unclear property rights or no mechanisms to create paper out of real assets. This slows down their growth. See Peruvian economist Hernando de Soto Polor's book *The Mystery of Capital: Why Capitalism Triumphs in the West and Fails Everywhere Else.*

7   I have been careful to use the term *financial investor* rather than *investor* because economists separate investment from saving. Firms invest and people save. The general public, however, doesn't differentiate between the two so talk about investing their money. I will therefore compromise and add the word *financial* in front of investor.

8   Taleb also recommends in his book to make use of serendipity by going to as many cocktail parties as possible.

asked in an interview about where he was parking his wealth in light of the recent financial crisis. Taleb's reply—"cash is king"—indicated that he wasn't ready to get back into other types of paper at that time.

Historically, money has had many forms. These include commodities such as gold or grain (cigarettes were used as money in German prisoner of war camps), coins, and bills, but these days the most important form of money is sitting in bank[9] accounts. Very few people keep their money as cash[10] under their mattress anymore—although I love finding cash when I do the laundry … particularly bills.

Money acts as grease for the wheels that turn the real economy, helping businesses to produce and consumers to buy. Grease is a good thing, except when it gets into your clothes and when companies start to hold lots and lots of money. This is a bad sign because it means that these companies are veering away from investing in real equipment, real inventories, and real buildings and choosing instead to hold cash that isn't real. Ultimately, money must buy real things to keep the real economy going. Really.

"Does it hurt?" asked the Rabbit.

"Sometimes," said the Skin Horse, for he was always truthful. "When you are Real, you don't mind being hurt."

Margery Williams Bianco (1881–1944), English-American author
Taken from *The Velveteen Rabbit or How Toys Become Real* (1922)

When an individual, business, or government buys the money of another country, the currency of the other country is called *foreign exchange*. While the origins of foreign exchange markets are found in international trade, the majority of buying and selling of foreign exchange nowadays is due to the buying and selling of financial paper. If a European wants to buy an American stock, it must do so with American dollars.

Foreign exchange markets connect buyers and sellers of currency with each other in order to trade their money.[11] The predominant players in this market are banks and central banks through two electronic networks—Reuters and Electronic Broking Service—that are computerized systems where dealers post bid (buy) and ask (sell) prices. The market clears automatically, which means that the computer matches the players who posted the same bid and ask prices. A minimum trade of $1 million of currency is required to play in this market, so I think it's fair to say that leaves most of us out of it. When the average person buys currency, he or she does so from a bank that buys the currency in this way.

Greasing the Wheels of Time

The importance of money flows from it being a link between the present and the future.
John Maynard Keynes[12] (1883–1946), English economist

---

[9] I will use the word *bank* to include institutions that act like banks. These include credit unions, savings and loans, trust companies, etc.

[10] In Canada, a little over 5 percent of money is in the form of cash when chequing, saving, and cash are added together. The situation in the United States isn't much different.

[11] The foreign exchange market is the largest financial market in the world. The *daily* turnover of currency is in the trillions.

[12] Keynes is probably one of the most influential economists of the last century. As Milton Friedman said in 1965, "We're all Keynesians now."

While money exists mostly in the form of bank accounts, money markets are about the buying and selling of short-term debt. So, what is the connection between the two? This might seem strange, but the only difference between them is a matter of time or (in financial terms) liquidity. Bank accounts—the most liquid of all financial assets—can usually be accessed 24/7 through the internet or bank machines, whereas money market debt can be as short as a day but can also be as long as one year. Because these assets are relatively short-lived and very common, they can be easily sold and converted into bank accounts. For all intents and purposes, they are as good as money, and economists call these financial assets *near money*.

This kind of short-term debt can be issued by governments in the form of Treasury bills[13] or by corporations in the form of Commercial Paper. Banks can also create such typical money market assets as Certificates of Deposit,[14] Banker's Acceptances,[15] or Repurchase Agreements.[16] While this list of financial instruments in the money markets sounds quite exotic, don't be too impressed. For visualization purposes, think of buyers and sellers exchanging pieces of paper created by governments, businesses, and banks that need to borrow for short periods of time. The pieces of paper are agreements to settle up sometime within a year. If people don't want to wait to settle later, they can sell the paper now in the money market to someone else who will settle with the borrower later. When you hear the term *money market*, this is what they are talking about. I guess the more accurate *near money markets* is a too much of a mouthful for the finance guys.

2. Debt

Creditors have better memories than debtors.

Benjamin Franklin (1706–1790), American politician and polymath
Taken from *Poor Richard's Almanac* (1758)

Debt is an IOU, or a promise to pay back—typically, with interest. This can be a loan, mortgage, or bond. Bonds have a term longer than one year and are publicly traded in bond markets. These are called over-the-counter markets, with market makers in the middle facilitating the trades. Market makers are usually investment bankers[17] in a brokerage division. In contrast, individual mortgages and loans are usually not negotiated in publicly traded markets. There are reasons for this that will become clear later in

---

[13] T-Bills are bonds sold with a promise to redeem them for $1000 in a year or less. They are sold at a discount to make a positive rate of return for the buyer.

[14] Certificates of Deposit are different from savings accounts in that a CD has a specific, fixed term (often three months, six months, or one to five years) and, usually, a fixed interest rate. It is intended that the CD be held until maturity, at which time it is cashed in for the principal and interest.

[15] A Banker's Acceptance, or BA, is similar to a certified cheque.

[16] In a repo, the borrower agrees to sell a security to a lender and also agrees to buy it back from the lender at a fixed price at some later date.

[17] Regular banks are called commercial banks and do the things that economists and the general public associate with banks. They provide the products that allow people to save and borrow. Investment banking deals only with very large financial investors and does such things as advising on mergers and acquisitions, underwriting a new stock offering, or speculating with derivatives. Underwriting connects businesses that need capital with financial investors who have it.

the chapter. We will see the vital role that regular banks[18] play in bringing borrowers and lenders together to create such things as car loans and home mortgages.

3. Equity

When I received the Nobel Prize, the only big lump sum of money I have ever seen, I had to do something with it. The easiest way to drop this hot potato was to invest it, to buy shares. I knew that World War II was coming and I was afraid that if I had shares which rise in case of war, I would wish for war. So I asked my agent to buy shares which go down in the event of war. This he did. I lost my money and saved my soul.

Albert Szent-Gyorgyi (1893–1986), Hungarian physiologist
Taken from *The Crazy Ape* (1970)

Equity is ownership in a company and can take the form of stocks or shares. If a company wants to raise financial capital by selling off ownership, it can list its company's stock on a stock exchange. This is done through an investment banker who has a seat on various stock exchanges. When a company issues stock for the first time, it is said to be going public with an initial public offering (IPO). If, at a later date, it issues more stock, these are known as secondary or seasoned offerings. The biggest job of these investment bank underwriters is to price the stock and facilitate the sale so that the issuing company will get the financial capital it needs to do its business in the real world.

Stock exchanges[19] have requirements for listing, and by necessity the businesses who list are large companies. It also costs a lot to be a part of an exchange, so only the biggest of these big players list on multiple exchanges. If a company cannot afford to list or fails to meet the requirements of the exchange, it can still sell shares in the over-the-counter market. For instance, penny stocks[20] are sold in this way. When General Motors filed for Chapter 11 bankruptcy protection, it was delisted from the various stock exchanges[21] but its stock was still available over-the-counter.

Since 1969, there has been a third option for buying and selling stocks. They now can be sold through electronic communications networks in much the same way currency is traded. A computer automatically matches buyers and sellers who give the same price. This is done for a small transaction fee.

4. Derivatives

The gambling known as business looks with austere disfavor upon the business known as gambling.

Ambrose Bierce (1842–disappeared 1914), American writer

---

[18] Other institutions offer bank-like services. These include credit unions, trust companies, and savings and loans companies. Finance companies like those associated with retail outlets (Sears, the car companies) provide loans without taking deposits. They create debt, then sell it to get the funds to lend.

[19] The top eight stock exchanges in the world are the New York Stock Exchange (approximately four times larger than any other), the Tokyo Stock Exchange, the NASDAQ, Euronext, the London Stock Exchange, the Shanghai Stock Exchange, the Hong Kong Stock Exchange, and, last but not least (at least from my perspective), the Toronto Stock Exchange.

[20] The terms *penny stock*, *microcap stock*, *small caps*, and *nano caps* are sometimes interchangeably.

[21] On November 18, 2010, a reorganized GM issued an IPO and was listed again. This allowed governments to sell off their shares and reduce their ownership of the company.

Derivatives derive their value from some other underlying asset. The most common types of derivatives available in the market are options, futures contracts, forward contracts, and swaps.[22] Derivatives can be sold over-the-counter like bonds or on special derivative exchanges[23] the way many stocks are traded. The most important role for derivatives is usually hedging,[24] a form of risk minimization. Think of hedging as an insurance policy against prices not going your way.

But, wait a minute. Aren't hedge funds partly to blame for the financial crisis? Then why did something that should reduce risk actually create a financial mess? Well, in reality, while risk reduction is the goal of hedging, hedge funds actually take the same derivative products and increase risk to generate above-average returns for their clients. They are speculators rather than hedgers. They are allowed to do so because only the very rich can play in this game, and governments don't regulate hedge funds to the same degree as other types of financial investments. In terms of regulation, it was felt that the big boys should be able to take care of themselves. Given the financial mess in hedge funds and the spillover effects on the economy as a whole, it looks like they aren't quite so independent and might need a diaper change. Often these funds borrow money[25] to buy derivatives, a practice known as leveraging, which accentuates the direction of the gains or losses. Needless to say, in the financial crisis of 2007–2009, it was the losses that got accentuated.

5. Pooling Assets

Undoubtedly, holding is risky.

Karen Burton Mains, American author
Taken from *Comforting One Another: In Life's Sorrows* (1997)

Assets can be created by pooling or combining any of the assets discussed above in some way. Normally, pooling is supposed to reduce risk, but you would never get that idea from the reporting on the financial crisis. Much of the excitement in the financial sector has been in this category. Here is where the fortunes of such companies as Lehman Brothers Holdings Inc. (which went bankrupt—interesting word[26]), Merrill

---

[22] Options are the *right* to buy or sell at a certain price some time in the future or to not buy or sell. Futures and forwards involve the *actual* buying and selling some time in the future. Swaps trade streams of income flow but the original assets remain with the original owners. Think of wife swapping: Everyone stays married to their spouses but they trade services with other partners.

[23] The world's largest derivatives exchanges (by number of transactions) are the Korea Exchange (which lists KOSPI Index Futures & Options), Eurex (which lists a wide range of European products such as interest rate and index products), and CME Group (made up of the 2007 merger of the Chicago Mercantile Exchange and the Chicago Board of Trade and the 2008 acquisition of the New York Mercantile Exchange).

[24] For example, a car company may agree to buy steel from a Chinese company for a particular price with delivery and payment due six months from now. If that price is quoted in U.S. dollars, the Chinese company is subject to exchange rate risk and could lose profits should the value of the U.S. dollar appreciate against the yuan. It may want to get rid of this uncertainty by entering into a contract that buys the U.S. dollar for a particular yuan price six months from now. This is called a forward contract.

[25] Sometimes called *buying on margin*.

[26] The word *bankruptcy* is formed from the ancient Latin *bancus* (a bench or table), and *ruptus* (broken). A "bank" originally referred to the bench on which the banker worked in the marketplace. Hence, when a banker failed, he broke his bank.

Lynch & Co. (which was bought out by Bank of America), and AIG or American International Group, Inc. (which needed massive bailout money to survive) played out. This category saw plenty of action during the fall of 2008.

These gourmet-sounding mixed bags include the following:

- Asset-backed securities, which include such things as asset-backed commercial paper[27] and collateralized debt obligations.[28] (I told you: Somebody has to have issues to make up names like these.) So, what do these things do? These products convert paper that is not tradable into something that can be traded in a public market. For instance, mortgages negotiated between individuals and their banks are not tradable but when banks repackage them in groups of mortgages, the mortgage-backed commercial paper can be sold on world markets. This process is known as securitization. The bank no longer owns the mortgages even though homeowners make payments to the bank. The bank services—for a fee, of course—the mortgage on behalf of the owners and is now just the frontperson. This allows banks that are heavily regulated to sell locked-in assets like mortgages and convert them to more liquid funds. The whole subprime mortgage market mess happened in this category of financial assets.

- Funds, whether they be managed funds, mutual funds,[29] investment funds, income trusts, or pension funds. Fund companies own a variety or portfolio of financial assets and allow small financial investors to buy units of the entire pool. These financial investors never directly own the assets in the pool. Rather, the investors are along for the ride with the fund company—and they hope it is a good one. Funds allow small-time investors to spread their wealth out over many assets and "not put all their eggs in one basket."

Gimme a Break

There are three kinds of men. The one that learns by reading. The few who learn by observation. The rest of them have to pee on the electric fence for themselves.

Will Rogers (1879–1935), American comedian and actor

In terms of broad asset groupings, we have hit most of the lingo found on the front cover of the business section. I know I have bombarded you with a lot of detail, but it was really unavoidable. It is precisely because of these minutiae that I find finance a bit over-the-top, so I can only image what you must be thinking. If you need to take a break, I completely understand. This is a good spot to do so.

---

[27] Asset-backed commercial paper (ABCP) is a form of commercial paper that is collateralized by other financial assets. In other words, this paper is backed by a collection of other types of paper. ABCP is used for short-term financing needs.

[28] Collateralized debt obligations are a type of asset-backed security based on a portfolio of fixed-income assets such as mortgages or car loans.

[29] A mutual fund is a professionally managed investment that pools money from many investors and invests it in all of the other types of financial assets. These assets can be bought, held, and sold by the fund manager.

Gossip Column

Merton Howard Miller (1923–2000) was the only child of Joel and Sylvia Miller. His dad was a lawyer who studied at Harvard, and while Miller followed in his father's footsteps by going to Harvard, he studied economics instead of law.

Throughout his academic life, Miller was surrounded by Nobel Prize winners in economics. Robert Solow (who won in 1987) was in the same introductory economics class at Harvard. After a career path that involved some government jobs, grad school at Johns Hopkins, and a brief stint teaching at the London School of Economics, he joined the faculty at what would become Carnegie Mellon University. It was there that Miller became colleagues with Herbert Simon (who won the Nobel in 1978) and Franco Modigliani (who won in 1985).

Merton Miller would see a whole new meaning to his initials, *MM*. In collaboration with Modigliani, their ideas about optimal financing of real corporations would become famous and taught in all corporate finance texts. Modigliani–Miller, known as M&M, isn't just candy. Their conclusions were revolutionary. They found that, as long as governments didn't distort one type of financing over another, there is no "one size that fits all" when it comes to acquiring financial capital to run a company. This was a new idea as "case study–type" business schools were teaching optimal debt-equity ratios on a case-by-case basis. When Miller was asked by reporters to explain why he won the Nobel Prize in 1990, he gave the following story. After a game, Yogi Berra was asked if he wanted his pizza cut in quarters or in eighths. Berra answered "in eighths," because he was really hungry. This cleverly and clearly demonstrated the fundamental idea of M&M. Financial assets are just about how you slice the pizza. This is not where the real action is. The size of the pizza has to do with how the company is doing as a profitable business.

Miller left Carnegie Mellon to go to Chicago and became colleagues with Milton Freidman (who won the Nobel in 1976), Theodore Schultz (who won in 1979), and George Stigler (who won in 1982). As each of these men were avid supporters of free market solutions to economic problems, Miller fit right in. He believed in the Efficient Market Hypothesis (more on this theory later in the chapter) and personally held his wealth in stocks that weren't actively managed. He did, however, play in the market from time to time as a gamble.

At Chicago, Merton taught Myron Scholes (who won the Nobel in 1997), who along with Fischer Black came up with a very mathematical theory for pricing options—a derivative. Miller also taught Sandy Grossman, who later worked with Joseph Stiglitz (who won the Nobel in 2001) on the effect that a few investors who search out information can have on the market as a whole.

Who knows? Maybe hanging out with all of these bright Nobel Prize winners gives off externalities. I should be so lucky as to catch it.

IN THE MARKET

Economic life should be definancialized.... Investments should be for entertainment.

Nassim Nicholas Taleb (1960–), Lebanese-born philosophical essayist, scholar, and practitioner of mathematical financial economics
Taken from *The Black Swan: The Impact of the Highly Improbable* (2007)

Now to the part I like: the underlying economics. It is all comes back to the simple idea of suppliers and demanders crossing paths in a market. Each of these financial assets has someone trying to sell or supply the asset and someone trying to buy or demand it. As discussed earlier in this chapter, they rendezvous in various kinds of markets, whether formal exchanges, over-the-counter markets, or electronic networks. The price of the asset changes if more people are selling (price will go down) or if more people are buying (price will go up). The financial pages of daily newspapers usually give you the results of the previous day's stock market trading. They tell you the opening price, the closing price, and the volume of shares traded for all stocks listed on the particular exchange they happen to cover. Basically, you are given the prices and quantities and it is up to you to figure out if there was a supply shift, a demand shift, or both. Usually, the commentary section will try to explain *what* happened that day in terms of what buyers or sellers were doing. Sometimes it will try to tell you *why* these participants did what they did. It all makes for interesting reading if that is what you are into. (I know, I know—some of you are thinking you'd rather read the obituaries.)

There are some common themes with respect to financial markets, and I'll give you a few of them so you see the connection between this chapter and the earlier Venti chapters—and hopefully you'll feel as if all of your hard work has finally paid off.

Normally, big buyers of financial assets such as pension funds own something from each category to get what they feel is a profitable "balanced" portfolio. If anything relevant changes, it may change the mix they want to hold. For example, if a pension fund manager wants to hold a few more stocks, he or she may sell some of the bonds to fund the purchase. Thus, the change in demand for stocks is the direct result of a change in the supply of bonds. The increase in the demand for stocks (demand shifts to the right) means that share prices go up. The sale or increased supply of bonds (supply shifts to the right) means that bond prices go down. If for some reason both stocks and bonds are unattractive, the managed fund will sell both types of asset and hold cash. This increases the supply of both stocks and bonds and each sees prices decline. The money market, however, will see an increase in demand, and those prices will go up. Anything that makes one type of asset more attractive relative to the others causes this kind of asset reallocation, which is really about changes or shifts in supply or demand for each type of asset.

All change is not growth, as all movement is not forward.

Ellen Anderson Gholson Glasgow (1873–1945), American Pulitzer Prize–winning novelist

This switching of assets could be due to a change in how different financial investments are taxed or regulated or to a change in their relative risk. If stocks get a tax break, the demand for stocks is up and the financial company sells bonds to raise funds. A government may regulate pension funds to hold more bonds, which will increase the demand for bonds and increase the sale of stocks by pension fund managers. If stocks are perceived by financial investors to be more risky, the supply of stocks goes up as they are sold off, and the demand for safer bonds goes up because everyone is buying them. Prices change until the benefit of switching is gone.

These markets are also affected by the state of the economy as a whole. This could include expected profits or changes in interest rates. If firms are doing well, they are issuing stocks and bonds to get the financial capital they need to buy real capital. This increases the supply of both stocks and bonds. Furthermore, these firms are expecting to make profits, which will be paid out to their shareholders. This increases the demand for these profitable stocks. Any bonds outstanding are now less risky because, given the buoyancy of the economy, the company is sure to pay them back. This will increase the demand for bonds. Therefore, when economies are growing, the volume of stocks and bonds traded tends to go up. Prices also tend to rise, which indicates that demand pressures are more than the supply increases.

On the other hand, if the central bank raises interest rates, this increases the cost of doing business. As a result, profits go down, and this decreases the demand for stocks. In addition, the interest payments on older bonds are now not enough to compete with other interest-bearing assets, so bonds take a capital loss. In other words, bond prices fall due to a lack of demand. When interest rates increase, the bond and stock markets tend to see lower prices.

> *Now that we have all this useful information, it would be nice to do something with it. (Actually, it can be emotionally fulfilling just to get the information. This is usually only true, however, if you have the social life of a kumquat.)*
>
> Unix Programmer's Manual

Buyers of these kinds of financial assets want to make informed decisions. Getting accurate information on a particular stock or bond means knowing details about that company (or, for some bonds, the government), the industry it is a part of, and the national and international economy in which it lives. This is a lot of information, but there are people out there looking for it. As long as the benefits of the information exceed the cost, analysts are motivated to go after it.

Markets That Get It Right

> *Where an opinion is general, it is usually correct.*
>
> Jane Austen (1775–1817), English novelist

If markets are functioning correctly they are called efficient. This means that the market price accurately reflects the opportunity costs of both buyers and sellers who know everything there is to know. With financial assets, opportunity costs are usually purely financial rather than mixed with personal preferences. No one in his or her right mind buys a financial asset because of how pretty the stock or bond looks. Personally, I get tons of mail from the mutual funds I own and, believe me, I don't look at all of those reports as a work of art in their own right. I usually glance at them to see how well my financial investments are doing and shove the papers in a drawer. (I confess: I sometimes just stuff the unopened envelope in the drawer.) I hold assets now because

I plan to sell them later, and later isn't here yet. Once I sell these financial assets, then I can go shopping.

The kind of assets people hold is of greatest indifference to most of us, but the return on those assets is not. This means that everyone wants to buy low and sell really high to make a big return. If markets are efficient, this should be difficult to do. Why? Well, let's suppose that there is this amazing publicly traded stock out there that is currently undervalued. Once people find out the stock is undervalued, they rush out to buy it. Normally, because the companies listed on stock exchanges are pretty well known to those in the business world (who are actively looking for this information), everyone gets this information at once and the stock price is bid up in minutes. The price is now "right" and no else will be able to pick this stock as a big "winner." Now suppose this happens for all stocks? Then they are all priced right.

If this is true, there are a couple of implications. The first is that you don't need any special skills to pick stocks. Pick any one you like. Pick one because you like the sound of its name. Throw darts on a board. Whatever. If they are all priced efficiently, then a monkey[30] could pick a portfolio and do as well as the average fund manager. Furthermore, you'd only need to pay the monkey in bananas. Believers in Efficient Market Hypothesis (EMH) believe that the best financial investments are low-cost index funds rather than high-cost managed funds. On average, the returns are similar but the costs are not.

It is hard to imagine that a fund manager who happens to do well five years in a row is just lucky rather than clever, but it's possible. Think of stock picking as tossing a coin. You have a 50–50 chance of heads or tails every time you toss. If you toss a fair coin and get heads five times in a row, this does not indicate a trend. There is no predictive power in your tosses. Next time you toss, you are no more likely to toss heads or no more likely to break the trend and toss tails. A completely random process can toss 100 heads in a row.[31] It is therefore possible for a fund manager to beat the average every year for 15 years, as William Miller did, and for the process of picking stocks be completely and utterly random. In fact, probability dictates that out of all the people picking stocks, somebody should fit this profile.

I Should Be So Lucky

There is no such thing as luck. There is only adequate or inadequate preparation to cope with a statistical universe.

Robert Anson Heinlein (1907–1988), American writer
Taken from *Time Enough for Love* (1973)

Others aren't quite so committed to the Efficient Market Hypothesis. They find it hard to believe that people like Peter Lynch (who made unbelievable returns when he ran Fidelity's Magellan Fund from 1978 to 1990), William Miller, and Warren Buffett are just lucky fellows. There is some research that indicates that these naysayers might be right and that strategies do exist to consistently and repeatedly outperform the market.

---

[30] Mr. Adam Monk, the *Chicago Sun-Times'* stock-picking monkey has beat the market for four years running.
[31] See *The Drunkard's Walk: How Randomness Rules Our Lives* (2008) by Leonard Mlodinow.

These approaches tend to fall into three categories, all looking at some part of the picking process. They include the following:

1. Having a genius or insider as the picker
2. Moving quickly once the information gets out
3. Understanding that smart people have biases and make systematic errors

1. In the Know

> *Anybody who plays the stock market not as an insider is like a man buying cows in the moonlight.*
> Daniel Drew (1797–1879), American financier

Without a doubt, there are some people who as a group consistently outperform the market. They are known as insiders and this is the reason why Martha Stewart[32] went to jail. If you trade on information not yet known to the public, you can do better than the market. However, be careful. It is precisely for this reason that insider trading is a crime in North America and that CEOs must announce when they are personally buying or selling their companies' stock. In Martha Stewart's case, it is still insider information if you get a tip from a broker (Peter Bacanovic) who also works for the CEO (Samuel D. Waksal) of another company (ImClone). Essentially, insider information is an example of asymmetric information that causes the market to become efficient once the information is out of the bag and in the public domain.

On the other hand, there may be individuals who are really good at interpreting the volume of information available on these companies, sorting out what is relevant, and seeing potential that others don't see. For example, Warren Buffett bought Coca-Cola stock in 1988 when it wasn't doing well. Somehow, he knew that the company had great untapped potential in overseas markets. He was right and, once Coca-Cola expanded into other countries, the stock took off. These great minds may exist, but one thing is certain. They are sort of like sports stars. They are not common, and the odds are that you and I are not part of that group.

2. A Mover and a Shaker

> *It is no use to keep private information which you can't show off.*
> Mark Twain (1835–1910), American writer and lecturer

As I mentioned earlier, if new information comes to light, the market can respond within minutes. But, for those minutes, the stock is undervalued or overvalued. Some investment banks have departments that specialize in fast trading. These traders watch computer screens for news and are always connected to securities dealers. If something comes in, they react immediately to make a profit.

Goldman Sachs went further with a computer program that looked for disequilibrium at the level of the millisecond. In July 2009, when employee Sergey Aleynikov supposedly stole the computer code, this created a financial sensation for two reasons.

---

[32] According to the U.S. Securities and Exchange Commission, Stewart avoided a loss of $45 673 by selling all 3928 shares of her ImClone stock. The day after her sale, the stock's value fell 18 percent.

Aleynikov was arrested by the FBI on industrial espionage charges, which is always titillating news to financial types, but, more importantly, the following statement was made by Assistant United States Attorney Joseph Facciponti: "There is a danger that somebody who knew how to use this program could use it to manipulate markets in unfair ways." This statement raised the interesting question of whether this practice is truly ethical. Needless to say, if you and I are leisurely reading the paper, picking stocks during our morning coffee break, we are a little too late.

3. Disturbing Behaviour

The difference between stupidity and genius is that genius has its limits.

Albert Einstein (1879–1955), German Nobel Prize–winning theoretical physicist

The final criticism of Efficient Market Hypothesis is much more fundamental. This research maintains that stocks can be overpriced or underpriced for a long time due to human predispositions. Dan Ariely, in his book *Predictably Irrational: The Hidden Forces That Shape Our Decisions*, outlines many of the ideas of this school of thought. Most of the applications to finance have to do with the underlying cognitive biases people may have.

Let me give you a few quick examples from the research:

1. It turns out that people have a very strong aversion bias against loss, even if the loss has a low probablitity and the gains are very probable. They are therefore "irrationally" unwilling to make those profitable investments.[33] This may explain why stocks of small firms tend to make higher returns. Fund managers are unwilling to hold them because of a fear of any loss, even if the probability of loss is very low.

2. People continue to work on projects doomed for failure if they have already committed resources to them. People don't want to lose when they should let it go. For example, a fund manager may hold a stock thinking it will have to turn around eventually.

3. Individuals have a very high opinion of their opinions. (Most people see themselves as above average, which of course is impossible on average.) If analysts have predicted that a stock will do well, they are unwilling to change their minds very quickly should bad news come in. This means that they don't react to the change fast enough and remain anchored to their previous opinion. The stock is not priced correctly until the anchor gives way.

4. Individuals exhibit an endowment effect. They value what they own more than they would if they were buying it new. This may keep stocks in a portfolio longer than is optimal.

5. Cognitive bias can also help to explain herding behaviour, which leads to bubbles. If everyone is buying, others buy; if everyone is selling, others sell. No one wants to look like the fool if something is a real trend. Besides, if you are foolish to buy high, the only ones who will lose are those at the cusp. You may be able to sell to an even greater fool.

---

[33] Israeli behavioural psychologist Daniel Kahneman (1934–) won the Nobel Prize in Economics for his work in this area. His writing partner, Amos Tversky, would undoubtedly have won as well but he died before the award was given. Nobel Prizes are never awarded posthumously. Both men moved into this area of economics because of their chance meeting with economist Richard Thaler. I guess you could call that good luck.

The implications of this work are the following. If a computer could be programmed to overcome these systematic cognitive issues, it should be a better stock picker. Richard H. Thaler, an American behavioural economist, has done just that, but the jury is still out on whether this approach does pick better or if it is just randomly lucky in the same way the monkey portfolio is. We will probably need about 200 years of data to know for sure.

Phew, here is another spot to stop if you need a break.

TOO BIG TO FAIL

The financial industry had always been intended to be something of an unseen backroom support for the broader economy, helping new businesses get off the ground and mature companies adapt and expand. Yet in the years leading up to the crisis, the finance sector itself became the front room. The goal on Wall Street became to generate fees for themselves as opposed to for their clients.

Andrew Ross Sorkin (1977–), American writer
Taken from *Too Big To Fail* (2009)

As discussed in the last chapter, externalities can cause market failures. This is a big deal in financial markets because, fundamentally, financial markets are all about the positive impact of paper markets on real markets. If it weren't for the positive spillovers that financial capital has on real capital, these paper assets would not have a raison d'être. It is precisely because we can't eat, wear, or live in stocks and bonds that the buying and selling of paper assets needs to be protected. If you have to choose between saving a major car company or saving a major investment bank, go for the bank. Cars are real and don't need to be saved. Paper, on the other hand, is the grease behind everything real in the economy. If that grinds to a halt, the entire real economy grinds to a halt as well. This is similar to the instructions given to parents on a plane. In the case of an emergency, make sure you put on your own oxygen mask first and then place the mask on your child.

Calling Information

The study of money, above all other fields in economics, is one in which complexity is used to disguise truth or to evade truth, not to reveal it.

John Kenneth Galbraith (1908–2006), Canadian-born economist and author
Taken from *Money: Whence It Came, Where It Went* (1975)

After all this talk of picking good stocks, you would think that stocks are the most important type of financial capital used to fund the real economy. Not true. Stocks account for less than 12 percent of the total funds. I can hear you gasp. So, what is the most important source of capital for business in the developed world? Let me give you a hint. It's not bonds. Rather, old-fashioned loans and mortgages through a bank (or something that acts like a bank) account for more than half of financial capital raised. This keeps the wheels of the economy turning. The question is, why? If stock markets can easily move funds from savers into the hands of investors, why isn't it the main conduit for this process? It turns out that financial markets face asymmetric information issues, transaction costs, and property right issues at every turn—all of the things we discussed in previous chapters—and that banks or near banks are uniquely positioned to solve these problems.

Picking a Lemon

I'll be with you in a squeezing of a lemon.

Oliver Goldsmith (1728/1730–1774), Anglo-Irish writer
From *She Stoops to Conquer* (1773)

So, what are the problems that banks and near banks can solve? Let's think about the dilemma of an individual saver who wants to park his or her life savings in order to have a comfortable retirement. How does one know if the borrower of these savings is good for the money, especially if he or she is a stranger? If you invest in a company, how do you know if it is a profitable one? You might pick a lemon and lose everything, or at least not do very well. This adverse selection problem is so worrisome that the lending market would be significantly smaller and only limited to large well-known companies if it weren't for bank-like institutions. The big companies can signal to financial investors across the country their creditworthiness and solve their own adverse selection problems. They do this when they hire expensive accounting firms to audit their books (although, as we saw with the Arthur Andersen–Enron scandal, this doesn't necessarily mean anything) and expensive investment bankers to do their IPOs. By law, both accounting firms and investment bankers must show due diligence as they certify their clients, thereby solving the asymmetric information problem. However, small and mid-size companies cannot afford this signal in order to sell their stock. These companies may be great investments but, because of "the lemons problem," private lenders cannot or will not risk lending to them. This is a loss on the real economy side.

All is not lost, however. Screening of smaller firms can be done fairly cheaply by banks. Banks can conduct interviews, look at a company's financial statements, visit its facilities, and check its credit rating to see if the business is a good risk for a loan. On the personal side, they can send someone out to see if a house is worth the mortgage they are putting on it, ask for tax returns, and check personal credit ratings. This allows individuals to get access to funds to buy a home. It also allows savers to know that their savings went to a good home.

Furthermore, these banks can use and keep the information private. Stock and bond markets cannot. For example, if a bond rating agency publishes bond ratings for its client who pays a lot for the reports, they cannot prevent others from free riding on the information and using it without paying for it. This means that less information gathering occurs than is optimal in these direct markets. On the other hand, banks have the incentive to get as much information as they can on would-be borrowers because they alone profit from that information.

Too Small to Play

A person's a person, no matter how small.

Theodor Seuss Geisel (1904–1991), American writer and cartoonist
Taken from *Horton Hears a Who!* (1954)

In terms of saving money, small-time investors (people like me) cannot directly play in the stock market cheaply. Each purchase or sale of a stock generates a brokerage fee or transaction fee, and the percentage is bigger the smaller the sale. Furthermore, in order to reduce risk, it is a bad thing to buy only one stock. (The pension funds of many U.S. companies have an overemphasis in those companies' stock. If a company goes bankrupt, this is a very bad thing indeed for its workers.) It is estimated that a person needs to hold at least 15 different stocks[34] in various sectors to minimize his or her exposure to undue risk. This becomes expensive in terms of transactions fees. Banks, on the other hand, often provide mutual funds, which are a cheaper way to buy multiple stocks. But even if they don't sell mutual funds per se, they hold a portfolio of loans and mortgages that spreads the depositors' (lenders') risk over many borrowers. Thus, banks act as a go-between for small firms and small financial investors to reduce risk at a low cost.

Hazardous to Your Financial Health

There is danger from all men. The only maxim of a free government ought to be to trust no man living with power to endanger the public liberty.

John Adams (1735–1826), American president

The other problem that needs to be solved in order for savers to part with their hard-earned savings is the problem of moral hazard. What if the borrower takes the money and spends it on jet planes, high-end parties, or expensive office equipment? This will not generate profits to repay the loan or pay stock dividends. Banks again can monitor their clients more cheaply than the average person can. They can add legal covenants to the contract restricting what the borrower can do with the money. If someone borrows to buy a house, the house is now held as collateral by the bank. To make sure that the borrower behaves appropriately, banks require the borrower to put in some of his or her own money in the form of a down payment or ask for a co-signer on the loan. The more the borrower has at stake, the less likely he or she is to fritter away the funds. (My parents would have killed me if I had defaulted on a loan they had co-signed.) Banks can put the incentives in the right place.

Moral hazard also explains why CEOs of large corporations are paid mostly in stock options rather than a salary. They now have something of theirs in the mix. It also explains why bondholders place restrictions on corporate boards or even have a seat on the board. If a board engages in very risky investments with the bondholder's funds, the only money it is losing is the bondholder's. But if things go well, the shareholders get the entire surplus. Bondholders have to watch for these incentives. Furthermore, shareholders are taking their revenge against CEOs who use their money in inappropriate ways. Canadian media baron Conrad Black was accused of corporate kleptocracy, which is a fancy way of saying that he personally took funds that belonged to all shareholders. He was charged with fraud and obstruction of justice and sentenced[35] to jail in the United States.

---

[34] See Wagner, W.H., & Lau, S.C. (1971). The effect of diversification on risk. *Financial Analysts Journal*, *27*(6), 48–53.

[35] Black appealed the ruling and, as of October 28, 2010, was left with only one count of mail fraud and one count of obstruction of justice. The court also ruled that he must be resentenced.

Law and Order

The world of antitrust is reminiscent of Alice's Wonderland: everything seemingly is, yet apparently isn't, simultaneously.

Alan Greenspan (1926–), American economist and chairman of the U.S. Federal Reserve
Taken from "Antitrust," published in *Capitalism: The Unknown Ideal* (1961)

Needless to say, given the importance of financial markets and all of the potential for market failure, financial institutions (banks, in particular) are some of the most regulated companies in the developed world. This is generally a good thing. Let's look at each market failure mentioned in the previous chapter and see what governments are doing about each.

1. Concentrated Markets
Governments try to keep the industry competitive with strict merger and acquisition regulations. However, the industry is still marked with TBTF, or the Too Big to Fail phenomenon.[36] In financial crises, governments actually encourage these kinds of mergers in order to keep the amount of bailout money required to a minimum. For example, in March 2008, as a result of the financial crisis, the Federal Reserve arranged the takeover of Bear Stearns (which had lost $3 billion in asset-backed securities of subprime mortgages) by JPMorgan Chase. Normally, banks like to merge because it reduces the cost of doing business due to economies of scale and scope[37] (which is a good thing) and because it gives them more market power (which is a bad thing). Governments have to weigh the pros and cons as they approve these mergers and acquisitions.

2. Externalities
As discussed, financial markets are all about positive externalities. If banks fail, the collateral damage can be horrendous. Even if banks are perceived to be failing, it can result in a bank run and shove good banks over the edge into bankruptcy. As people rush to get their deposits out of a bank they fear might fail, it causes that bank to actually fail. Therefore, deposit insurance is required by law because it gives confidence to savers that their money is fine where it is. Take a deep breath. There's no need to have a bank panic attack.

3. Asymmetric Information and Information Gathering
Information is critical to efficient financial markets, but information suffers the problem of being a public good. On publicly traded assets like stocks or bonds, there is no means to exclude non-payers from using information once it becomes available. Therefore, not enough information is collected on the whole. Governments help by legislating mandatory disclosure laws, forcing the information to be acquired and made public. These could include standardized accounting practices across the G-10 countries, rules of board governance, and requirements for CEOs to publish their trading activites, including any potential conflict of interests.

---

[36] First used in 1984 to bail out the Continental Illinois National Bank and Trust Company.

[37] Economies of scale is about producing more of the same thing (e.g., loans) at a cheaper price. For example, larger banks can have a lawyer on staff to handle all of the mortgages. Economies of scope is about producing related products (loans, mutual funds, life insurance, etc.) with the same agent. This again reduces the cost.

4. Government-Legislated Prices

Governments can also legislate interest rates. Interest rates are really prices on borrowing and lending money, so this is paramount to legislating a price. Typically, this is not a big problem in developed countries because the laws are usually about very specific unusual loans, such as payday loans[38] or loan shark activities. However, the United States created difficulties for normal banks with Regulation Q,[39] which started out with the best of intentions. This regulation prohibited banks from paying any interest on chequing accounts. Needless to say, once less-regulated saving alternatives hit the market, it became hard for banks to get people to save with them, especially when the competition from money market mutual funds paid interest. Not to be left in the cold, these banks developed other products that got around this rule. Regulating interest rates is generally a bad idea.

5. Asymmetric Information and Moral Hazard

We looked at asymmetric information problems extensively already, so I won't repeat myself. Here I just want to note that moral hazard can be created by regulations. For instance, if a bank knows that it is too big to fail or that, if it does fail, deposit insurance will clean up the mess, it could choose to engage in very risky behaviours. To prevent this, governments require the banks to hold reserves of cash or other short-term capital. Furthermore, all financial institutions are monitored by various government agencies and must submit reports on a regular basis. Governments also criminalize and prosecute white-collar financial fraud such as Ponzi[40] schemes, hiding of losses[41] or falsifying trading records,[42] insider information, and conflicts of interest such as front running.[43] The hope is that the severity of the punishment will deter others from trying the same types of fraud. One thing is certain: Even with government intervention, moral hazard is difficult to eliminate in the financial sector.

Abnormal Behaviour

> *Every normal person, in fact, is only normal on the average. His ego approximates to that of the psychotic in some part or other and to a greater or lesser extent.*

Sigmund Schlomo Freud (1856–1939), Austrian psychiatrist

---

[38] According to the Criminal Code of Canada, any rate of interest charged above 60 percent per annum is considered criminal.

[39] Regulation Q was put in place by the Glass-Steagall Act of 1933 but phased out by the 1980s. The key provision of Regulation Q that remains is that banks cannot pay interest on chequing accounts.

[40] The term *Ponzi scheme* is a widely used description for any scam that pays early investors returns from the investments of later investors.

[41] In 1995, Nick Leeson of Barings LLC, without anyone's permission, started to bet on derivatives. He hid his activities from his superiors and succeeded in bankrupting the company, but not before he lost $1 billion. He went to jail and wrote a memoir. He is now out of jail, speaking on the dinner circuit, and is the CEO of an Irish football club.

[42] In 2008, Jerome Kerviel of Société Générale made bets on the futures market. He falsified documents and lost the company 4.9 billion euros. He was arrested for fraud.

[43] Front running means that a broker buys for himself before he buys for the client whose order is large enough that it may change the price.

In many ways, the subprime mortgage crisis of 2007–2009 is counter to the normal functioning of banks. This crisis only happened because banks (or near banks) were giving ninja mortgages (no income, no job or assets) to people who were therefore very risky. This was partly the result of a political push to encourage home ownership among low-income earners. Furthermore, the banks were willing to provide these mortgages because the loans were taken off the banks' books through the process of securitization, creating asset-backed securities of these subprime mortgages. The loans were then no longer the bank's problem, so they didn't worry about them. It appears that the scene was ripe for a little moral hazard. The incentives were huge to provide as many bad loans as possible because they were so profitable with little liability. Down the line, other international financial investors bought these asset-backed securities because they were first bought and then sold by Fannie Mae and Freddie Mac,[44] which were receiving affordable housing credits from the U.S. government for buying and repackaging these subprime securities. Here, the government was trying to increase home ownership in the United States. Rating agencies perceived the implicitly government-backed securities as very safe and gave them high ratings.

All was well as long as housing prices continued to rise. The assets backing the paper were worth something; therefore, the paper was worth something. However, once housing prices started to plummet, the paper followed suit. That, of course, was bad, but it gets worse. Hedge funds leveraged themselves to buy these asset-backed securities, so any decline in value of this paper was magnified. Furthermore, these asset-backed securities were downgraded by the rating agencies, which led to the downgrading of AIG, an American insurance company, on September 16, 2008. AIG, which previously could engage in the derivatives markets without collateral, was suddenly required to come up with collateral for all of its deals. Of course, AIG didn't have it and encountered a liquidity crisis. To add insult to injury, on October 22, 2008, the creditors of Lehman Brothers—who had bought derivatives (credit default swaps) from AIG to hedge against a Lehman bankruptcy—settled their accounts when the bankruptcy happened. AIG will never be the same. All of this happened because the initial bank managers were no longer left holding the bag. The moral of the story is this: If banks get stuck with bad loans, they usually solve the adverse selection problem. If the incentives are thoughtless, moral hazard happens.

Closing Markets

One sees qualities at a distance and defects at close range.
Victor Hugo (1802–1885), French writer and statesman

As I end this chapter, I don't want to give the impression that financial markets are such a mess that we should just give up on them. That would be a mistake. Financial markets

---

[44]   The Federal National Mortgage Association, commonly known as Fannie Mae, was founded during the Great Depression as a government-sponsored enterprise. Its mandate is to keep the number of loans flowing to the lower-income public by agreeing to buy these loans from the banks, thus removing them from the banks' books. Fannie Mae then repackaged the loans into groups and resold them to investors. These are called asset-backed securities in general and collateralized debt obligations in particular. Freddie Mac does basically the same thing but is not constrained to mortgages of low-income families.

are the main reason that the Western world has such a high standard of living, and that point should never be lost. One of the best things about humans is that we can learn and make improvements to our systems. Furthermore, small changes can make a big difference. I am optimistic that the financial crisis of 2007–2009 will result in a few regulatory changes for the better and that we will weather the storm.

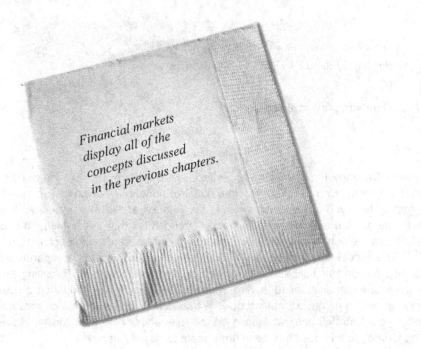

Financial markets display all of the concepts discussed in the previous chapters.

Conclusions: Tying Up Loose Ends

It is the loose ends with which men hang themselves.
Zelda Sayre Fitzgerald[1] (1900–1948), American writer

The retirement party invitation reads:

Cocktails at 6 p.m.

Dinner at 7 p.m.

You arrive early for the evening's festivities at 5:35 p.m. In fact, you get there so early that the room is empty except for the guest of honour—your boss—and his family. After greeting him, you turn your attention to his entourage. His wife, a banker, looks lovely in her little black dress and genuine pearls. You can tell that she is pleased and proud that all four of their children are in attendance. You shake hands with each in turn.

The oldest daughter works in advertising but is currently on parental leave. She stands beside her husband, who is holding their adopted son. Recalling the numerous stories of expensive, failed in vitro treatments, a complicated adoption process, and the mix-up over a neighbour cutting down a tree during their adoption celebration party, you offer your heartfelt congratulations on the new addition to their family. However painful the journey to this point has been, they seem to be very happy.

The next oldest—a son—is a partner in an accounting firm. You can tell that he is very much like his dad in both looks and temperament. Recently, his wife thought she had discovered a Jackson Pollock painting at a garage sale. So far, no one in the art community will authenticate the painting, and she continues to work at a local art gallery. Their two children—a boy and a girl—are in elementary school. The boy appears to be discreetly putting a spider down his little sister's back.

The third oldest looks very theatrical ... and very pregnant. You know that this was not a planned pregnancy and that her career as a Shakespearean actor is on hold for a while. Looking closely at her face, it appears that she has come to terms with her situation. She holds hands with her husband, who is sporting a happy grin. What great teeth. Of course—he's a dentist.

Last, but not least, is the youngest son, a boyishly handsome young man. He plans to squeeze four years into six in order to max out his football eligibility and still get a degree. His dad worries that he parties a bit too much and studies too little. His date for the night is the most drop-dead gorgeous blonde you have ever seen, except for maybe in the movies. He must be doing something right!

---

[1] Wife of writer F. Scott Fitzgerald. Theirs was a tempestuous marriage.

As the room fills up, the wait staff bring around complimentary glasses of wine. Should guests want anything other than wine, they can buy it from the bar along the back wall.

Oh, no! You notice that, in the corner, two senior partners have already started to talk politics. They can never agree on anything, let alone politics. You make your way over to save the day but your attempt turns out to be unnecessary. They are interrupted by a young woman with a prosthetic shoe. She gushes, "Thank you so much for the scholarship. I can't tell you what this means to me now that the cost of my final year is covered. What a luxury to be able to quit my bartending job and focus completely on my studies. Thank you. Thank you." The gentlemen are obviously delighted that their contributions to the linguistics endowment fund are so greatly appreciated. They both reiterate the sentiment that the money couldn't have gone to a better recipient. You think, wow, at last, something they agree on!

The cocktail hour is coming to an end and the master of ceremonies issues a call for guests to take their seats. You quickly and surreptitiously check your BlackBerry for text messages. There's nothing important.

A BIG ENDING

What is written without effort is in general read without pleasure.

Samuel Johnson (1709–1784), British writer and lexicographer

We have come to the end of this book, and it is time to retire this baby. According to websites that specialize in giving advice on how to give a good speech, construct a good essay, or pen an effective non-fiction book, the conclusion is very important. It should summarize all of the major points, restate some thesis found in the introduction, and leave the audience wanting more. In my case, the more would be another Cocktail Party Economics book. To be honest, I don't see how repeating myself would make you want to read another book. It sounds so boring that, frankly, I just can't bring myself to do it. So here's what I'm going to do instead. I will give you what I think are a couple of major implications of markets. These may seem like new ideas, but hopefully they will make sense given what you have read so far.

Get to the Points

There ain't no such thing as free lunch.

Taken from *Economics in Eight Words*[2]

First, economics is mostly about exchange. This is in contrast to the answer I get when I ask people: "What do you think economics is all about?" Most people answer "money." Granted, money is often involved, but it doesn't have to be. For example, I don't think it would be a good idea if, after a pleasant evening spent in bed, the husband or wife (depending on who "demanded" and who "supplied") left a little cash on the night table to finalize their transaction. On the other hand, there is an economic theory postulated by

---

[2]   *El Paso Herald-Post*, June 27, 1938, but often attributed to Milton Friedman.

some academics that marriage is an arrangement whereby women and men trade sex for security. I will leave you to debate who is getting what.[3]

Furthermore, in a recent book called *Catching Fire: How Cooking Made Us Human*, primatologist Richard Wrangham outlines another exchange theory that suggests that the responsibility traditionally shouldered by women for meal preparation has its roots in an implicit contract whereby the male protects the food supply of the woman in exchange for her culinary skills. Today's markets with explicit prices are just a more sophisticated version of that exchange. Now the food chain has more complicated contracts between complete strangers and women who want to eat out.

Second, don't be scared of markets. They are not inherently evil. Rather, a well-functioning or efficient market brings many buyers and sellers together to give everybody what they want: a better life than the one they've got. In order for life to be truly better, all individuals must ultimately be consumers. Adam Smith, the granddaddy of economics, couldn't have said it better when he wrote, "Consumption is the sole end and purpose of all production; and the interest of the producer ought to be attended to, only so far as it may be necessary for promoting that of the consumer."

Furthermore, virtually all buyers and sellers exchange freely and without compulsion. They do what they do because they want to. Nobel Prize–winning economist Milton Friedman summarized this point when he said, "The key insight of Adam Smith's *Wealth of Nations* is misleadingly simple: if an exchange between two parties is voluntary, it will not take place unless both believe they will benefit from it."[4]

Third, incentives matter.[5] Markets generate prices, and these prices act as reference points in decision making. For consumers, price represents the opportunity cost against which they evaluate their marginal values. Only if the marginal value exceeds the price is the item worth buying. For producers, the price embodies the marginal benefit of taking their products to market. As long as the marginal benefit covers the opportunity cost of production, the firm has an incentive to make it. It doesn't matter if prices are explicit or implicit; all exchange is ultimately about opportunity costs and marginal values. Prices just take the guesswork out of what those final numbers are. As a result, only those items that have a higher value in the minds of the consumers than the opportunity cost paid by the producers actually get bought and sold. This is a good thing. Society should never use scarce resources to make something if people do not value it enough. If marginal values or opportunity costs should happen to change ... no problem. Buyers and sellers will get the message through the price signal and react accordingly. The system works.

Fourth, markets aren't sacred and therefore shouldn't be worshipped. Usually, markets offer a great way to allocate scarce resources, and fortunately they usually get it right. But—and this is a big but, I cannot lie—sometimes markets get it wrong. If a market can solve its own problems, great—leave it alone. But if it can't, it is up to governments to ride in on their big horse and save the day. However, governments should be

---

[3]   For an interesting economic discussion about this topic, read Tim Harford's book *The Logic of Life*, page 71.

[4]   Taken from *Free to Choose: A Personal Statement*, by Milton and Rose Friedman. *The Economist* hailed Milton Friedman as "the most influential economist of the second half of the 20th century ... possibly of all of it."

[5]   This is the main point of the bestselling books *Freakonomics* and *Super Freakonomics*.

careful to not create bigger problems than the ones they are trying to solve. They need to keep in mind the law of unintended consequences. If governments institute policies that, unbeknownst to them, change either opportunity costs or marginal values, then people will change their behaviour, and not always in the ways hoped for.

By now, I hope you realize that the discipline of economics is really a way of thinking about anything that involves choice. Most economists aren't too confident that governments can come up with a better system than the free market to assist in those choices. This may be why we are so committed to it.

I'M SO GLAD WE HAD THIS TIME TOGETHER

Oddly enough, it is the market—the least overtly spiritual of concepts—that delivers a profoundly spiritual message: that it is through exchange that difference becomes a blessing, not a curse, enrichment, both sides gain.

Baron Jonathan Henry Sacks (1948–), British Chief Rabbi
Taken from *The Dignity of Difference* (2003)

Well, there you have it. A few big ideas and a lot of small talk about markets. I hope you feel more confident during cocktail party conversations. Even if these kinds of conversations aren't your thing and you would rather discuss the latest movie or novel, there are still some benefits to knowing this material. If you happen to be a woman, remember that an educated understanding of a subject viewed as a typically male one is like fantastic underwear. No one has to see it, but you can feel the difference and it changes how you carry yourself. If you are a man, lightly chit-chatting on these matters with *savoir faire* is very attractive, especially if you know when to stop. Remember, the marginal value of anything—even economics—diminishes.

GOSSIP COLUMN WITH SPECIAL FEATURES AND END CREDITS

An author who speaks about his own books is almost as bad as a mother who talks about her own children.

Benjamin Disraeli, 1st Earl of Beaconsfield (1804–1881), British prime minister

Throughout the pages of this book, I have told you a lot about economics and economists and a little bit about myself. It's time to reverse those proportions. Here is my opportunity to give you a behind-the-scenes look at the creation of this book, as well as to give credit where credit is due.

Look Who's Talking

One of the best decisions I made at the absolute beginning of this project was to have a writing partner who could actually write. Rick Maranta and his wife, Judy, also happen to be long-time friends of my husband, Martin, and me. One of the amazing things about working with Rick is his ability to fundamentally change every paragraph of the book, yet keep my voice. When people who know me read the final manuscript, they felt as if it was me talking.[6] *I* felt as if it was me talking. As the Brits would say, "Brilliant."

I have to tell you that this book would never have seen the light of publishing day without my friend Rick. It wasn't just a comma here and a verb tense there. His editorial comments made me work twice as hard to get it right. Let me give you one example of a comment he wrote to me on Chapter 6: "A real-world example of this situation is really important. You are tending to veer into the abstract without any tangible example that people can relate to. A book like this must have lots of examples." Rick improved the entertainment factor of the book and, because of that improvement, dare I say improved the educational value of it as well. It is our wish that you can read this book on the beach, at the cottage, or on public transit.

The Readers

Economists are generally negligent of their heroes.
John Kenneth Galbraith (1908–2006), Canadian-born economist
Taken from *The Age of Uncertainty* (1977)

I started out with many readers for the first chapter of this book, but the field quickly narrowed to two women who stayed with me every step of the way. I would like to express my profound thanks to Patricia Swidinsky and Mary-Jane Davison. Essentially, I wrote and they read. Furthermore, they were always positive and excited about what I way trying to do but gently let me know when they didn't understand what I was saying. I pictured their faces as I typed on my QWERTY keyboard. Both are intelligent, educated, and interested in learning more about economics. I couldn't ask for a better first audience.

My sister Marian Van Calbi started reading for me near the end of the writing process, but she had great ideas. She asked me to tell her what happened to all of the people in the various cocktail party vignettes. She wanted to know more about these fictitious people. This chapter's opening story is a direct result of that request. I didn't incorporate the busy retirees who participated in the car rally and attended the opera. Needless to say, our guest of honour is a friend and plans to participate in their future adventures. I haven't sorted out whether his wife is going to take early retirement to join him yet. I also didn't know how to tell you that the bride's family store did go out of business, but thankfully the dad works as the local store manager for the new big-box store.

I wish to thank my good friend Brenda Murray for her lovely drawings of Rick and myself. We decided that a book like this needed a bit of glamour and a picture of us probably wouldn't "cut it." Brenda promised to make us look great without the necessity of surgery!

I would also like to thank my colleagues in the Economics department at the University of Guelph. Many of them read a chapter in their area of expertise and gave me valuable feedback. They are Asha Sadanand, Atsu Amegeshi, Michael Hoy, Laurent Cellier, Francis Tapon, Bram Cadsby and former colleagues Ray Rees, Louis Christofidies, Graeme Wells, and Merwan Engineer (who saved me from a very

---

[6]   To hear Rick speak in his own voice, please read the Afterword.

embarrassing mistake). Economists can be a picky bunch when it comes to economic theory and the last thing I wanted was to get slammed by the broader academic community. Therefore, I asked Professor Brian Ferguson to read the gossip columns. Brian is very much like the featured early economists: well read—his library is legendary and his memory encyclopedic—and a bit of a quirky dresser. When he wears bifocals, it is really two pairs of glasses! These economists kept me from sacrificing accuracy in order to make things readable. Any economic errors are certainly not their fault. On the creative side, our former graduate secretary Anne Bolger told me that I needed to add a summary (the napkin notes) at the end of each chapter. Lastly, my chair, John Livernois (who co-teaches introductory microeconomics), agreed to use this book as part of our curriculum. To all of them, my fulsome thanks.

Counting the Cost and Paying the Price

A woman must have money and a room of her own if she is to write fiction.
Adeline Virginia Woolf (1882–1941), English writer

Usually, the last individuals to get thanked are family members. Furthermore, they are usually thanked for enduring all manner of trials and tribulations imposed upon them during that the writing of the book. While I have things for which I wish to thank my husband and two sons, in all honesty the price they paid for me to write this book is not one of them. Let me explain. Martin owns an environmental consulting company and has a home office in the basement of our house. He has had this home office since our youngest child was a year old, and that child is now a teenager. Martin works a minimum of 60 hours a week and, frankly, I don't think my new busyness really registered because his nose was to the proverbial grindstone.

Probably my oldest son has the biggest beef with me, but only because the desktop computer I really like to use is in his room. (We bought him an expensive laptop.) On a regular basis he would say, "Mom, can I have my room back?" to which I would reply "Give me 15 more minutes." I will admit that he was slightly inconvenienced, but I don't really think it was that big of a deal.

Last but not least, my youngest son should thank his lucky stars I was so engrossed in writing this book. I no longer had time to nag him about cleaning his room, practising his guitar, doing his homework, and wasting countless hours playing video games. (I do feel somewhat guilty about this lapse in parenting.) Both of us hope—for very different reasons—that there will be a sequel.

If you have to ask how much it costs, you can't afford it.
John Pierpont Morgan (1837–1913), American financier and banker

The person who paid the price to write this book is fortunately the person who economists say should pay if this is an efficient market. That person is me. I paid in hours and hours of sitting in front of a computer screen, giving up nights, weekends, and some holidays over what turned out to be a couple of years. There were three costly side effects. First, I gained 10 pounds. All of my cute little cocktail dresses fit a tad more snugly and seem a little more revealing. *Sigh.* Second, my house and garden are a mess. (In our family, due to differences in marginal values and comparative advantage, Martin does the cooking and I do the cleaning. I think the fact that I don't clean or garden as much as I used to may have been a contributing factor to the weight gain.) Third, I dropped many of my volunteer activities to focus on writing this book. It is my sincere hope that what you hold in your hands is worth the price I paid.

So, if they didn't sacrifice in the production of this book, why am I grateful to my family? Well, my family believes that I can write a bestseller. My kids say such things as, "Mom, when you make royalties on your book, can I have …?" This has been said so often that I have come to believe that royalty cheques are inevitable. Martin proudly tells people that I am writing a book. When writing got hard, I partly kept at it because of their great expectations.

Publishing Phenomenon

One of the most terrifying aspects of publishing stories and books is the realization that they are going to be read, and read by strangers. I had never fully realized this before, although I had of course in my imagination dwelt lovingly upon the thought of the millions and millions of people who were going to be uplifted and enriched and delighted by the stories I wrote.
Shirley Jackson (1916–1965), American author
Taken from *Come Along with Me* (1968)

I never wanted to self-publish, because as an economist I firmly believe in the vital role of "middlemen." The basic tenet of this belief is that publishing houses add value when they guide the process of getting a book from writer to reader. I was right. I would therefore like to express my appreciation to Pearson Education Canada in the person of Gary Bennett, for saying yes to this book. His "yes" was the critical one I needed to get. Even though I haven't "laid eyes" on any of the people I am going to mention, their eyes have combed this book many times. Each pass had a slightly different focus, which improved the quality of the book. Karen Townsend, the developmental editor, decided what stayed in and what had to go. The nip and tucks were worth it. Susan Broadhurst was both the production editor and the copy editor, fixing all of the spelling, grammar, and style errors. Patricia Jones proofread the final pages to make certain that mistakes didn't make their way into the published book. If I had self-published, the quality of this book would not have been the same.

You hold in your hands my book, my baby. A lot of me has been passed on, but so has something of an economics heritage. I hope you found it to be a good read. If not, remember that it is my baby and you should never tell a mother that her child is ugly … at least not to her face. Ciao.

Afterword: Rick's Postpartum

As Evie has said, in your hands you hold her "baby." Let me just say that I am honoured to have been able to participate in its happy delivery. (I'm not quite sure what that makes me in this analogy, but whatever it is, I want you to know that her husband, Martin, is okay with it.) As with childbirth, producing a book like this must entail a sometimes painful process. For me, writing always has its struggles, frustrations, and times of pain when you want to bang your head on the desk because you just can't express something the way you would like to. However, you press on with the thought that hopefully you are bringing something of value into the world, something that everyone will love as much as you do. As a writer, before I embark on such a laborious venture I make sure, like any good economist, to count the costs and insist that there is a good enough marginal benefit associated with the effort. I am happy to say that I think *Cocktail Party Economics* was well worth the effort it took to write for a number of reasons.

First, whenever you get a chance to write a book with a bright, passionate, Type A person with something important, entertaining, and interesting to say, you go for it. Evie is one of those people. She has been a friend of mine for many years, and what I love about her most is her enthusiasm and willingness to work through things with people, through good and bad, to get things done. In humility, she realizes the importance of community and that only by combining the complementary skills of different people can we achieve something better than what one could have done on our own. Now, she may say that she is simply being a pragmatic economist, but I don't think you can get that sort of wisdom from graphs.

Second, I enjoy the challenge of making a topic that is perceived as complex accessible to a wider audience. I love the phrase *it's not rocket science* because I don't think most things really are as complicated as rocket science (however, now I'm really not sure that rocket science is all that complicated after I read that a father and his son successfully sent their iPhone into space and recorded video with it). In any event, the point is that sometimes people go out of their way to make things sound more complicated than they really are. I don't like that. I never have. I want to help people understand things at whatever level they are at. I think this book goes a long way toward making the subject of economics, which touches us all, accessible to a larger audience.

Third, I never turn down an opportunity to appear smarter than I am. I am not an economist by profession, but you know what? After working with Evie to write this book, I now realize that I am exercising my inner economist every time I choose a Venti Caffè Mocha instead of a Tall Caffè Latte at Starbucks. It's all about opportunity costs, baby, and that's pretty sweet!

But you know what is even sweeter? My wife, Judy, who enabled every opportunity for me to work on this book with encouragement and patience. Thanks so much, honey!

Index